BORDER
AND
CONNECTIVITY

North-East India and South-East Asia

BORDER AND CONNECTIVITY

North-East India and South-East Asia

Editors

K. Vidya Sagar Reddy

C. Joshua Thomas

PENTAGON PRESS LLP

Border and Connectivity: North-East India and South-East Asia
Editors: K. Vidya Sagar Reddy, C. Joshua Thomas

First Published in 2019

ISBN 978-93-86618-80-1

Published by
PENTAGON PRESS LLP
206, Peacock Lane, Shahpur Jat
New Delhi-110049
Phones: 011-64706243, 26491568
Telefax: 011-26490600
email: rajan@pentagonpress.in
website: www.pentagonpress.in

Printed at Aegean Offset Printers, Greater Noida, U.P.

CONTENTS

Foreword *vii*

Introduction *ix*

I. ACT EAST POLICY IN CONTEXT

1 Conversations Beyond the Centre: India's Border Regions as Drivers of the Act East Policy 3
Nimmi Kurian

2 Preparing the North East Region of India for an Effective Act East Policy 14
P. Lazarus Samraj and James Ralte

3 Act East Policy for North East India: Prospect, Ethnicity, Soft Power 32
Lalengkima

4 Consociating India with ASEAN: Prospects and Challenges in Look East Policy 41
M.N. Singh

5 CLMV and Act East Policy: Exploring New Avenues 52
Pankaj Jha

6 Trade Potential of North East India with ASEAN1 62
Sunetra Ghatak

II. BORDER AND CONNECTIVITY

7 A Political Economy Analysis of Growth Episodes in the North-Eastern Region 81
Debajit Jha

8 India's Connectivity with ASEAN: A Micro-Level Study of Socio-Economic Connectivity and Its Impact on Border Trade at Zokhawthar (Mizoram) 95
Ruatdiki Hmar

9 Importance of Myanmar in Act East Policy 107
Lalrinngheta

10 Enhancing Indo-Myanmar Trade with Special Reference to Zokhawthar–Rih Border Sector 117
Lily Sangpui

11 India-Myanmar Sub-regional Cooperation 130
Pradip Phanjoubam

12 Act East Policy from Perspectives of Soft Power Engagements and Connectivity between Northeast India and ASEAN 139
Suwa Lal Jangu

13 Prospects of India-ASEAN Relations in the Light of Myanmar's Political Reforms 156
Jonathan Zodintluanga

14 Connecting Lives on India-Myanmar Border: Issues in Migration and Public Health Hazards 169
Anasua Basu Ray Chaudhury

III. NORTHEAST INDIA AND ASEAN

15 Look and Act East: View from the Northeast Region and Mizoram 183
Jagadish K. Patnaik

16 Developmental Implications of the Act East Policy: A Case of Tourist Promotion in Mizoram 194
K.V. Reddy

17 Process of Look East Policy and Its Perspectives in Manipur and Nagaland 206
Jangkhongam Dounge

Contributors 221

Index 223

FOREWORD

I am delighted to present the book, *Border and Connectivity: North-East India and South-East Asia*, which is an outcome of the national seminar organised by the Department of Political Science, Mizoram University, in collaboration with the ASEAN Studies Centre, Shillong, on 23 and 24 March 2018.

While the themes of culture, commerce and connectivity are cornerstones of India's Act East policy, this volume captures the essence of infrastructural development, human capacity building and soft assets as pillars to connect Northeast India and Southeast Asia. Northeast India's soft power assets will play a critical role in India's relations with ASEAN through the CLMV countries (Cambodia, Laos, Myanmar and Vietnam).

I trust that this volume will provide valuable information to policy makers, researchers, students and the public on the Act East Policy and Northeast India.

Anurag Bhushan
Joint Secretary (ASEAN-ML)
Ministry of External Affairs
Government of India, New Delhi

INTRODUCTION

India-ASEAN relations form the core of India's foreign policy shift from 'Look East' to the Act East Policy (AEP). There has been considerable progress in India's economic and strategic relations with Southeast Asia. Several regional partnership initiatives such as the Bay of Bengal Initiative for Multi-Sectoral Technical and Economic Co-operation (BIMSTEC), the Mekong-Ganga Cooperation (MGC), Bangladesh, Bhutan, India, Nepal Forum (BBIN), Bangladesh, China, India and Myanmar Forum (BCIM), etc., engage directly or indirectly with ASEAN. In India's engagement with ASEAN, which includes the Regional Comprehensive Economic Partnership (RCEP) with ASEAN+6, much focus has been placed on trade and connectivity which are likely to have positive implications on landlocked India's Northeastern region as well. This calls for India-ASEAN's enhanced cooperation in shaping the regional economic and security architecture.

The year 2017 marked the completion of 25 years of India's dialogue partnership with ASEAN, 15 years of Summit-Level partnership and five years of India-ASEAN strategic partnership. This defines a dynamic trajectory for India-ASEAN relations. Against the background of the growing relations between India and ASEAN, there is a need to review the progress, problems and prospects of India-ASEAN relations.

This volume broadly focuses on the following themes:

1. Impediments in India's Act East Policy with respect to India's Northeast and the way forward
2. Identifying strengths and weaknesses of each Northeastern state to be a facilitator and benefactor in India's AEP
3. Significance of Cambodia, Laos, Myanmar, Vietnam (CLMV) in India's AEP
4. Border trade, cultural exchanges and tourism between India's Northeast and Southeast Asia
5. Northeast as an investment destination for ASEAN

The first section of the volume has a collection of articles examining the opportunities, challenges and implications that India's Act East Policy towards Southeast Asia has ushered in the North-Eastern region. The thematic outline of border trade, connectivity and soft power is discussed in context to India's Act East and the Northeastern region. In this section, Nimmi Kurian in her article *Conversations Beyond the Centre: India's Border Regions as Drivers of the Act East Policy* argues that if *it is to succeed, India's Act East policy has to be framed first and foremost as a sub-regional experiment in co-governance which* will in turn hinge essentially on two overlapping concerns, namely, the extent to which the policy acknowledges that communities and sustainable tourism resource management are co-travellers.

P. Lazarus Samraj and James Ralte in their article *Preparing the North East Region of India for an Effective Act East Policy* underline the importance of empowering the people of the Northeastern region with modern high-tech education, providing them entrepreneurial and skill development training by involving higher educational institutions. Lalengkima in his article *Act East Policy for North East India: Prospect, Ethnicity, Soft Power* argues that India's Act East Policy towards its Northeastern region and extended neighbouring countries should firstly work towards ethnic integration of the inhabitant tribes of the region and rectify ethnic tensions there. M.N. Singh in his article *Consociating India with ASEAN: Prospects & Challenges in Look East Policy* examines the fundamental factors that propel India to inch towards the ASEAN countries in the present global scenario. It further explores the potential prospects and challenges inherent in the Look East Policy, especially with Northeast India.

Pankaj Jha in his article *CLMV and Act East Policy: Exploring New Avenues* argues that the CLMV countries have emerged as a bloc that can create political synergies and has seen relatively stable regimes. This paper highlights the complementariness and the development of synergies between India and the CLMV countries. Sunetra Ghatak in her article *Trade Potential of North East India with ASEAN* makes an assessment of the volume and composition of the trade pattern between India and ASEAN and provides an enumeration of economic potential and facilitating factors for economic integration of the NER with ASEAN. The author further discusses critical bottlenecks that need to be addressed for realizing trade potentials between India and ASEAN.

The second section of the volume clubs together a set of articles that explore the growth potentials of border trade between India and Myanmar through India's Northeast. These growth potentials will have to be substantiated by addressing the geopolitical and socio-ethnic peculiarities in cross-border areas. Debajit Jha in his article *A Political Economy Analysis of Growth Episodes of the North-Eastern Region* identified that the Northeastern region has experienced two episodes of growth acceleration. The episode of the first growth acceleration had begun in 1993 and lasted until 2007. Although, the growth rate of the region during this period accelerated, the region has grown slower than the national average. The second episode of growth acceleration began in 2007 and lasts until the end of the period of our study. Ruatdiki Hmar in her article *India's Connectivity with ASEAN: A Micro Level Study of Socio-Economic Connectivity and Its Impact on Border Trade at Zokhawthar (Mizoram)* argues that India's Act East Policy has transformed the perception of India's Northeastern region from a sensitive border area to a prospective economic zone. The Indo-Myanmar border is perceived in the context of a two-nation affair but as a via-media for closer economic integration of India's relations with the East and Southeast Asian nations.

Lalrinngheta in his article *Importance of Myanmar in Act East Policy* argues that the internal political development of Myanmar, democratic set-up, peace and stability of the civilian government and the Rohingya crisis will be crucial factors for India's Act East Policy towards Myanmar. Lily Sangpui in her article *Enhancing Indo-Myanmar Trade with Special Reference to Zokhawthar–Rih Border Sector* examines the various aspects of the Zokhawthar-Rih trade sector situated along the Indo-Myanmar border and argues that socio-economic cooperation could be extended in order to change its transit nature which could substantiate to some extent India's imbalance of trade across the Indo-Myanmar trade zone.

Pradip Phanjoubam in his article *India-Myanmar Sub-regional Cooperation* holds that with the return of democracy in Myanmar, India is now making a fresh approach and the Northeast is eagerly and hopefully waiting to see this new approach take a shape that would benefit the region. The author further argues that there will be hurdles, some historical and some as a consequence of the new world economic order and geopolitics. Suwa Lal Jangu in his article *Act East Policy from Perspectives of Soft Power Engagements and Connectivity between Northeast India and ASEAN* examines the soft power engagements and connectivity between India and Myanmar. The author argues that some of the issues that need to be addressed are building institutions, addressing coordination gaps, improving the cooperation-based planning, implementation process and addressing diverse geopolitical and socio-ethnic peculiarities in cross-border areas.

Jonathan Zodintluanga in his article *Prospects of India-ASEAN Relations in the Light of Myanmar's Political Reforms* argues that owing to the recent political reforms taking place in Myanmar, India-ASEAN relations in one way or the other is expected to reach the next level through greater enhancement of India's Look East/Act East Policy. The prospects of India-ASEAN relations from the perspective of Myanmar's recent reforms seems to be promising, positive as well as challenging. Anasua Basu Ray Chaudhury in his article *Connecting Lives on India-Myanmar Border: Issues in*

Migration and Public Health Hazards argues that any cross-border regime for the free flow of goods, services and capital will remain plain untenable until India moves in to neutralise health security threats in the region. Within the above context, this paper considers the cases of Mizoram and Manipur to highlight and identify correlation between migration and the spread of border diseases and evaluates the existing status of disease among the bordering states of Northeast India and Myanmar. Lastly, it addresses the collaborative efforts between both the nations for an effective border health infrastructure, management and disease control strategy.

The third section of the volume locates the political, economic and cultural landscape of Mizoram in the context of India's Act East Policy towards Southeast Asia. The collection of articles weighs the ideational and aspirational against the potentials and implications of positioning Mizoram as a stakeholder in India's Act East Policy.

J.C. Zomuanthanga in his article *India's Act East Policy: A Trajectory for Northeast India* argues that as the Act East policy takes shape, India–Southeast Asia relations stand poised to shift to a new trajectory. The Northeast of India has been positioned as a priority in the Act East Policy (AEP). It has given an impetus to local economies and bilateral trade and in the long run could transform the economic profile of Northeast India. Jagadish K. Patnaik in his article *Look and Act East: View from the Northeast Region and Mizoram* argues that India's Act East Policy has a two-pronged objective of politically integrating India's northeast with the rest of the country and India with the wider East Asia in another direction.

K.V. Reddy in his article *Developmental Implications of the Act East Policy: A Case of Tourist Promotion in Mizoram* identifies developmental problems such as the Inner Line Regulations (ILR) among others that undermine tourist development in the state of Mizoram. Jangkhongam Doungel in his article *Process of Look East Policy and Its Perspectives in Manipur and Nagaland* traces the genesis of the Look East Policy and process of its development. It attempts to critically analyse the perspectives of the Policy in Manipur and Nagaland with objective observation.

While the themes of culture, commerce and connectivity are the cornerstones of India's Act East policy, this seminar will focus on the premise that India's Northeast will play a critical role in India's relations with ASEAN through the CLMV countries (Cambodia, Laos, Myanmar and Vietnam). The geographical positioning of India's Northeast is an asset to physical, cultural and commercial connectivity between India and Southeast Asia. Therefore, understanding the internal and external challenges requires taking stock of the perspectives of the stakeholders of the region which will enhance the region's effective participation in India's AEP. However, the positioning of India's Northeast as the hub of physical/digital connectivity with

Southeast Asia calls for pinning down specific issues to transform infrastructural and capacity-building mechanisms in the region. This also requires linking the complementarities in trade and connectivity between India's Northeast and the CLMV within the ambit of India's 'Make in India' initiative and establishing a foothold in the country's global supply value chain with East Asian countries. The respective Assam and Manipur governments have designated departments on AEP affairs constituted in 2017, which is a first-of-its-kind in the region. A bottom-up approach towards understanding the strengths and weaknesses of each Northeastern state's ability to effectively partner and be a benefactor in India's AEP has to be critically examined.

This volume is the outcome of the national seminar titled *Border and Connectivity: North-East India and South-East Asia* organized by the Department of Political Science, Mizoram University, Aizawl, held during March 23-24, 2018. We are thankful to ASEAN Studies Centre for sponsoring the event and Mizoram University for providing the necessary space. We would like to express our appreciation to all participants and support staff—contributors, resource persons, commentators and others—for making it such an intellectually stimulating event.

We are thankful to Smt. Preeti Saran, Secretary (East) and Shri Anurag Bhushan, Joint Secretary (ASEAN-ML), Ministry of External Affairs, Government of India; Professor S.K. Srivastava, Vice-Chancellor, North-Eastern Hill University (NEHU) & Chairman, ASC and ICSSR-NERC, Shillong; and Professor K.R.S. Sambasiva Rao, Vice-Chancellor, Mizoram University, Aizawl, who has been a great source of strength in organizing this important seminar. We thankfully acknowledge the help received from Professor R.K. Satapathy, Honorary Director, ICSSR-NERC, the staff of ASC, ICSSR-NERC, Mizoram University, for the success of the entire event. Lastly, Mr. Rajan Arya of Pentagon Press deserves special thanks for bringing out this book.

K. Vidya Sagar Reddy

C. Joshua Thomas

I. ACT EAST POLICY IN CONTEXT

1

Conversations Beyond the Centre: India's Border Regions as Drivers of the Act East Policy

Nimmi Kurian

India's sub-regional diplomacy is clearly beginning to produce a modest but valuable space for sub-national actors to become (active partners in framing and fashioning the terms of India's engagement with its neighbourhood. This is part of a longer shift in Indian foreign policy towards a greater sub-regional engagement with its neighbourhood. While regional trading blocs and arrangements have been a common phenomenon, both the bilateral and regional levels have tended to bypass the sub-regional level with its local governance particularities and stakeholders.[1] Sub-regional cooperation represents a novel extension of this larger idea in that the unit of cooperation becomes the geographically proximate sub-regions within two or more countries as important sites of transnational cooperation. (See Map 1)[2] A striking aspect of this growing international engagement is the diversity and expansion of issues beyond trade and investment to include cross-cutting concerns such as environment, land use planning, housing and infrastructure among others.[3]

At the outset, the normative potential of sub-regionalism can be evaluated against three possible benchmarks. Firstly, the sub-regional turn in Indian diplomacy marks an interesting discursive shift in Indian foreign policy and its engagement of the Asian neighbourhood. It brings a long-overdue attention to the borderlands both as a missing level of analysis and as a level of governance (Kurian 2015:1). The idea of projecting Northeast India as a gateway to the wider dynamic Asian neighbourhood has found an increasing measure of rhetorical importance under India's Look East policy, the rechristened Act East policy. Through a host of sub-regional initiatives like the BIMSTEC (Bay of Bengal Multi-Sectoral Initiative for

Technical and Economic Cooperation), the Mekong Ganga Economic Cooperation (MGC), and the Bangladesh-China-India-Myanmar Economic Corridor (BCIM EC) India has attempted to signal the growing priority it attaches to integrating its eastern region with the wider Asian neighbourhood. Bottom-up economic processes are today resulting in the rise of a new set of sub-regional stakeholders with stakes in trans-border cooperation. These dynamic processes constitute subterranean sub-regionalism; a form of integration that mainstream research and policy has so far not paid adequate attention to. (Kurian 2016). These shifts bring interesting methodological and conceptual insights to rethink the role of the border region not as a passive location but as a foreign policy actor with agency. There is a need to systematise the diversity of this growing engagement by border states with reference to its nature (formal or informal); activities (social, economic, cultural, political); duration (sustained or episodic) and actors (public or private). This paper argues that the success of India's Act East policy will turn on Delhi's capacity to recognise and engage with the complex range of these processes. Addressing this gap could add much-needed content and cohesion to India's foreign policy initiatives by making it more responsive to both domestic and sub-regional developmental priorities. This also has the potential to recognise the border actor as a critical stakeholder on a range of shared trans-border issues such as trade, energy, environment, land use and transport.[4,5]

Secondly, India's (re)engagement with sub-regional Asia offers at the outset the potential for a critical re-engagement with the notion of the 'international' itself by going beyond a limited geopolitical understanding towards a sociological one. The borderlands, far from being the 'periphery,' are uniquely positioned at the intersection of national and cultural crossroads and bring several crossover disciplinary and policy insights. If these are dismissed as illegal or worse, as irrelevant, such rich narratives would have no hope of finding entry points into the mainstream discourse. The lived experiences of border communities have to be at the centre of any new rethinking on borderlands. Delhi's discourse on borders runs the risk of becoming a marginalised narrative if it fails to connect with the lives of the people. If it is to succeed, it will need to cross the discursive line and reimagine the border as verb. The role of transnational ethnic social networks in a border region needs to be recognised as a form of social capital. Transnational social networks based on ancestral and kinship ties and interpersonal trust networks constitute a form of social capital that is integral to a trans-border sub-region, resting on a highly place-centric sense of self and community identity. A social history of trans-Himalayan trade reveals how trans-border exchanges were characterised by highly personalised trust-based relationships. These performed a crucial economic function by helping to reduce transaction costs, given the arduous challenges involved in conducting long-distance trade. Highly personalised trust-based informal networks characterised trans-Himalayan long-distance trade. Trade ties were underwritten by trust-based ritual practices such as *gamgya* and *netsang*, unwritten contracts that *inter alia* included preferential terms of barter besides access to grain and shelter. This personalised trust-based contract was mutually beneficial and its success can be measured from the fact that these often lasted for several generations, being passed on from trader to the next of kin. (Kurian 2017).

Thirdly, a bottom-up Act East policy driven by the border regions can help locate Indian IR within the larger historical template of social, economic and cultural flows that constitute the lived experiences of border communities. It is these 'connected histories' that have to be at the centre of any new rethinking on borderlands. It is time to turn the page back and recall these 'histories of Asian cosmopolitanism' to remind ourselves that the contemporary notion of Northeast India as a landlocked region has little or no historical credence. The sub-regional project as a narrative aimed at transforming economic geographies has today been raised to the highest levels (of rhetorical importance in India's policy discourse. At the (core of this vision stands a series of trans-border infrastructure projects that India has initiated in the sub-region. (See Map 2).[6] These projects involve the restoration of key road and rail (links between India and its immediate neighbourhood, many of which were operational even till the late 1960s. (Kurian 2014). For India's Northeast, transit connectivity through Bangladesh offers quicker road, rail and inland water transport options. India is funding the construction of a $51 million, 14-km long rail project that will connect Tripura's capital, Agartala, with Akhaura, the south-eastern border town of Bangladesh. Akhaura, a prominent jute-trading centre during the British period, is today an important railway junction in Bangladesh with links to Chittagong, Sylhet, Mymensingh and Dhaka. The Agartala-Akhaura project promises to bring multiple benefits to the Northeast. The rail link will drastically reduce the distance between Agartala and Kolkata and allow for freight movement between the two capitals. For example, the distance between Agartala and Kolkata through Guwahati is 1,650 km but the link through Bangladesh will reduce this to just 350 km. India and Bangladesh have also agreed in principle to revive the rail link between Chilahati, a border railway station in Bangladesh, with Haldibari in West Bengal. Some sections of this rail route are already functional and require relatively modest (costs to re-establish connectivity. This route will also provide Bangladesh much-faster connectivity with Bhutan and Nepal. Another proposed link between Kulaura in Bangladesh and Mahishashan in Assam will open a trade route between Assam's Barak valley and Bangladesh. India is also building three rail lines to Bhutan linking Assam and West Bengal with Bhutan. The two lines from Assam (are a 51-km track linking Pathshala and a 57-km track from Kokrajhar to Bhutan's Nanglam and Gelephu, respectively. A third rail line will link Hashimara in West Bengal to Phuentsholing in Bhutan through a 17-km track. Another link is a 16-km track connecting West Bengal's Naxalbari to Kankarvitta in Nepal and a 15-km track from Bihar's Jogbani to Nepal's Biratnagar. India is also pursuing an East-to-West road corridor linking Moreh in Manipur through Bagan in Myanmar to Maesot in Thailand. The highway will further be extended to Singapore, Malaysia, Cambodia, Laos and Vietnam holding the promise of seamless continental connectivity with Southeast Asia. Trial runs for the Trilateral Highway project are scheduled to begin by December 2015. The Motor Vehicles Agreement signed between Bangladesh, Bhutan, India and Nepal in June 2015 is also a major transit agreement with clear potential. There are also plans to improve internal rail connectivity within the Northeast. As part of a long-standing programme of rail upgradation, the Union Budget of 2017-1018 set a target of achieving broad-gauge rail connectivity to all capitals of the Northeast by 2020. (*Economic Times*, 2017).[7]

The Road Less Travelled: Borderlands Tourism

India has been underscoring the transformative potential of cross-border partnerships in the field of tourism for the Northeast. It is not difficult to understand why. The Northeast presents a picture-postcard collage with its rich fare of festivals, monasteries, temples and churches, verdant tea gardens, mighty rivers, deep forests, diverse ecological zones and even more diverse peoples. From the only floating national park in Keibul Lamjao in Manipur to the high-altitude biosphere reserve park in the Khangchendzonga in Sikkim to Gyaker Sinyi, the natural lake in Arunachal Pradesh, to Sibasagar, the ancient capital of the Ahoms in Assam or the Krem Mawmluh caves in Meghalaya, marketing the Northeast offers spectacular choice. There are plans to connect Northeast India to the well-established tourism networks of Southeast Asia. The Greater Mekong Sub-Region represents an example of a successful transnational tourism regime designed for joint marketing of tour programmes in the region.[8]

While the promotion of a model of mass tourism has undoubtedly seen an expansion of tourism revenues and footfalls, interventions that do not respect the supply potential of mountain ecologies are creating and reinforcing interlocking webs of environmental and socio-economic vulnerability. The fixation with the economic potential of tourism has also meant that this growth has often sidestepped the lives of borderland communities, bringing few economic opportunities to the region.[9]

If (re)designed as an alternative model of borderlands tourism, it has the potential to bring tourism-generated revenues directly to the rural communities and help diversify and restructure mountain economies. For instance, well-planned, rural home stays can be designed in winter months so as to not disrupt rural agricultural calendars as well as also provide rural folk with additional income-generating activities. (*Sikkim Now* 2009). This can effectively alleviate the otherwise enormous pressure on local infrastructure during the peak summer seasons. Such community-based tourism projects hold the potential to look into questions of income generation, job creation, safety and crime and underline the need for 'situated development' that responds to local particularities. A unique conservation initiative launched in Arunachal Pradesh in 2008 promotes sustainable wetlands tourism by making monasteries take the lead in the preservation of high-altitude wetlands like the Bangajan. The three-year WWF project called *Saving Wetlands Sky High* also engages the monasteries in waste disposal activities so as to ensure that tourism does not impact the wetlands adversely. It is only when tourism as a sector begins to address such questions that it can create enabling spaces for communities to partake of these opportunities as well as benefits.

There is scope for the Northeast to institutionalise cross-border cooperation in marketing, transit, research, training and a variety of imaginatively conceived package tour programmes. Such an integrated approach can be extended to cover the entire region including Bhutan, Nepal and Sri Lanka. Meghalaya, for instance, is set to launch a week-long tourism festival in Dhaka by the end of 2009 to expand partnerships in the tourism sector. An interesting initiative that India and other countries in the region could join is the *Tourism Earth Lung Initiative* launched by Sri Lanka in 2007. The initiative aims to make the country a carbon-neutral destination by 2018 and plans to put in place a research and development programme to engage all stakeholders in the public and private sectors, local communities, NGOs, tourists, researchers as well as liaise with the forestry, environment and energy departments. Similarly, the Buddhist circuit special train that was launched by the Indian Railways in 2007 is expected to connect major Buddhist pilgrim centres in India and Nepal such as Bodh Gaya, Nalanda, Rajgir, Varanasi, Shravasti and Lumbini. A campaign *Come to India—Walk with the Buddha* was also launched in several Southeast Asian countries to promote tourism to Buddhist heritage sites across the country.

There also exists good potential to connect Northeast India and Southwest China to the well-established tourism networks of Southeast Asia. The South-eastern and East Asian countries have been aggressively marketing themselves as tourist destinations and across the region tourism is a big revenue earner. The entire region could be promoted as a tourist destination and skilful marketing can imaginatively project its natural beauty and immensely rich cultural and ethnic diversity. The Greater Mekong Sub-Region represents an example of a successful transnational tourism regime, with tourism being one of the major growth engines among the 11 flagship programmes of the regional cooperation. The Mekong Tourism Development Project has been so designed for joint marketing of tour programmes in the region. The Heritage Necklace Circuit today links the six heritage sites of Siem Reap in Cambodia, Hue in Vietnam, Luang Prabang in Laos, Bagan in Myanmar, Sukhothai in Thailand and Lijiang in Yunnan, China. There are also efforts to promote the GMS as a single destination and move towards harmonisation of regulations and procedures. The six countries have agreed in principle to move towards a GMS visa that could be like the Schengen to facilitate travel from outside the region.

Sub-regional Dialogues on Sustainable Development

Cross-border partnerships in conservation become the natural and critical corollary to sustainable tourism in a border region. Trans-boundary governance challenges point to the limitations of decision-making processes that operate within straitened territorial frames of reference. (Kurian 2014). This also raises larger questions of defining the limits of acceptable use, particularly given the recent surge that the Northeast has seen in domestic tourist arrivals.

National efforts to safeguard a sub-regional resource base will prove to be sub-optimal and end up operating within fractured frames. Efforts in one part of the region to conserve resources can quickly unravel in the absence of similar laws and policies in another area in the neighbourhood. While there is growing recognition of the need for sub-regional cooperation within the BCIM region, there have been limited collective learning opportunities to share information, experiences and lessons on sustainable development. A predominantly economic reading of the sub-regional initiative has meant that the ecological sustainability of the BCIM initiative remains largely under-theorised and under-studied. What are the prospects for India to forge issue-based linkages with its sub-regional neighbourhood on a range of regional public goods?

There are compelling reasons for initiating conservation conversations within the BCIM region given the interlinkages between environmental goods and services in the region. Resource degradation is becoming a common feature afflicting the region and interventions that do not respect the supply potential of mountain ecologies are creating interlocking webs of environmental and socio-economic vulnerabilities. Water management issues, ecological imbalances in the form of rising temperatures, retreating glaciers and droughts caused by indifferent rainfall are increasingly finding their way to parts of the extended sub-region. Climate change is exacerbating the spatial and temporal variations in water availability with the annual runoff in mega deltas such as the Brahmaputra and Indus projected to decline by 14 per cent and 27 per cent respectively by 2050. The growing pace of forest fragmentation, land conversion and habitat loss will require targeted policy and institutional support since these directly impinge on livelihood chances of the rural poor. Of all the effects of these multiple stresses to the ecosystem, its social impact on the lives and livelihoods of local communities who depend on a range of ecosystem services will be the most serious.

Any meaningful debate on questions of benefit sharing and tradeoffs will need to address three key challenges. Firstly, establishing a baseline database for different biodiversity and ecosystems components will be an essential prerequisite to informed public policy on sustainable development. For instance, the lack of reliable data adds to the uncertainty concerning Himalayan glaciers and the possible adverse impact on the 1.3 billion people of the region and the demands for irrigation, drinking, sanitation, industrial and other uses. Gaps in the knowledge base regarding transition of land use also need to be plugged as they have far reaching socio-economic as well as ecological impacts. Studies in China's Yunnan province have shown that in order to better monitor changing land use, national level monitoring has been abandoned in favour of a more subnational scale of analysis. Multi-scale and multi-actor frameworks with coordination among all stakeholders will be required to build these databases at sub-regional levels.

Secondly, sub-regional platforms to share experiences, knowledge and forge sectoral and cross-sectoral linkages will be valuable. Such a BCIM-wide sub-regional networking platform could connect what may otherwise remain disparate dots in the conservation effort. There are nascent efforts at transnational institution building in the sub-region that are beginning to plug gaps in the knowledge base and bringing together local, national and regional stakeholders. For instance, there are trans-boundary environmental networks that focus on various aspects related to environmental protection such as the Asian Environmental Compliance and Enforcement Network (AECEN), South Asian Biosphere Reserve Network (SeaBRNet), Asian Network of Sustainable Agriculture and Bioresources (ANSAB), Freshwater Action Network South Asia (FANSA), Himalayan Conservation Approaches and Technologies (HIMCAT) and South Asian Network on Environmental Law (SANEL) among others. Similarly, landscape approaches to conservation have the potential for improved management of shared bio-cultural diversity. Fledgling efforts at trans-border institution building include the Kailash

Sacred Landscape Conservation and Development Initiative by India, China and Nepal; the Brahmaputra-Salween Landscape Conservation and Development Initiative by India, China and Myanmar and the Kanchenjunga Landscape Conservation and Development Initiative between India, Nepal and Bhutan. Initiatives such as these could help mediate competing interests of diverse institutional actors.

Thirdly, strengthening non-structural risk reduction measures could be a potential area of cooperation within the BCIM region. More effective risk identification techniques can go a long way in reducing loss of life and uncertainties that climate change and extreme weather events bring in their wake. Strengthening local innovation systems within the BCIM region will be key to the success of many of these measures since the kind of specialist knowledge that mountain communities acquire in the course of their lives constitutes an oral knowledge base that is almost unique and without parallel. Enhancing citizen contributions to biodiversity science could also be an important tool of public policy. Citizen biodiversity monitoring systems could help track variations as well as provide accurate assessments of the state of biodiversity within the sub-region. The manner in which these choices are made can help redraw the conceptual toolkit to facilitate more effective governance of regional public goods within the BCIM region. If handled creatively, these hold the potential to rethink the sub-region as an ecological space, and not merely as an economic one.

If it is to succeed, India's Act East policy has to be framed first and foremost as a sub-regional experiment in co-governance. This will, in turn, hinge essentially on two overlapping concerns, namely, the extent to which policy acknowledges that communities and sustainable tourism resource management are co-travellers and that cross-border partnerships constitute a critical corollary to sustainable tourism. Tourism, like myriad other flows, will hinge critically on how a border region is (re)imagined in the national narrative. Borderland tourism needs to evolve beyond the simplistic mix-and-stir model of throwing resources at a region and merely charting spikes in tourist arrivals. An apt imagery for borderlands tourism would be to imagine the road ahead, not as a linear one but one with several forks and bends, each replete with local narratives.

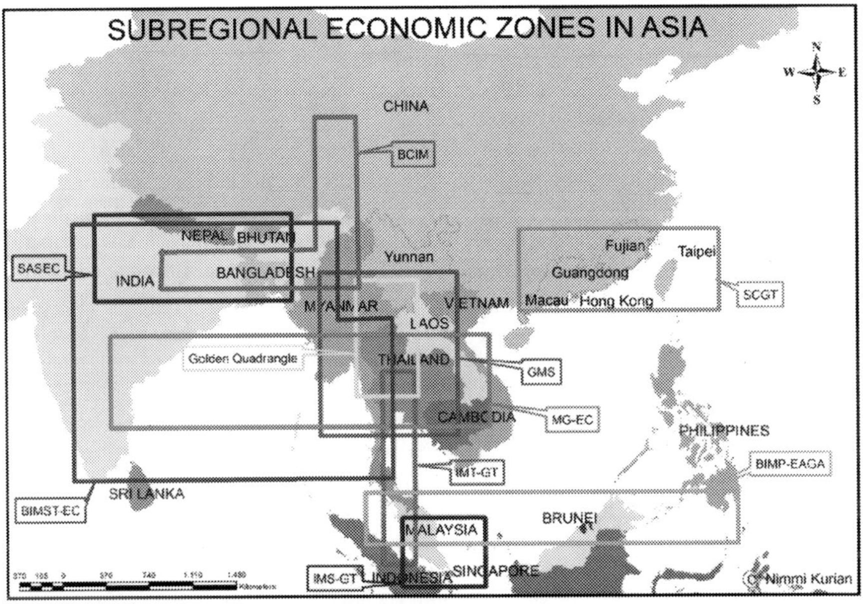
SUBREGIONAL ECONOMIC ZONES IN ASIA
CHINA
BCIM
NEPAL
BHUTAN
SASEC
INDIA
BANGLADESH
Yunnan
MYANMAR
VIETNAM
LAOS
Fujian
Taipei
Guangdong
Macau
Hong Kong
SCGT
Golden Quadrangle
THAILAND
GMS
CAMBODIA
MG-EC
PHILIPPINES
IMT-GT
BIMP-EAGA
SRI LANKA
BIMST-EC
BRUNEI
MALAYSIA
IMS-GT
INDONESIA
SINGAPORE
© Nimmi Kurian

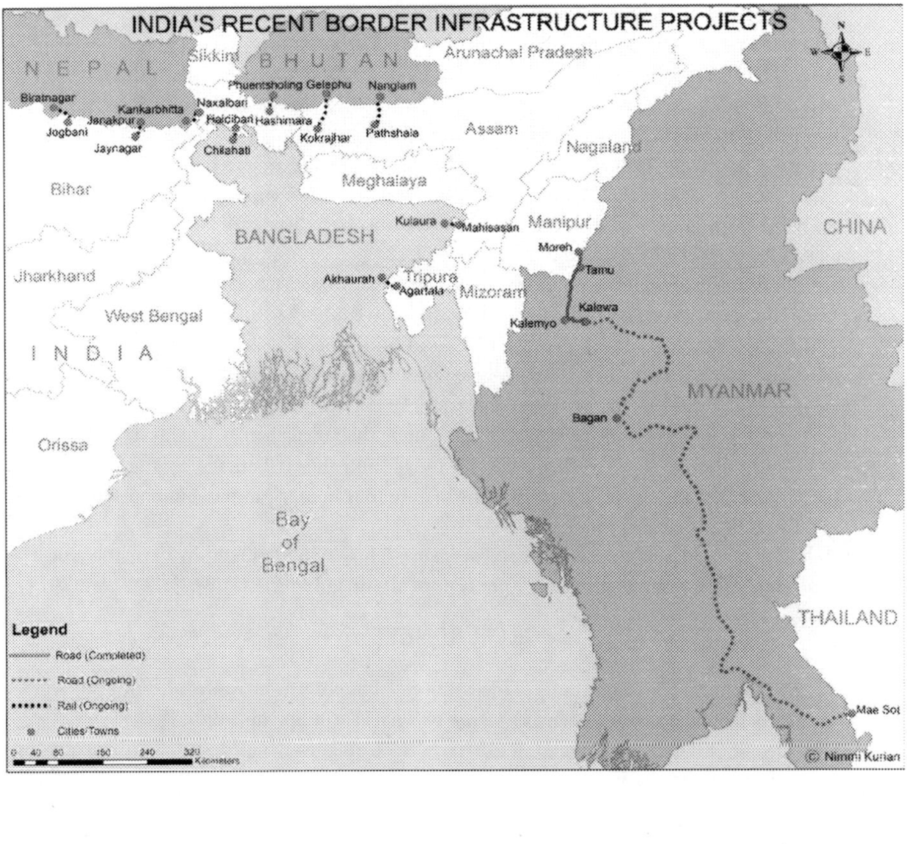
INDIA'S RECENT BORDER INFRASTRUCTURE PROJECTS
NEPAL
Sikkim
BHUTAN
Arunachal Pradesh
Biratnagar
Jogbani
Janakpur
Jaynagar
Kankarbhitta
Naxalbari
Haldibari
Chilahati
Phuentsholing
Gelephu
Hashimara
Kokrajhar
Nanglam
Pathshala
Assam
Nagaland
Bihar
Meghalaya
Kulaura
Mahisasan
Manipur
BANGLADESH
CHINA
Moreh
Tamu
Jharkhand
Akhaurah
Tripura
Agartala
Mizoram
Kalewa
Kalemyo
West Bengal
INDIA
MYANMAR
Bagan
Orissa
Bay of Bengal
THAILAND
Legend
Road (Completed)
Road (Ongoing)
Rail (Ongoing)
Cities/Towns
Mae Sot
© Nimmi Kurian

ENDNOTES

1 The growing international engagement and involvement by states has been a growing area of scrutiny and interest. (Duchacek, 1990, Michelmann and Soldatos, 1990, Blatter et al., 2008, Marks and Hooghe 2005); Duchacek I. 1990).

2 Source: Nimmi Kurian, *Conversations Beyond the Centre: India China Borderlands*, Sage, 2014.

3 For instance, the Subnational Global Climate Leadership Memorandum of Understanding (or the Under 2 MOU) brings together subnational governments from 32 countries willing to commit to achieving a per capita emissions target of less than 2 metric tons by 2050. The International Council for Local Environmental Initiatives (ICLEI) is another such initiative established in 1990 that brings together more than 1,200 cities, towns and counties spread over 70 countries. Five cities from BRICS countries—Rio de Janeiro, Saint Petersburg, Mumbai, Qingdao and Durban—established a partnership in 2008 to share experiences as well as to study strategies to deal with processes of urbanisation and the proliferation of mega-cities.

4 India's border states are beginning to establish direct links with local authorities of neighbouring countries. India and Bangladesh recently held District Magistrate-level meetings to discuss strategies towards more effective coordinated border management and tackling trans-border crime. (*Nagaland Post* 2015) District Magistrates and officials from Mamit and Lunglei districts of Mizoram met their Bangladeshi counterparts from the Rangamati and Bandarban districts to discuss more effective border management mechanisms in March 2015. The Deputy Commissioner of Rangamati district led a nine-member Bangladesh team to Mizoram to work towards greater coordination between district administrations on both sides. A meeting of district-level officials from Tripura and Bangladesh was also held in January 2015 at Agartala, Tripura's capital. The meeting was attended by officials from Tripura's four districts, namely, Sipahijala, Gomti, South Tripura and Dhalai and from Bangladesh's five districts—Comilla, Feni, Rangamati, Khagrachari and Chittagong.

5 The Damodar Valley Corporation is expected to start exporting power to Bangladesh after winning a global tender for cross-border power supply. The short-term supply of 300 MW is likely to commence from June 2018 and is to be evacuated through the 500 MW Bahrampur transmission line to Bheramara in Bangladesh. (*The Hindu* 2018).

6 Source: Nimmi Kurian, *Conversations Beyond the Centre: India China Borderlands*, Sage, 2014.

7 This is imperative since far more forbidding than the landlocked status of the Northeast is the fact that each of these states suffers the double disadvantage of being 'internally locked', 'themselves locked and locking out others, unable to connect with each other physically in terms of poor transport links, and more seriously unable to make connections intellectually and emotionally with their closest neighbours, or even with and among their own people.' (Prabhakara 2004:4606)

8 For instance, the Heritage Necklace Circuit today links the six heritage sites of Siem Reap in Cambodia, Hue in Vietnam, Luang Prabang in Laos, Bagan in Myanmar, Sukhothai in Thailand and Lijiang in Yunnan, China.

9 While India hosted 8.89 million tourists (as against China's 56.9 million) in 2016, the Northeast region received only an estimated 0.5 per cent of all foreign tourists. (*Northeast Today*, 2017).

REFERENCES

Blatter, J., M. Kreutzer, M. Rentl and J. Thiele. 2008. "The foreign relations of European regions: Competencies and activities," *West European Politics* 31 (3): pp. 464-490.

Chakraborty, Sujit. 2014. "70 Indian border markets to be open to Bangladeshis," *Business Standard*, 10 October.

Criekemans, D. 2008. 'Are the Boundaries between Diplomacy and Paradiplomacy Watering Down?' Paper presented at the Second Global International Studies Conference/WISC, Ljubljana, Slovenia, 23-26 July.

Duchacek, I. 1990. 'Perforated Sovereignties: Towards a Typology of New Actors in International Relations' in H. Michelmann and P. Soldatos P., eds. *Federalism and International Relations*, Oxford University Press.

Economic Times, 2015. 'Indo-Bangla Joint Conference to Begin on February 3,' 1 February.

Hocking, B. 1993. *Foreign Relations and Federal States*, London, Leicester University Press.

Kurian, Nimmi, 2018. 'Leaping Over Potholes? The Road Ahead for Tourism in India's Borderlands,' *CPR Policy Brief*, March.

Kurian, Nimmi, 2014. *India China Borderlands: Conversations Beyond the Centre*, Sage.

Kurian, Nimmi, 2015. 'Indian IR's Subregional Moment: Between a Rock and a Hard Place?' CPR Policy Brief, November.

Kurian, Nimmi, 2014. 'Conservation Conversations: Subregional Dialogues on Sustainable Development,' *TheSARCist*, June.

Kurian, Nimmi, 2017. 'Crossing the Line: The Border as Verb', *Live EncountersNortheast Today* 2017. 'What Ails Tourism to Northeast India?', 22 December.

Prabhakara, M. S. 2004. 'Is North-East India Landlocked?', *Economic and Political Weekly*, 16 October, pp. 4606-08.

Shyam Kishor 'Mizoram and India's Act East Policy,' Paper presented at the National

Sikkim Sunday Now 2009. 'Winter's the Ideal Season,' 18 January, p. 4.

The Economic Times 2017. 'Broad gauge connectivity to all NE state capitals by 2020 on target: Budget 2017,' 01 February 2017.

The Telegraph, 2015. 'Bihar Cry for More Power,' 10 April.

2

Preparing the North East Region of India for an Effective Act East Policy

P. Lazarus Samraj and James Ralte

ABSTRACT

The growth of a nation in international politics as well as regional politics to a large extent depends on the foreign policy it envisages in pursuance of its own national interest. The Indian Government's Act East policy is one of those foreign policies that have been envisaged way back in the 1990s as Look East Policy, which aimed at forging and establishing closer ties and relations with India's eastern neighbours like Myanmar and the ASEAN countries. This attempt of India in establishing a closer and concrete relation with Myanmar and the ASEAN countries through the Look East Policy has been found wanting in many aspects as with the passage of almost 22 years there has been very little achievement on various fronts. Thus, in November 2014, at the 12th ASEAN-India Summit and 9th East Asian Summit held at Naypidaw in Myanmar, Narendra Modi, the Prime Minister of India, formally enunciated the Act East Policy, which is a redefinition of the Look East Policy of 1991 aiming at forging economic, political, cultural and security cooperation with Myanmar and ASEAN countries. And for this, the development and restructuring of the Northeast region and its people should be a priority for the Indian Government, as the region with its strategic location and cultural proximities of the people with the population of Myanmar is the gateway for 'looking east' and for actively engaging with East ASEAN countries.

In this context, this paper underlines the importance of empowering the people of the Northeast with modern high-tech education and providing them entrepreneurial and skill development training by involving higher educational institutions. At present, only Assam is having an IIT and the rest of the NE regions are neglected in terms of technical education. Before starting the smart cities project it is necessary to set up technical educational institutions to achieve the Make in India vision of the present Union Government. For that, it is necessary to take the initiative to build confidence-building measures by assuring the NE people that their cultural identity will be protected in spite of celebrating pluralism. The highly popular English education may be helpful for the policy makers to reach the unreached. Moreover, NE higher education institutions can take initiatives to start courses on understanding the East Asian region's culture, business environment, language, sensitivities and other economic priorities and opportunities so that the people of NE could serve as bridges and change agents for a better India-ASEAN cooperation. Above all, the Central Government with the cooperation of the state governments should take the initiative to address the causes of insurgency to achieve a peaceful NE, to move towards a pro-active Look East and Act East Policy.

This paper intends to analyse the important areas the central and state governments should concentrate on for winning over the people of NE without alienating them before aggressively pursuing frontier expansion, for any external aggressive policy without the wholehearted cooperation and involvement of the local population will be a disaster.

Introduction

Policy shifts and policy priorities are part of any nation-state, which are based on so many factors. The Look East and Act East policies, the innovative policy shift of India established with the intention of expanding its strategic and economic interests towards ASEAN is a compelling necessity. Obviously, East Asia is witnessing political stability and consistent economic growth and is emerging as a more strategically important region when compared to the highly disturbed and unstable eastern and northern neighbours of India. Consequently, India's ambitious Act East Policy is a compelling economic as well as strategic necessity. However, it is a well-known fact that any policy without the active cooperation and involvement of the people will be a self-defeating initiative. For instance, China and most of the developing countries are facing a lot of resistance from the local people against the so-called developmental initiatives by governmental enterprises or MNCs. Therefore, it is necessary to involve the North-East people by educating, empowering and involving, them in the positive agenda of Act East. In this context, this paper intends to analyze the challenges of the North East for the successful execution of the Act East Policy. The authors have also come up with potential policy suggestions and remedies for effectively making use of the North Eastern region of India for garnering the desired fruits of India's ambitious Act East Policy.

Act East Policy

The Act East policy of 2014 was launched at the 9th East Asia Summit in Myanmar by the Prime Minister of India, Narendra Modi. In simple terms, the Act East Policy of 2014 is a refined version of the Look East Policy of 1991 which aims at improving economic relations with the East Asian neighbours of India. Besides, it also aims to improve India's ties with the East Asian countries in terms of culture, politics and strategic cooperation in different dimensions.

The Act East Policy of India recognizes the strategic importance of its North-Eastern region as the gateway to the East Asian nations and, for that, the development and process of strengthening the North Eastern region in terms of the economy and infrastructure is a priority in the policy. Understanding the strategic importance, successive Indian governments intend to have a strong relationship with ASEAN nations in all areas—political, cultural, energy and defence fields. Consequently, the Act East Policy emphasizes the importance and viability of having a concrete relationship with Myanmar, Thailand, Cambodia, Laos and Vietnam in particular and ASEAN and Pacific countries in general, as they are also developing nations like India and also have great potentialities in the areas of business, agricultural production, defence sector as well as mineral reserves, which are all very important for the growth and further development of India's economy. While answering a question in Parliament, the Minister of State for External Affairs Gen. Dr. V.K. Singh (Retd.) said,

> *"The Objective of "Act East Policy" is to promote economic cooperation, cultural ties and develop strategic relationship with countries in the Asia-Pacific region through continuous engagement at bilateral, regional and multilateral levels thereby providing enhanced connectivity to the States of North Eastern Region including Arunachal Pradesh and other countries in our neighbourhood. The North East of India has been a priority in our Act East Policy (AEP). AEP provides an interface between North East India including the state of Arunachal Pradesh and the ASEAN region. Various plans at bilateral and regional levels include steady efforts to develop and strengthen the connectivity of Northeast with the ASEAN region through trade, culture, people-to-people contact and physical infrastructure (road, airport, telecommunication, power, etc.). Some of the major projects include Kaladan Multi-modal Transit Transport Project, the India-Myanmar-Thailand Trilateral Highway Project, Rih-Tiddim Road Project, Border Haats, etc."*[1]

Strategic Importance of North-East India

It is a well-known fact that North-Eastern region states of India shares 98 per cent of its border with various neighbouring countries.[2] Obviously, the unique location and highly sensitive neighbours, mainly China, Myanmar and Bangladesh, suggest that this area is strategically very important for India. The North-Eastern region is facing intra-regional and extra-regional challenges. Infiltration, drug trafficking, arms smuggling, cross-border terrorism, dumping of substandard Chinese goods, chemically contaminated variety of foods, poor border management, growing trust deficit among the people, excesses of Indian military forces and insecurity among the women and youth are some of the major strategic challenges.

Potentialities of North-East India

For more than six decades, the North-East has been one of the most neglected areas. This is due to the short-sighted policy of the Union Government which concentrates on border areas for only aggressive and repressive policies towards the problem of insurgency, which is alienating a majority of the people of the region. Moreover, the North-East people have been denied higher educational facilities and job and business opportunities. Consequently, in spite of a huge potential for generating hydroelectric and thermal power, this area has been witnessing frequent power cuts and poor connectivity.[3] However, when compared with the rest of India, the people of the North-East are blessed with English education. The credit for this goes to the English missionaries who established English medium schools. Given an opportunity with adequate entrepreneurial training, the North-East people have a tremendous potential to compete with East Asian economic tigers because of their familiarity and fluency in English. Moreover, untapped natural resources like uranium, coal, natural gas and oil with proper infrastructure for better connectivity can convert the whole North-East into a prosperous and developed gateway of India.

Problems Faced by North-East India

So far, the North East is one of the most volatile and sensitive regions of India beset with numerous types of problems including a spate of insurgency and inability to generate own financial resources.[4] At present, the North-Eastern states are getting grants from the Union Government in the ratio of 90:10.[5] Poor governance, poor industrialization, drug trafficking, human trafficking, fragile ecosystem, poor infrastructure, trust deficit, parallel governments, corruption, poor connectivity, economic isolation, power deficit, absence of credible leadership, unemployment, under-employment and underdevelopment in spite of abundance of natural and human resources are making the North-Eastern region problematic. Above all, the separatist and ethnic insurgencies and local chieftains who do not want connectivity, modernization, industrialization tap the existing resources with the help of the so-called outsider-Indian Government.[6]

Democratic governments tend to delay when it comes to decision-making. Authoritarian and totalitarian governments are known for quick decisions and implementation. Multi-party and multi-ethnic democracies are known for very slow decision-making when it comes to deciding on policy matters. The Act East Policy is one such example, where the Government of India is concerned. While a totalitarian one party-controlled China is aggressively pursuing its expansionist agenda taking advantage of common identities (Han dynasty 92 per cent of the total population[7]), India, a multiparty democracy, is struggling to achieve its aim of economic growth and development. India's North-Eastern region is unique with 98 per cent of its border with other countries and 2 per cent with India. Moreover, the North-East is beset with so many intra- and inter-tribal rivalry and unresolved problems of insurgency. Frequent human rights violations and inward looking and sluggish mentality of youth are bottlenecks for the overall development of the North-East.

At present, insurgents and local businessmen control and run businesses by forming an alliance and conveniently blame the central and state governments for their economic backwardness. Moreover, the people of the region are very suspicious of outside entrepreneurs and consider them as intruders and polluters of their long-cherished cultural tardyons. In this context, attracting outside entrepreneurs and businessman towards the North-East to invest their hard-earned money will be a day dream. Therefore, it is necessary to initiate joint business collaborations involving local and educated entrepreneurs and win their support. To overcome the trust deficit, the Central Government can come up with a new policy initiative of providing entrepreneurial training to local youth involving higher educational institutions and financing them to set up small-scale and medium scale industries.

Solutions and Suggestions

- *Managing inter- and intra-tribal Rivalry*

The North-East is known for people with multiple identities based on their cultural roots. They are highly possessive and inward looking and fond of preserving their geographical and cultural identities and political rights and privileges.[8] Managing diversity is one of the greatest challenges of any transitional democracy. The sensitiveness and trust deficit has instigated so many bloody violent activities in the North East between the major and minor groups, for instance, the Naga and Kuki violence in the 1990s. The deep-rooted conflicts and mistrust cannot be easily healed and erased through commercial or economical gain alone. It is necessary to take a positive humanistic approach to help the younger generation. A unique mechanism may be created to initiate confidence-building measure to overcome the trust deficit among the major players. The people of the North East should go for a paradigm shift by learning from Vietnam, America and now the North Korea-America détente. Higher educational institutions can take the lead in organising conciliating programmes with the support of NGOs and leaders of tribal and religious heads. The possible problem-solving mechanism should include the formula of sharing and utilizing funds and enjoying the fruits of innovation. There may be an inter-tribal coordination committee consisting of panchayat leaders, state representatives, committed NGOs, educationalists and human rights activists to identify problem areas and finalize the problem-solving paradigm. Without such a mechanism, phase two of the Look East policy will not be a success and instead the region will face more strikes, blockades, violence and bloodshed.

One of the ways of addressing inter- and intra-ethnic rivalry is advocating pluralism and positive humanism. The varied ethnic groups should be taught secular democracy where multi-cultural, multi-religious and multi-linguistic communities exist. The racial attacks by super racists reveal the failure the American education system and family foundation.[9] One of the purposes of the Act East policy is to remove all barriers by means of technological innovations and technical educations so as to promote interaction and exchange of ideas. It is necessary to teach the youth and children of the North-East the art of accepting the people of other identities as equals so that they could grow with maturity to deal with the problems, for the quality of maturity alone creates credibility and contact. The quality of credibility and contact will gradually attract investments with a wide network. There is a saying that the best city is one that attracts the best brains of the world. The worst state is the one that exports human resources and imports coolies. Now most of the North East-educated youth are keen on getting jobs elsewhere, preferably in South India, and are even ready to settle there as they are not assured of jobs and peace in their homeland. Resolving inter-tribal problems in a mature way, celebrating diversity, promoting pluralism, connecting the people of the North-East through road, air and water, creating job opportunities and promoting an entrepreneurial culture will attract more and more intelligent people from the rest of the world.

- *Addressing Militancy*

Insurgency is one of the reasons that is affecting the normalcy and development of North-East India. There is nothing wrong in saying that insurgency is one of the reasons for the continuous disturbance of the entire North-East. It has been reported that there are many major and minor insurgency groups actively involved in different areas with different reasons.[10] Most militant groups are known for maintaining their identity and superiority against other groups working for a similar cause. However, they are astutely adapting the strategy of getting technical and weapons support from other militant groups working against India with an objective of subserving their own interests. Inter-militant group coordination is a great challenge facing the North-East. Second factor is the level of support they are receiving from the locals without which no extremist group can survive for a longer time. Thirdly, the militant groups are getting support from across the border to establish their camps and get various types of assistance. Fourthly is the backing of extra-territorial support, mainly by China, which is pursuing a strategic agenda of containing India within the subcontinent by assisting extremist groups like Maoists, red corridors and all the North-Eastern groups and Pakistan in the west. In this context, it is necessary to address the menace of extremism by formulating multifaceted strategies. The insurgency of militants and human rights violations by the Indian military has placed ordinary people between both of them. One of the objectives of any separatist movement is to disrupt the peace and be offensive about the development agenda of the State and Union governments in order to justify their stand that the governments will never deliver to the people but instead exploit their resources with the iron hand of the military.

It has been reported that 5,000 militants are holding 23 lakh people of Manipur in constant fear.[11] It is the same situation in Nagaland which is facing constant blockades by the Nationalist Socialist Council of Nagaland. It's a greatest challenge to bring the militants back to the table to address their genuine concerns. Unless, there are coordinative efforts by the state and central governments to win the militants back to the mainstream and join in the developmental agenda, the so-called economic projects and other developmental packages will be considered a trap by both the natives as well as the militants. At present, the so-called counter-insurgency policies are military centric or police centric as established available evidence.[12] The rebels have close contacts with their counterparts in Myanmar and Bangladesh and are also getting weapons from China. The policy-makers should take the utmost care to address the issue. Firstly, the Government should take the initiative to convince the citizens that the Act East Policy would bring good tidings to the people of the North-East. There should be series of negotiations with the insurgent leaders about the problem-solving attitude of the central and state governments. Secondly, ensure opportunities for the militant leaders to take part in elections and decision-making. Thirdly, the government should initiate a flexible judicial instrument policy as adopted by the Italians in the 1960s[13] to address the terrorist groups by pardoning all the fighters and guaranteeing them educational and employment opportunities. Not knowing the development opportunities is one of the causes of under-development. Both the centre and state governments should utilize the services of all educational institutions, particularly teachers, to organise confidence-building programmes and convey the message of peace, prosperity, cooperation and development. Though it is a tough challenge to win back the highly opinionated and committed militant groups that have internal as well as intra-territorial and extra-territorial support, the collaborative and positive efforts of committed NGOs, dedicated teachers and positive humanists may give dividends in the long run. It is necessary to give the message of Abraham Lincoln that "United we stand and divided we fall."[14]

Confidence Building amongst the People about the Indian Military

Representative democracy is an incomplete democracy and participative and inclusive democracy with transparency and accountability alone can win the support of the people. It is a well-known fact that in any democracy, without the support of the people, it is very difficult to implement even an ideal policy by outsiders. Unlike the Chinese authoritarian system, Indian democracy is known for its open dissent. Obviously, wining and involving the people of the North-East as stakeholders and beneficiaries of the cake of development alone will help the central and state governments to achieve their targets of Act East. Allowing international and mainland greedy corporates to establish their enterprises without addressing social responsibility will not bear fruit. Even though it is a Himalayan task to cure the deep-rooted wounds of the North-East women and the youth who are looking at the Indian military as intruders, outsiders and agents of Indian imperialism, the state and union governments should organize seminars, workshops, symposiums and outreach programmes to win the support of the people.

- *Skill Development and Entrepreneurial Training Programmes*

It is a well-known fact that one of the causes for the fall of the Soviet Union was its failure to invest in higher education with all the disciplines for innovation including the Humanities and Social Science.[15] America continues to be a super power for more than a hundred years in spite of so many challenges. Whenever America faces a crisis, one group of more than 430 universities would come up with innovative and problem-solving techniques.[16] Understandably, any nation that is blessed with strong higher education institutions with committed and foresighted faculty will definitely last long. It is true that, compared with the rest of India, the North-Eastern region is ahead in literacy rate, thanks to the efforts of missionaries. However, the present education system is producing clerical job-oriented graduates. When Soviet Union sent its first satellite into orbit, John F. Kennedy was instrumental in changing the curriculum from top to bottom and set a vision of sending a man to the moon within 10 years.[17] Similarly, the North-East should think about a new common curriculum from bottom to top to face the new situation. School children may be adequately trained in work culture, entrepreneurial training, managerial skill and well-disciplined behaviour like cleanliness, interpersonal relationship, maintaining health and protecting social capital like the Japanese, Koreans and Taiwanese school children.

For training the trainers, all the schools should be equipped with necessary labs and teachers with technical skills. It is high time to go for a Memorandum of Understanding for exchange programmes for teachers with Korean and Japanese educational institutions and student education programmes. It is necessary to go for a massive paradigm shift in the education system to pluck the fruits of the Act East Policy to create new hope. At present, the North-East lacks higher educational institutions; there is only one Indian Institute of Technology located in Guwahati, Assam. The North-East with financial assistance from the Central Government and technical help from South East Asia should think about establishing engineering colleges in all the states to meet the requirements of the changing scenario. All higher educational institutions should establish study centres in the countries of East Asia so that scholars of different institutions gather together for understanding and solving problems collectively. Without a strong think tank, it is impossible for the bureaucracy or the military or election-oriented political leaders to imagine a successful Act East Policy. Higher educational institutions should also strengthen the Humanities and Social Science disciplines in order to protect the culture of the North-East from the onslaught of the negative forces of globalisation. Skill development will also liberate the youth from the clutches of drugs and other bad habits.

Consensus about Policies and Programmes

In most of the transitional democracies, the first or second generation leaders are known for their super ego and dominating and dictating policies. When they are in power, they neglect, under-estimate, condemn, humiliate and harass opposition party leaders. This kind of arrogance and short-sighted mentality of charismatic regional leaders creates problems and hurdles not only for the government exchequer but also paralyzes all the programmes initiated by previous governments. For instance, Tamil Nadu, which is known for its cinema-crazy and egoistic leaders, has paid a heavy price because of the negativity of its leadership. For example, the Karunanidhi government invested more than Rs. 1,500 crore for a new Assembly building and many more crores of rupees for the Anna Library building. But they were systematically downgraded by the egoistic Jayalalitha government.[18] Therefore, the people of the North-East should be ready to learn from the mistakes made by other states if they want to enjoy the fruits of the Act East Policy.

They should develop a culture of consultation, cooperation and consensus for policy formulation. The broad policy should be formulated at the higher levels involving all political party leaders and committed NGOs with credibility who are working among the ordinary people of the state, media persons, intelligentsia, bureaucrats and, above all, scholars from higher educational institutions. It is impossible to formulate a uniform policy to address the needs of all the people for the whole of North-East India is highly sensitive and deeply polarized. The Central

Government should be careful before taking policy decisions. The Delhi-centric armchair-ivory tower bureaucrats should not be allowed to impose their short-sighted and self-defeating agenda without consultation with the local intelligentsia. Any policy without systematic consultation will be a self-defeating one and it may convert the seven sisters into seven enemies and among these seven enemies there may be the possibility of another seventy enemies because of so many identities. Consequently, the Look East and Act East policies may be considered as unwanted and uninvited trouble-making intruders into the homes of the North Eastern population. It is necessary to prepare the mindset of the people to accept the innovative changes as heavenly angels coming with heavenly manna to uplift their standard of living on par with other developed states like Taiwan, Singapore and Malaysia. The government should take special initiatives to prepare the minds of the people to accept the change as positive since any innovative programme without the wholehearted involvement of the people will create more problems than solve them. Weaning the people away from inward-looking parochialism, self-contentment, lazy, sluggish, indifferent, pleasure seeking, procrastinating mentality towards outward-looking entrepreneurs and skilled-workers is the need of the hour.

- ***Smart Villages Apart from Smart Cities***

According to most environmentalists and human rights activists, the so-called smart cities and economic free zones are self-serving innovative ideas of corporate giants which systematically sidelined, alienated, discriminated and ignored the masses and their rights justifying their wrongs in the name of the so-called economic free zones and smart cities.[19] Moreover, they are creating environmental problems—polluting the air, water and the soil because of massive construction programmes, excavations, etc. It also created a security zone, displaced so many sons of the soil and resulted in the emergence of a new class within each and every state. Therefore, the so-called smart cities and special economic zone may be replaced with self-contented, self-reliant, self-empowered well-connected villages in the North-East. All the villages should be connected with proper roads, water supply, uninterrupted power and educational facilities. Policy-makers can think about establishing small manufacturing units in each and every village to create healthy completion so that they will produce competitive high-quality products to sell in the international market. Power generation may be initiated through non-conventional sources, solar and windmills instead of thermal plants that pollute the environment.

- ***Common Power Grid and Non-conventional Resources***

Energy is the basis of successful economic activities. Uninterrupted and guaranteed power supply is the backbone of any manufacturing unit apart from technology, finance and human resources. At present, most of the North-East is suffering because of serious power cuts for so many years.[20] If policy makers are really interested in implementing a successful Act East Policy they should give top priority to meet the energy needs of all the states. The North-East is has a high potentiality for hydro-solar and wind energy. There should be a North-Eastern state power grid to achieve surplus power within 10 years to supply power to all remote villages. It needs statesmanship, commitment, far-sighted thinking and wholehearted cooperation of all the North-Eastern states and Union Government. If each and every policy initiative is politicised, the North-East will face more darkness than light. The leadership should show maturity in the form of their ability to cooperate.

- *Sharing the Cake of Development*

One of the negative impacts of the present phase of globalisation is that all development-oriented initiatives have become skewed in favour of the few rich. Consequently, the ever-growing monstrous inequality is making a mockery of the so-called developmental policies. On one side, the government is privatizing profits and nationalizing losses. On the other, the number of unemployed is growing day by day. According to statistics, one per cent of Indians own 58 per cent of the country's wealth.[21] The purpose of the first generation capitalist was profit-making with a humanist face. However, the present crony capitalism is number one enemy of welfare and believes in accumulating wealth by any means. If the policy makers intend to formulate policies to sub-serve only the interests of MNCs at the cost of the middle class and the poor, it will damage the reputation of North-East India. It is high time to think about a new model of inclusive growth of a win-win situation by sharing the cake of development.

- *Strong Consumer Movements*

US President John F. Kennedy once said, "If properly organized, consumer forums are the most powerful body in this world."[22] He also said that the biggest organization is that of consumers. Consumer forums with educated and well-informed consumers are sources of strength for any quality-centric industry or sources of destruction for any manipulative unit. At present, the majority of consumers in transitional countries are not aware of their rights and privileges and are also not aware of the choices of their products. Consequently, they become easy prey to tricky, manipulative, greedy corporates. In this context, the people of the North-East should form strong consumer forums. Further, to protect consumer rights, it is necessary to form a strong consumer forum to create awareness about the rights and privileges of consumers. At present, corporates are adapting all the manipulative techniques possible to colonize people's minds to sell their sub-standard products including food items at the cost of high-quality and time-tested traditional foods and medicines. The Jallikattu movement in 2017 was an eye-opener in Tamil Nadu to boycott the chemical bottle and plastic packet products of corporates and youth were encouraged to drink traditional drinks like lemon juice, coconut water, etc.[23] It is the responsibility of the North-Eastern states to learn and explore their traditional food habits and time-tested traditional medicines. In South India, unlike allopathic medicines, traditional Siddha and Ayurveda are preferred for treatment. Now in Tamil Nadu and other southern states, people are creating awareness about environment-friendly, health-friendly, wealth-friendly habits through social media. Each and every North-Eastern state should establish tribal-herbal research units to abandon chemical-oriented Western medical practices. The people of the North-East should be ready to learn from the bitter experience of other states and should think about forming strong consumer forums and popularizing consumer rights and privileges to protect them from the evil designs of greedy corporates. The educated in the North-East should take a systematic initiative to create awareness about health-damaging corporate bottled drinks, preservative-oriented packed foods, Western processed meats and factory-centric preservative tinned foodstuffs.

It is a well-known fact that most of the corporate food items cause many health issues like diabetics, blood pressure, obesity, digestion problems, skin disease, liver problems and cancer.[24] Consequently, corporates will establish many so-called health centres to sell their highly-priced pharmaceutical items to loot the public. The people of the North East should carefully prepare themselves to face the new challenge by promoting healthy, time-tested food habits. Western corporates are also known for producing substandard items by using popular labels just for Indian consumers, justifying that it suits Indian conditions. It is necessary to create awareness about the comparative quality of products supplied by the corporate and available in India and elsewhere. Connecting India with other East Asian countries is an advantage to the North-East as they can compare the quality of products sold in Singapore with those in the North-East. The consumer forums can mobilise and create awareness through social media so that the public can easily boycott substandard products. Here also, committed NGOs, human rights activists, teachers and consumer forums can form a grand alliance to safeguard their interests against manipulative, greedy corporates.

- ***Protecting Human Rights and Women Empowerment***

In general, the women from the North-East enjoy better education, greater mobility and visibility than women of other parts of India.[25] However the unemployment rate, domestic violence against women, alcoholism, sexual violence and harassment by security forces and local chieftains are the growing challenges they are facing.[26] Unless they are properly educated, economically empowered and adequate protected it is impossible to formulate a win-win policy in the North-East. It is necessary to provide leadership skill to the women to face the new changes brought about by connectivity. One of the victims of modernization is the family foundation which has been shaken by the negative forces of technological innovation. Materialism and extreme individualism has resulted in many social problems like divorce, alienation, deserted parents, drug addiction and all forms of violence that are compromising highly nurtured family values. Women are the real home builders and are the first teachers of their children and are expected to teach them moral and ethical values by practising them at home. The ultra-modern feminism, individualism, don't care attitude, etc., will destroy the highly precious, irreparable social capital. The North-Eastern women should be taught in the higher educational institutions and by committed NGOs the importance of family foundation, moral ethical values and the importance of investing their time in their children apart from entrepreneurial training, for materialism without moral values will swallow everything.

- *Strengthening Panchayati Raj and Good Governance*

In general, the latest phase of Liberalisation, Privatisation and Globalisation is considered by most socialist scholars, residents and local people as an uncontrollable, unregulated monster intruding into their territory and destroying their culture, identity, local economy, and colonizing the minds of the people through highly manipulative market techniques using the latest media to sell their products. The dissent in the tribal areas of Andhra Pradesh, Odisha and Bihar reveals that the tribals are not only losing their lands and livelihood but also their constitutional privilege of tribal identity because of forced migration from their comfort zone to the mainland. Consequently, MNCs with the help of the central bureaucrats and other agencies are exploiting the mineral and natural resources and creating under-development in the name of modernization and industrialization. As mentioned elsewhere, the highly sensitive and unprepared people of the North-East should be cautious before implementing projects of Act East. Inclusive growth or capitalism with a human face is the other side of the same coin. If policy makers are particular about sharing the cake of development, it is necessary to involve local people in policies at all levels.

To achieve this objective, the local Panchayati Raj should be strengthened financially and higher educational institutions should organise leadership training for Panchayati Raj Institutions and help them to formulate policies and programmes to meet local needs. At present, the Delhi-centric armchair policy makers are outsourcing their job to multinationals. Consequently, the research wings of multinationals are drafting their policies and programmes and trying to formalize them with the tag of the Central Government policies and programmes without addressing the genuine needs of the local people. This Delhi-centric and corporate-centric approach will be considered neo colonialism, which will never yield any results to the people. The North East population has a great record of maintaining clean villages as a role model as is evident in the case of Mawlynnong, in the state of Meghalaya, which is being proclaimed as Asia's cleanest village and is a popular tourist destination because of its cleanliness and well-maintained environment. Given an opportunity with adequate training, job opportunities and entrepreneurial skill, they will know the art of governance efficiently. As Mahatma Gandhi dreamt, the self-reliant village is the real asset of India. An empowered Panchayati Raj Institution may take so many positive initiatives like restricting drug trafficking, human trafficking, illicit arms trade, discouraging militancy, maintaining law and order, protecting the environment, preserving and promoting traditional products, nurturing their traditional medicines, safeguarding their cultural values, guaranteeing women's rights and encouraging youth to acquire entrepreneurial skills. Certainly, only an empowered Panchayati Raj Institution can play a role of positive change agent in the whole of the North-East. Unlike rest of India, North-Eastern states like Manipur, Nagaland and Assam are known for frequent bandhs, blockades and boycotts in addition to regular power cuts.

The empowered Panchayati Raj Institution will definitely go a long way in addressing the much-needed decentralization of administration in the region. If the present government fails to strengthen Panchayati Raj Institutions, the people of the North-East may never be empowered and there may be a danger of more and more insurgent groups citing the governmental failures. Women representation in periodic elections, adequate funding for local infrastructure, small scale industry, settling disputes, youth empowerment programmes, skill training for manufacturing and exports, protection of youth from drugs, etc., can be better managed and understood through the initiatives of empowered Panchayati Raj Institutions, which will have a further positive impact on the credibility and success of the Act East Policy.

- ***Creating Connectivity and Promoting Tourism***

One of the secrets of success of the American dream is that the citizens there have succeeded in laying down strong spacious strategic roads connecting the north, south, west and east through railways and air for quick transportation of goods, commodities and people. Consequently, Americans love travelling comfortably without much difficulty. The taxpayers' money is utilised by the federal government for helping the people move from place to place. India's North-Eastern region is known for its natural beauty and should be a tourist hotspot and could be converted into a hub of immense business potential. Prime Minister Modi repeatedly assured the people of the North-East to connect all the states by air, road and waterways. The BJP success in the recently-held elections in the North-East may be a moral boost for the government and it may generously finance multibillion dollar projects to connect the states in the North-East. The tall promises of central and state governments should be met with adequate resources and meticulous execution of plans with people's participation. If all the 'seven sisters' are well connected, they will attract more and more investors as well as tourists not only from India but also from East Asian countries. Further, higher educational institutions may be encouraged to set up tourism and management departments to meet the need of tourists.

Conclusion

The Act East Policy is a historical necessity for India to expand its political, economic and strategic outreach. To reach the East Asian countries, the 'seven sisters' of the North East should be beautified, empowered, equipped and prepared to receive the bridegroom of development. Winning the hearts of alienated, disconnected, underdeveloped people in the North-East who suffer from a deficit of trust is a Himalayan task. At present, the BJP electoral managers have succeeded in forming their governments with their coalition partners in almost all the North-Eastern states and that is an added advantage. The Modi government's tall promises of connecting the North-East, building infrastructure and empowering the people need a lot of cooperative, collaborative efforts of the centre and the state with the people of the North-East. It is necessary to go for a paradigm shift in policy-making involving the people of the North-East, guaranteeing them a share in the cake of development. Without preparing them for a new positive change, it will be nearly impossible to achieve the desired results of the Act East Policy.

ENDNOTES

1 Retrieved from *http://pib.nic.in/newsite/PrintRelease.aspx?relid=133837* on 16 March, 2018

2 Retrieved from https://www.sevendiary.com/single-northeast-state-shares-international-borders/ on 16 March 2018

3 Pranjal, Kumar & Phukan (Dec 04, 2015) Conflict in Northeast India: Issues, Causes and Concern, *Nelive* Retrieved from https://www.nelive.in/north-east/opinion/conflict-northeast-india-issues-causes-and-concern on 16 March 2018

4 Ranabir Samaddar, Peace Studies: An Introduction to the Concept, Scope, and Themes, Sage Publications, 2004

5 Barua, A. & Das, S. K. (2008). Perspectives on Growth and Development in the Northeast: The Look East Policy and Beyond. *Margin: The Journal of Applied Economic Research*, 2(4), 327-350.

6 Chaudhury, Roy Dipanjan (January 24, 2018) India's Act East policy complements Asean's Act West strategy, *The Economic Times*. Retrieved from https://blogs.economictimes.indiatimes.com/et-commentary/view-indias-act-east-policy-complements-aseans-act-west-strategy/ on 16th March 2018

7 Retrieved from http://tiansheng.expertscolumn.com/article/why-are-majority-chinese-called-han-peoplenationality on 16 March, 2018

8 Retrieved from https://in.boell.org/2009/02/28/conflict-northeast-india-issues-causes-and-concern on 16 March 2018

9 Retrieved from https://www.nytimes.com/2018/01/20/opinion/racism-america.html on 16 March 2018

10 Retrieved from https://www.tandfonline.com/doi/abs/10.1080/1057610X.2013.842132?src=recsys&journalCode=uter20 on March 16, 2018

11 For details see: Madan B. Lokur (2016), "Judgment on Extra Judicial Execution Victim Families Association (EEVFAM) & Anr", [http://supremecourtofindia.nic.in], Accessed on 10 March 2018. URL:http://judis.nic.in/supremecourt/qrydisp.aspx?filename=39896

12 Retrieved from http://www.thehindu.com/opinion/lead/For-a-review-of-counter-insurgency-doctrine/article16366244.ece on March 16, 2018

13 Retrieved from https://scholarship.law.cornell.edu/cgi/viewcontent.cgi?article=1059&context=ijli on March 16, 2018

14 Retrieved from https://apessay.com/order/?rid=56311004f456c5a6 on March 16, 2018

15 Retrieved from https://www.cogentoa.com/article/10.1080/2331186X.2017.1399968 on March 16, 2018

16 Retrieved from https://www.ed.gov/news/speeches/education-only-solution on March 16, 2018

17 Retrieved from https://history.nasa.gov/moondec.html on March 16, 2018

18 Retrieved from http://www.thehindu.com/news/cities/chennai/karunanidhis-dream-building-begins-functioning-as-hospital/article4362068.ece on March 16, 2018

19 Retrieved from https://my.vanderbilt.edu/greencities/files/2014/08/King-built-environment.pdf on March 16, 2018

20 Borah, Pallabi (September 2007), Power and Energy Scenario of the Northeast, *Dialogue* Vol. 9, No. 1

21 Retrieved from http://www.thehindu.com/business/Economy/Richest-1-own-58-of-total-wealth-in-India-Oxfam/article17044486.ece on March 16, 2018

22 Retrieved from http://www.consumerssa.com/consumer-rights/ on March 16, 2018

23 Retrieved from http://www.livemint.com/Politics/4yTp3306JCVDee2CXhPdTO/Riding-on-Jallikattu-protests-Tamil-Nadu-traders-look-to-ba.html on March 16, 2018

24 Retrieved from https://articles.mercola.com/sites/articles/archive/2008/01/12/what-happens-to-your-body-within-an-hour-of-drinking-a-coke.aspx on March 16, 2018

25 Das, Jogdesh (Sept-October 2012) Women's Human Rights in North East India, *IOSR Journal of Humanities and Social Science (JHSS)* Vol. 3, issue 4, pp. 34-35

26 Ibid

REFERENCES

Agrawal, P., Gokarn, S., Mishra, V., Parikh, K., & Sen, K. (2016). *Economic Restructuring in East Asia and India: Perspectives on Policy Reform.* Springer.

Asher, M. G. & Sen, R. (2005). India-East Asia integration: a win-win for Asia. *Economic and Political Weekly*, 3932-3940.

Baruah, S. (2009). *Beyond counter-insurgency: Breaking the impasse in northeast India.* New Delhi: OUP.

—— (2007). Postfrontier blues: Toward a new policy framework for Northeast India. *Policy Studies*, (33), I.

Batabyal, A. (2006). Balancing China in Asia: a realist assessment of India's Look East strategy. *China Report*, 42(2), 179-197.

Bhaumik, S. (2009). *Troubled Periphery: The Crisis of India's North East.* Sage Publications India.

Barua, A. & Das, S. K. (2008). Perspectives on Growth and Development in the Northeast: The Look East Policy and Beyond. *Margin: The Journal of Applied Economic Research*, 2(4), 327-350.

Bhattacharjee, J. B. (2007). *Roots of Insurgency in Northeast India.* New Delhi: Akansha Publishing House.

Das, S. K. (2010). India's Look East policy: Imagining a new geography of India's Northeast. *India Quarterly*, 66(4), 343-358.

Downie, E. (2015). Manipur and India's Act East" Policy. *The Diplomat.*

Grare, F. & Mattoo, A. (Eds.). (2003). *Beyond the rhetoric: the economics of India's Look East policy,* (Vol. 2). Manohar Publishers.

Ghoshal, B. (2007). Some New Thoughts on India's Look East Policy. *IPCS Issue Brief,* 54(1).

Haokip, T. (2015). India's Look East Policy: Prospects and Challenges for Northeast India. *Studies in Indian Politics*, 3(2), 198-211.

Haokip, T. (2015). *India's Look East policy and the Northeast.* Sage Publications India

Jaffrelot, C. (2003). India's Look East policy: an Asianist strategy in perspective. *India Review*, 2(2), 35-68.

Jia, R. (2007). India's "Look East" Policy and its Development [J]. *South Asian Studies Quarterly*, 4, 004.

Jianrong, C. (2006). Look East Policy and Strategy of Balance of Great Powers: Perception Change in India and ASEAN [J]. *Southeast Asian Studies*, 3, 011.

Lacina, B. (2009). The problem of political stability in Northeast India: Local ethnic autocracy and the rule of law. *Asian Survey*, 49(6), 998-1020.

Ladwig III, W. C. (2009). Delhi's Pacific ambition: Naval power, "Look East" and India's emerging influence in the Asia-Pacific. *Asian Security*, 5(2), 87-113.

Lee, L. (2015). India as a nation of consequence in Asia: The potential and limitations of India's 'Act East' policy. *The Journal of East Asian Affairs*, 29(2), 67.

Levesque, J. (2007). Mekong-Ganga Cooperation Initiative: India's Underused Soft Power Tool. SAEA Group.

Maini, T. S. (2014). India's "Look East" Policy Begins with Myanmar. *The Diplomat*, 8.

McDuie-Ra, D. (2008). Between national security and ethno-nationalism: The regional politics of development in Northeast India. *Journal of South Asian Development*, 3(2), 185-210.

Mehrotra, L. (2012). India's Look East Policy: Its Origin and Development. *Indian Foreign Affairs Journal*, 7(1), 75.

Mero, M. K. (2005). Indo-Myanmar border trade in the light of India's Look East policy. *Indo-Myanmar border trade, status, problems and potential*, 64-73.

Mishra, R. (2018). From Look East to Act East: Transitions in India's Eastward Engagement. In *International Relations and Asia's Southern Tier* (pp. 321-340). Springer, Singapore.

Naidu, G.V.C. (2013). India and East Asia: The Look East policy. *Perceptions*, 18(1), 53.

Nanda, P. (2003). *Rediscovering Asia: Evolution of India's Look-East Policy.* Lancer Publishers.

Pant, H.V. (2007). India in the Asia–Pacific: Rising ambitions with an eye on China. *Asia-Pacific Review*, 14(1), 54-71.

Pattanaik, K. Jajati. (2015). Act East Through the North-East. *Mainstream*, Vol. LIII, No. 16. Retrieved from http://www.mainstreamweekly.net/article5596.html

Ram, A.N. (Ed.). (2012). *Two Decades of India's Look East Policy: Partnership for Peace, Progress and Prosperity.* Institute of Southeast Asian Studies.

Rajendram, D. (2014). *India's New Asia-Pacific Strategy: Modi Acts East.* Lowy Institute for International Policy.

Sajjanhar, A. (2016). Taking Stock of India's Act East Policy. *ORF Issue Brief* (142).

Singh, Niranjan & Lairenjam. (2017). Geo-Politics & Role of Skill Development in India's Act East Policy. *India Foundation Journal*, Vol. V, No. 4.

Sridharan, K. (2005). The ASEAN Region in India's 'Look East' Policy. *India and ASEAN: Foreign Policy Dimensions for the 2Ist Century.* London: New Centuries Publications.

Strachan, A.L., Kang, H.K. & Sinha, T. (2009). India's Look East policy: a critical assessment. Interview with Ambassador Rajiv Sikri'. New Delhi: *Southeast Asian Research Programme, Institute of Peace and Conflict Studies.*

Thomas, C. J., Singh, N.B. & Das, G. (2013). *Indo-Myanmar border trade: Status, problems and potentials.*

Verghese, B.G. (2013). *India's Northeast resurgent: Ethnicity, insurgency, governance, development.*

3

Act East Policy for North East India: Prospect, Ethnicity, Soft Power

Lalengkima

Introduction: From Look East to Act East

India's search for economic development resulted in the creation of its famous 'Look East Policy' in the early 1990s. The Look East Policy has today matured into a dynamic and action-oriented 'Act East Policy'. External Affairs Minister Sushma Swaraj announced at Hanoi, Vietnam, in August 2014 that the time was ripe for India to adopt an Act East Policy, not just 'look' but to 'act' accordingly (*India News*, 2014). The Prime Minister of India at the 12th ASEAN India Summit and the 9th East Asia Summit held in Nay Pyi Taw, Myanmar, in November 2014, formally enunciated the Act East Policy (Parameswaran, 2014). Nevertheless, the Look East was converted to Act East; India already began border connectivity with East Asian states like Myanmar. Cooperation like the Mekong-Ganga Corporation covering Thailand, Myanmar, Cambodia, Laos and Vietnam on the one hand; and the Bay of Bengal Initiative for Multi-Sectoral Technical and Economic Cooperation (BIMSTEC) on the other had already became a strategic cooperation for India which includes tourism, trade, technology, investment, culture, education, transport, etc. (Overview, 2018).

Moreover, India already had become a Sectoral Dialogue Partner of ASEAN in 1992, Dialogue Partner in 1996 and Summit Level Partner in 2002. In 2012, the relationship between ASEAN and India was upgraded into a Strategic Partnership (ASEAN India, 2018). Since the implementation of the Look East Policy, ASEAN has been an important business partner for India on the global stage. Table 1 highlights the growth of trade between India and ASEAN for the last two years.

Table 1

Sector/Particulars	*2015-16*	*2016-17*
India's total trade with ASEAN	US$ 65 billion	US$ 70 billion
India's export to ASEAN	US$ 25 billion	US$ 31.07 billion

Source: Ministry of External Affairs, http://mea.gov.in/aseanindia/20-years.htm

Investment flows are also substantial in both ways, with ASEAN accounting for approximately 12.5 per cent of investment flows into India since 2000. FDI inflows into India from ASEAN between April 2000 to August 2017 was about US$ 514.73 billion, while FDI outflows from India to ASEAN countries, from April 2007 to March 2015, was about US$ 38.672 billion. The ASEAN-India Free Trade Area has been completed with the coming into force of the ASEAN-India Agreements on Trade in Service and Investments on 1 July 2015 (ASEAN India, 2018).

Trade, investment and the flow of technology was benefited between India and East Asian Nations. Thereby, the Act East Policy is one of the most crucial aspects of the foreign policy of India and yet there are so many difficulties in implementing it. The major doorway of the policy, that is North East India, happens to be a home of different tribes having distinctive cultures and traditions which in turn create some problems for implementing the policy smoothly. The issues of migration, ethnicity, distinctive political culture and divergent socialization, border disputes, transportation and connectivity are becoming some of the hindrances for the smooth functioning of the Act East Policy. Keeping all these in mind this paper intends to focus on some of the problems and prospects of the Act East Policy especially from an ethnic perspective.

The main objectives of this paper are divided into:

1. To highlight the problem of ethnic integration with the mainland.
2. To find cultural similarities between North East India and East Asia.
3. To set the North East as an example of ethnic harmony through the Act East Policy.

Problem of Integration

The problem of ethnic integration of North East India with the mainland is one of the biggest tasks faced by the Indian government in the post-independence period. Ethnic consciousness rose steadily since the beginning of the twentieth century. It culminated during the late 1980s and early 1990s which found its expression in the rise of various insurgent movements demanding ethnic homelands ranging from autonomy to secessionism from India.

The history of North East India during the medieval period was already linked with the South and East Asian nations rather than the mainland. The connectivity of trade, travellers, scholars and pilgrims between North East India and East Asia has already become famous among scholars of the present era. The historical ties of North East Indian ethnic groups such as the Tai-Ahoms and the Khasis with Southeast Asia—including China's Yunnan province are well known (Ludden, 2003).

After the independence of India, the age-old issues of integration still persist. Many scholars believe that the cultural gap between the people in the North-East and those of the mainland is so deep that the region is unlikely to be psychologically integrated with India in the near future. The reason behind this issue of integration began from the medieval period in which the moral connection with the East Asian countries is stronger than with the mainland. As a result, it is alleged that the people of the Northeast are alienated from the rest of India.

As such, the Government of India pursues different inclusive policies like seat reservation in public offices, schools and other institutions; a separate autonomous body for most tribes in the region and scholarship and compensation; but all these inclusive policies still fail to totally integrate the people of North-East India with the mainland. To find the reason behind all these issues, one must look from the perspective of political theory and philosophy such as the issue of reverse discrimination and the like...which is not the intention of this paper.

Anyhow, since the integration issue still persists in India, the Act East Policy which meant to transform North-East India to a whole new level of development could not run smoothly as expected. Some thought that the integration problem intensifies secessionist feeling among the people in the North-East who in turn hindered not only the development of the erstwhile Look East Policy but also some of the major government policies.

Cultural Ties as 'Soft Power'

If India looks for immediate benefit of the Look East policy it should involve the deepening of India's cooperation in trade and investment, technology, transport and communications and energy and tourism with its eastern neighbours. Sanjib Baruah, a staunch proponent of a continental Look East policy, advocated that "India should take more advantage of North-East India's history and culture as a soft power resource" (Baruah S., 2003). This involves reviving the shared historical and cultural ties between the people of Northeast India and Southeast Asia.

The concept of soft power in international politics and the concept of soft power in this paper are not the same. Having a few similarities, the soft power of this paper is the cultural similarities between the North-East and East Asia. However, the concept of soft power was defined by Nye as the ability to do or command another country by making use of cultural and other social values to connect people. He describes the determinants of soft power as growing out of "a country's cultural...out of our values—democracy and human rights, when we live up to them" (Nye Jr., J., 2004). Power is the ability to alter the behaviour of others to get what you want. There are basically three ways to do it: coercion (sticks), payments (carrots), and attraction (soft power) (Nye Jr., J., 2006).

Accordingly, the cultural similarities between North-East India and East Asia could be used as a 'soft power' to strengthen the relationship with South East Asian nations. In order to boost the national economy, it is imperative for a country to cultivate cultural exchanges with people and have direct contact with them. As already mentioned, the cultural ties between the North-East and the East Asian nations had been already a part of a bond, a sentimental bond between them which could be benefitted in terms of trade and flow of technology. This bond could be transformed or converted as part of the backbone of the Act East Policy so that there could be a robust economic development for India and East Asian nations.

During the last couple of years, there were movies from East Asian states that highlighted the cultural similarities between the North-East and South East Asia. For example, the movie called 'Warriors of the Rainbow' depicted such similarities in terms of social life, political life; even in the way they dress and sing. All these similarities could be transformed into a sentimental tie which in turn will create people-to-people direct contact, and, lastly, in turn, boost the nation's economy. The Act East policy should make sure of it. There is no other Indian foreign policy that could benefit the ethnic similarities between the North-East and East Asia.

A Home of Ethnic Harmony and Tourist Destination

Different writers, scholars and journalists often used to describe the location of the North-East as landlocked, situated between international borders, locked from almost all sides except the Chicken's Neck in Siliguri. However, being a landlocked area, the place is a home of different ethnic tribes with some tribes having a close resemblance to each other. Divergence in the ethnic tribe could be an example for the whole world. There were talks on ethnic violent activities, looting, arson, militancy, etc.; all these activities have threatened the whole of North-East India for a long period. But now peace has begun to prosper in the region (of course, there are still some issues) and the Government must see that ethnic peace and harmony in the North-East must be retained as far as possible so that the region could become an example of peace and tranquillity for the world.

The region could become an image of ethnic harmony and the Act East Policy must look forward to seeing or making sure of it. Bordered by four countries and facing towards southern China and Southeast Asia, India's North-East can work as a driving force for regional development and send a political message of ethnic harmony to a diversified world in an era of globalisation. B.G. Verghese observes that the "Northeast cannot ignore its immediate neighbourhood, which is far more international than national." (Verghese, 2002). The border of the North-East which is international rather than national is a part of its culture. This border shares more values than the 'Chicken's Neck' in Siliguri because of ethnicity. Therefore, ethnic issues must be solved as far as possible.

Different writers and scholars believe that the Government of India must actively involve itself in solving the age-old ethnic problems in the North-East region (Sundaram, 2013). Until and unless this age-old ethnic issue is solved by the Government, there can be any active foreign policies for the region which would likely boost a nation's or region's economy. Therefore, the Act East Policy must also address the North-East's immediate neighbourhood keeping in mind the region's ethnic divergence and solving unsolved tribal issues.

Once the ethnic issues within the region are solved, the North-East could attract more tourists, especially from Asia, because there are cultural similarities between the two which could become the main reason for tourist attraction. The revenue from the tourism departments of the North-Eastern states is meagre in comparison with the other parts of India. For instance, with respect to outbound tourism, a total of 3.1 thousand people living in Mizoram undertook foreign trips during 2010-11. This is 0.03 per cent of the total outbound tourists of India. In 2015-16 the overall (direct+indirect) share of tourism in the state Gross Domestic Product (GDP) was 5.27 per cent. And the overall (direct+indirect) share of tourism employment in the total state was 6.62 per cent (Ministry of Tourism, 2016). The revenue earned by the Tourism Department for the same period reached Rs. 222.01 lakh (Government of Mizoram, 2017).

Moreover, the number of tourists in Mizoram declined during the last five years. Not only in Mizoram but also in other parts of the North-East, the number of tourists from foreign places does not increase as expected by many policy framers who dreamt about the North-East becoming a tourist destination of India. The numbers of tourists in Mizoram for the past five years can be seen in Table 2.

Table 2

Year	*Domestic*	*Foreign*	*Total*
2013-13	64,631	712	65,343
2013-14	64,583	906	65,489
2014-15	67,554	862	68,416
2015-16	66,583	830	67,413
2016-17	38,648	405	39,053

Source: Government of Mizoram: Mizoram Economic Survey 2016-17

In Mizoram alone, the share of tourism to the state GDP in 2015-16 is too low. The reason behind this may be the location and climate of the region. But most tourists want to visit a landlocked area having strange weather and climate with divergent ethnic groups like North-East India. But still, the vision of the region's politicians was to make the North-East a destination for tourists from all over the world. Some arguments stem from issues like Inner Line Regulation which somehow makes tourists reluctant to visit some parts of the region, namely, Mizoram. The Act East Policy must seek to rectify all these errors in the social setting of the region. It might be difficult to change the social life of the people through certain policies, but it could be done to attract more tourists which could be a way to maintain ethnic prosperity in the region.

Conversion of Conflict to Sentiment

The problems of Naga and Bengali infiltration in Assam, the Bodo movement, BRU issues in Mizoram and Tripura, Chakma refugees in Arunachal and Mizoram, Hajong refugees in Arunachal, etc., are some of the unsolved issues of the North-East region. Many ethnic communities like the Kukis, Mizos, Nagas, etc., were divided into two by the separation of Burma and British India in 1937 (Haokip, 2015). The partition of India in 1947 by the British has alienated numerous ethnic communities of the region. The imaginary political boundary was drawn by Cyril Radcliffe in Delhi before partition divided the Garos and Khasis. Thus, these borders forced the ethnic communities to live in different countries. It also disrupted old trade routes and deprived the communities in North-East India of trading with the other side of the international boundary.

However, the feeling of tension between tribes of the North-East and of its neighbours still persist. For example, the infiltration of Chakmas and Chins from Bangladesh and Myanmar to Mizoram creates a feeling of tension and conflict between Bangladeshis (including all inhabitants like Bawm, i.e., a part of the Mizo tribe) and Mizoram on the one hand and between Mizoram and the Myanmarese (including Chin, Kuki and any other Mizo sub-tribe or kin) on the other. All these feeling of tension, hatred towards each other and conflict could be transformed or converted into a sentimental feeling that could integrate the people regardless of their international territories. For example, the Government of India through its Act East policy, could intensify ethnic integrity of the North-East with that of its neighbours as well as with other parts of East Asia. The Government must sponsor ethnic integration like holding a famous festival in other parts of East Asian.

The partition of India in 1947 caused the extreme geo-political isolation of the North-East, making it emotionally, though not quite physically, South Asia's third landlocked state along with Bhutan and Nepal. The loss of connectivity and market access all around set its economy back by at least a quarter century. The impact of this was not fully understood (Verghese, 2002). The old trade routes between the immediate neighbourhood of the North-East which are international have been tempered down since independence. Therefore, some persons argue that it is more difficult to reach the neighbourhood of the North-East than to reach another part of the world, one writer observes:

> *"Hostilities between India and Pakistan have cut old routes of communication and mobility across new national borders more dramatically than almost anywhere in the world. The Bengal-Assam railway tracks from Guwahati to Dhaka were torn up at the Cachar-Sylhet border, in 1965. Now it is much easier to communicate by phone or mail between Dhaka and London than between Dhaka and Guwahati" (Ludden, 2003).*

If the above argument is correct, it means that trade and the flow of capital, as well as technology between immediate neighbours (like Myanmar, Bangladesh, China and Bhutan) is far less difficult than anticipated. Equally, the entire North-East must be treated in all strategic respects as a single, unified entity, a federation within a federation. While the distinctive identities and concerns of the 'Seven Sisters' plus Sikkim must be respected in every way, they cannot prosper without regional integration. This alone will ensure cohesion, overall development, coordination and economies of scale. This understanding too has to dawn fully on all concerned (Verghese, 2002).

In the last few decades since the liberation of Bangladesh in 1971, there have been powerful economic and environmental push factors in Bangladesh that combined with politically and economically motivated pull-factors in India leading to an unending influx of Bangladeshis into the border states of North-East India. Due to atrocities committed by the majority Muslims, displacement by the Kaptai Dam reservoir in 1964 and the non-payment of compensation by the erstwhile East Pakistan government in the Chittagong Hill Tracts, thousands of Chakmas were displaced and sought refuge in India. In 1964, the Government of India temporarily resettled about 35,000 Chakmas in Lohit, Changlang and Papumpare districts of the North East Frontier Agency (present-day Arunachal Pradesh). Others ended up in Cachar, Mizoram and Tripura. The recipient communities, especially the students' unions, in Arunachal Pradesh and Mizoram often expressed their resentment and protest over the demographic change. There are an estimated 40,000 to 50,000 Chin refugees in Mizoram who fled there to escape abuses after 1988 when the Myanmarese government cracked down violently on the pro-democracy movement. There are also recent instances of the Meiteis of Manipur being concerned about the immigration of Chin refugees into different parts of the hill districts especially Churachandpur, Bangladeshi Muslims in Jiribam sub-division bordering Cachar and migrant labourers and Marwari businessmen in Imphal Valley who are mainly from Bihar and Gujarat. In Meghalaya, the Khasi Students' Union, from time to time, expressed their resentment over the influx of migrants from Bangladesh and Nepal. Although Nepali and Chakma migration had stopped after a certain period of time, the migration of Muslims from Bangladesh continues till date. All these ethnic violent activities that stem from threat, tension, hate, etc., must be converted into sentimental feeling. This is the task of the Government through its policies to support ethnic integration.

Conclusion

Since the implementation of the Look East Policy in the 1990s, there were developments in terms of infrastructure and capital flow which began from trade and investment. The cooperation initiatives like Mekong-Ganga and other measures could be implemented only if there is peace and harmony between India and other South-East Asian states. To build good relations with neighbours rapidly, it is imperative to attain cultural ties through which there could be a strong bond between countries which in turn will create economic development.

If the Act East Policy is to benefit the North-East, there must be ethnic integration between the tribes of the region; there must be moral ties and integration between the mainland and people of the North-East; there must also be a sentimental feeling between North-Eastern tribes and East Asian states. When all these integrational ties are fully achieved, only then, will the Act East Policy be successful. So, the policy must also seek to rectify ethnic errors in the North-East.

REFERENCES

ASEAN India. (2018, March 3). Retrieved from Ministry of External Affairs: http://mea.gov.in/aseanindia/20-years.htm

Baruah, S. (2003). Between South and Southeast Asia: Northeast India and the Look East Policy. (S.

Baruah, Ed.) *Centre for Northeast India South and Southeast Asia Studies (CENISEAS) Papers* No. 4, p. 46.

Baruah, S. (2003, December 12). Look East, but via the Northeast. *The Indian Express.*

Government of Mizoram. (2017). *Economic Survey 2016-17.* Aizawl: Planning & Programme Implementation Department (Research & Development Branch).

Haokip, T. (2015). *India's Look East Policy and the North East.* New Delhi: Sage Publications.

India News. (2014, August 25). Retrieved March 2, 2018, from NDTV.com: https://www.ndtv.com/india-news/time-to-change-look-east-policy-to-act-east-policy-sushma-swaraj-653063

Ludden, D. (2003). Where is Assam? Using Geographical History to Locate Current Social Realities. (S. Baruah, Ed.) *Centre for Northeast India South and Southeast Asia Studies (CENISEAS)* Paper 1, p. 22.

Malone, D. (2011, September 3-9). Soft Power in Indian Foreign Policy. *Economic and Political Weekly,* 46(36), 35-39. Retrieved August 3, 2017, from http://www.jstor.org/stable/41719935

Ministry of Tourism, G. (2016). *Regional Tourism Satellite Account Mizoram, 2015–16 (Phase III).* New Delhi: National Council of Applied Economic Research (NCAER).

Nye Jr., J. (2004, Winter). Soft Power: The Means to Success in World Politics. *Political Science Quarterly,* 680–681. doi:10.1002/j.1538-165X.2004.tb01291.x

Nye Jr., J. (2006, Feb 23). Think Again: Soft Power. *Foreign Policy.* Retrieved March 8, 2018, from http://foreignpolicy.com/2006/02/23/think-again-soft-power/

Overview. (2018, March 11). Retrieved from BIMSTEC: http://bimstec.org/overview/

Parameswaran, P. (2014, Nov 17). *ASEAN Beat.* Retrieved from TheDiplomat.com: https://thediplomat.com/2014/11/modi-unveils-indias-act-east-policy-to-asean-in-myanmar/

Sundaram, A. (2013, May). Look East Policy. *International Journal of Advancements in Research & Technology,* 2(5), 169-185.

Verghese, B. G. (2002, April 18). Unfinished Business in the Northeast: Pointers towards Restructuring, Reform, Reconciliation and Resurgence. *Kamal Kumari Memorial Lecture delivered in Guwahati.* Guwahati, Assam. Retrieved March 3, 2018, from http://www.bgverghese.com/northeast.htm#Top

4

Consociating India with ASEAN: Prospects and Challenges in Look East Policy

M.N. Singh

ABSTRACT

India has not had a phenomenal relationship, at least not in political and economic, with the Southeast Asian countries for long although they are located in the same continent. Despite sharing strong cultural affinities with many of these countries, the Indian government has not developed a robust foreign policy towards these countries for various reasons. After Independence, historically, India has adopted NAM and it had put into practice a kind of controlled economy, not opening to the global market. India was also somewhat inclined towards the erstwhile Soviet Union and these countries were not coming forward towards India. For years, post-independence, India's focus has been emphatically towards the West.

Today, the scenario is completely different and the Indian market, after the daring economic reform pioneered in 1991, is open to the world market. For the emerging economic and strategic ends, India began looking towards Southeast Asia. With a sizable Indian Diaspora in the region, coupled with the looming rise of China in Asia, there are several economic and strategic possibilities and India cannot afford to overlook these countries.

On the part of Southeast Asian countries, there is a constant fear about the overarching power of China. It is only natural that these countries look up to India as a potential power to balance the hegemonic rise of China in the region. More than anything else, after the Chinese invasion of India 1962, there have had been rigorous strategic changes in these two Asian giants. As China is boldly befriending the immediate neighbours of India and encircling it, it becomes a necessity for India to counter the Chinese move by embracing collaborative ties with Southeast Asian countries.

It is after 1991 that India began to focus keenly on these countries for all possible ties and the most pragmatic result of this initiative is the Look East Policy. Profoundly conceptualized under the visionary leadership of former Prime Minister P. V. Narasimha Rao, the Look East Policy, while mapping the North-east region of India as the corridor, is shaping up steadily. In recent times, India has not only signed the ASEAN-India Free Trade Area Treaty among some countries, it has also been accorded observer status to the ASEAN Inter Parliamentary Assembly. As a matter of fact, the Look East Policy is not just about economic ties, but is also for strategic purposes in the Asia Pacific. However, the Look East Policy inherits lots of challenges and significances in the North-east region.

The present paper seeks to examine the fundamental factors that propel India to inch towards ASEAN countries in the present global scenario. It further explores the potential prospects and challenges inherent in the Look East Policy, especially with reference to North-East India.

Keywords: *Gateway; Economy; Export; Power; Potential; Trade*

Geo-Historical Genesis of the ASEAN Organisation

The ASEAN, formed in 1967, has demonstrated, despite other imperfections, the multitudinous virtues of regional cooperation and understanding. By the time of its inception, the world was under the wave of the Cold War between two superpowers. The world was virtually divided into two blocs—Soviet-led communist bloc and the U.S.-led capitalist bloc. Then there are the NAM countries. While many countries were either pro communism or pro capitalism, there were some who were neutral. Likewise, the Southeast Asian countries had different ideological affiliations and regional wars supported covertly by rival superpowers have been witnessed. It was indeed a sagacious move steered by some of the pioneering leaders of Southeast Asia to forge a regional organisation that will bestow advantages upon themselves.

The objectives of the ASEAN are multidimensional. It is to promote collaboration on a wide range of fields—economic, cultural, social, technical and administration in order to boost economic growth, cultural development and overall social progress in the region (ASEAN Declaration, 1967). Not the least in the economic realm, these countries form the ASEAN organisation to minimise economic barriers and develop economic collaboration among themselves. It promotes mutual trade and free trade areas. The ASEAN is supposed to be a non-military, non ideology, and non-confrontationist organisation.[1]

India and Southeast Asian countries have had a long connection in the past. India and Southeast Asia are maritime neighbours and there is ample proof of their age-old economic and cultural ties. Before the British rule, India had a long tradition of trade relations with these countries. It was when European colonialism manifested in Asia that the old course was reversed. The maritime link between India and these countries was dominated by European countries (Baru, 2001, p. 5). In the formative years of the ASEAN, India was not too keen to associate with it. There are some observable reasons which compelled India to be indifferent. First, during the Cold War period India, along with some like-minded countries, had adopted NAM and India wanted to maintain an independent foreign policy. But some of the ASEAN countries had ideological affiliations with either of the superpower blocs. And India got entangled in the political conundrums spewed by its neighbours. Some countries also perceived India to be leaning towards the Soviet Union. So, the geo-political environment was not conducive for India to develop better ties with ASEAN countries. Second, India has a geographical disadvantage to have land connectivity with the ASEAN. India can connect with the ASEAN through Bangladesh and Myanmar. But India's relations with Myanmar and Bangladesh are not good enough to avail the much-needed transit facilities. It is because Myanmar, apart from being a closed country, has not enjoyed political stability for decades. For Bangladesh, it always has a fear psychosis, given India's size and vast resources. Third, the foreign policy of a country is also largely shaped by the ruling elite. In India's case, the ruling elite have been inclined towards the West thereby ignoring its relatively poor Southeast Asian countries. This is proven from the fact that Nehru was so idealistically busy in world politics that he hardly had any distinct foreign policy for Southeast Asia. More than anything else, until 1991, the Indian economy was not liberalised and it was insular. India had no practical inclination to foster trade relations with Southeast Asia.

Even when there was the stupendous economic rise of certain Asian countries like Singapore, Hong Kong, Taiwan and South Korea, commonly known as the Asian Tigers in the 1970s, the unprecedented success did not inspire India to look towards them for better economic ties. One reason often argued is favour is that the success of these countries is based on an export-oriented market system. For a large country like India, the model was not suitable as economic reform did not take place during those years. It is also quite obvious that India did not have the capacity and equipment to tie up with Southeast Asian countries. As a matter of fact, these ASEAN countries are every competitive and efficient in the economic sector. The region has abundant natural resources with high technical skills and productivity. On the part of the ASEAN, India has lost both confidence and prospect after it suffered a humiliating defeat at the hands of China in 1962.[2] But afterwards, some countries too had reluctance allowing India to associate with the ASEAN. In fact, India did not enjoy good relations with some of the ASEAN members. For example, Indonesia, the main member country of the ASEAN initially, had not shared a good rapport with India. It was after the ouster of president Sukarno that relations between the countries have become normal.

Changing Foreign Policy of India and the ASEAN

As argued earlier, India's relations with South Asian counties in the early years of its independence was somewhat distant. It was after 1991 that India began to extend its overture of engaging with the ASEAN vigorously. In 1991, the disintegration of the USSR took place and that ensued in the end of the Cold War. India's focus on the international level got widened with the collapse of the USSR. More importantly, India also undertook historic economic reforms that heralded the opening up of its economy to the world. Earlier, Indian economy was inward-looking and India was tilted towards the former Soviet Union. With the liberalisation of its economic policies, India felt the need to expand its ties in Asia. The Government of India embarked on free market policies abroad. In terms of land connectivity, with the joining of Myanmar in the ASEAN, there is a direct connection with the Southeast Asian countries. Moreover, India's geo-political position demands closer relations with its south Asian neighbours.

For the fulfilment of its dream of becoming a regional power as well as a global player, India needs to heighten its economic and strategic might in the globe. It becomes imperative for India to engage with these countries. For all economic and strategic moves, India can no longer afford to ignore them. Today, India is a nuclear power and its status plays to its advantage. As a nuclear power, the ASEAN countries can look up to India to balance China in the region. To stabilise the region, there is always a need for a regional power balancer and India naturally fills the void. These countries nurture a fear about a single hegemonic power in the region. In other words, the hegemonic rise of China in Asia can pose a big threat to some of these countries and it becomes necessary to have an equally powerful country to balance power in the region.

There has been an ever-increasing importance of the Indian Ocean for economic and strategic reasons in the world. It becomes obligatory for both India and Southeast Asia to bolster cooperation with each other. These littoral countries have maritime trade activities across the Indian Ocean and they see the need to establish a zone of peace in the Indian Ocean because it is a highly militarised zone. Today, India's military ties with some ASEAN countries are growing and India regularly holds military exercises and conducts patrolling in collaboration with some of the ASEAN countries. This definitely builds up the mutual trust between India and these countries. The idea of reinforcing an 'Indian Ocean Community' is catching up fast.

India has a core interest in the South China Sea like many other countries. The South China Sea is strategically very important for many countries including India. It has a huge reservoir of gas, oil and other resources. It is also very active in world shipping activities. India's multiple interests include oil exploration, freedom of navigation, freedom to trade freely with the Asia Pacific region, etc. Having a foothold in the South China Sea is not only important for India's economic development, it could also serve as a better platform for bargaining against China's increasing presence in the Indian Ocean. With the growing aggressive Chinese influence in the South China Sea, the maritime interests of many stakeholders are likely to be jeopardised. China is also trying to restrict India's activities in the region. So the viable option for India is that has to forge stronger ties with Southeast Asian countries politically and economically to counter China.

India and ASEAN share some common interests apart from economic ends. There is a huge Indian Diaspora in the region and there are close cultural affinities between the two. Both intend to combat international issues like global terrorism, drug trafficking, smuggling, transnational crimes, diseases, piracy, etc. In fact, there is no history of direct confrontation or war between India and any of the ASEAN countries. They were also under colonial powers. So it becomes clear that India and ASEAN can only reap rich dividends through cooperation.

Today, India's equation with the ASEAN is fast moving forward. It is argued that Singapore has played an important role in bringing India into the circle of ASEAN (Sikri, 2016, p. 120). For Singapore, having a close engagement with India will boost its economy and security. India also responds favourably towards Singapore and both countries have expanded their cooperation beyond trade and commerce. In 1995, India was accorded the status of a full Dialogue Partner of the ASEAN. In 2009, India signed the Free Trade Agreement in goods with ASEAN and with huge potential facing them, both can reap dividends. Today, the trade between India and South East Asian countries is soaring. Moreover, with the not so encouraging initiatives of SAARC in recent times and India's frustrating experience with it, it makes better sense to invest more in ASEAN (Khanna, 2007, p. 247).

There is better air connectivity between India and the ASEAN countries. With increasing people-to-people contact, tourism in both the regions has shot up. There are plans to construct railway links from India to Hanoi via Myanmar, Thailand, and Cambodia. The India-Myanmar-Thailand highway project is on the anvil. Most notably, Mekong-Ganga Cooperation is a promising initiative to foster better ties between India and ASEAN. MGC is an organisation having potential for cooperation in the fields of tourism, culture, transport, education, etc. Besides, there is BIMSTEC which aims at cooperation in the fields of trade, investment, technology, transport, energy, agriculture, tourism, fishery etc.

Expanding Eco-Strategic Horizon and Look East Policy

India formally launched its Look East Policy in 1991 under the leadership of P. V. Narasimha Rao. The Look East Policy was initially focused towards South East Asian countries and later on it was expanded to China, Japan and South Korea. Therefore, the vision of this policy is truly large. It is a paradigm shift as far as

Indian foreign policy is concerned towards Southeast Asia and East Asia. India's Look East Policy from the beginning has been to expand both its economic and strategic reach to Asia-Pacific countries. There are three observable factors that pushed India to embark on the promising Look East Policy. First was the collapse of the former Soviet Union and India's diversifying its foreign policy in search of new alternatives. The second reason was the historic and bold economic reforms carried out in the year 1992. The third reason is SAARC not becoming a vibrant option for the expansion of the Indian economy at the global level. Hence, India is setting its eyes towards Southeast Asia and East Asia.

On the domestic front, India intends to develop its landlocked North-Eastern region as part of the Look East Policy. The North-Eastern region is definitely a gateway to foster economic relations with these countries. The region provides the only workable option to develop land route connectivity with these countries. India is aiming to have direct access to Southeast Asia and East Asia through the North-Eastern region. With this view, road links and railway connections are under construction.

Among the vital prospects, the Look East Policy can open up immense economic opportunities for India. India can utilise this to export its goods and services to the world market. For instance, India can export its software products and professionals to the international market, particularly in Asian-Pacific markets. It can also definitely enhance India's strategic security in the Asian region. The Look East Policy can enable India to tighten its hold in the Indian Ocean through pragmatic initiatives. Further, India can establish its foothold in the South China Sea in collaboration with some ASEAN countries. And by strengthening its economic and strategic positions, India can deal with the rising China on an equal footing.

There are formidable challenges for India. China is wary about India's growing proximity with ASEAN countries. In any case, China cannot digest India's rise and it will use all possible means to block India. With the ever-advancing 'string of pearls' endeavour, China can be expected to be more aggressive with India. There is also a bigger threat of illegal migration in the North-east and eastern states of India. With the increasing extent of people-to-people contact and free movement, this demographic problem may worsen. Also, ever since the implementation of FTA in 2010, India has been experiencing a trade deficit. There has been an increasing rise in imports from ASEAN countries, but the same cannot be said about India's export. India has to ensure that it does not suffer a trade deficit by negotiating with the ASEAN countries on better terms.

Look East Policy and the North-Eastern States of India

There are numerous challenges concerning the North-Eastern region that face the Look East Policy. With the landlocked geographical location, the North-Eastern region of India is considered to be the periphery of the country. When the Look East Policy actually takes place, it remains to be seen whether the core and the periphery will share the benefits or is it the core that is going to exploit the periphery. Applying Immanuel Wallerstein's core-periphery analogy (Wallerstein, 1974, p. 401) if the gap between the core and periphery is not bridged, it is the mainland states and not the North-Eastern states that are going to reap the benefits. Ultimately, it may be likely that the North-Eastern region can be converted to conduits of goods for markets in Southeast Asia.

In India's Look East Policy, there are two contesting points. One is the global ambition for which India intends to extend its strategic and economic ties with Southeast Asian and East Asian countries. Another is the local ambition that people of the North-East to bargain for the elevation of its political set-up and economy (Chakraborty & Ray, 2014, p. 88). The visible ways to solve this intricacy in the context of the Look East Policy are still myriad. But the overall success of the LEP in the North-East region will be contingent upon the modalities in which these two glaring ambitions are balanced.

The region is insurgency-hit and many developmental works are not moving forward smoothly. There is also constant political instability arising out of the ethnic conflicts, nationality issues and questions of sovereignty and nation state. As the result, there is a lack of infrastructure and political stability is needed to able to capitalise the fruits of the Look East Policy. The region is still stuck with the traditional economic model and without promoting modern skills and enterprises, the opening of its economy to the already-developed economies in Asia is likely to bring much hardship. In fact, it is the big companies and MNCs that are likely to sweep the region's economy and deprive the locals of the benefits of the LEP.[3] Moreover, there is the high possibility of cheap Chinese goods flooding the region. There are bigger fears that the local markets in the region will be swamped by big business houses and big enterprises from within and outside the country. Without developing the required business acumen, skill and entrepreneurial spirit, the region may not reap the rich dividends that would flow from the Look East Policy. There is an enormous urge to develop infrastructure and human resources in the region. The region needs to get rid of its dependent economic model.[4]

For India, the dominant link with Southeast Asia has been through the sea route and the plan to link with these countries through a land route has not taken off. There are difficulties in linking with these countries through the neighbouring country of Myanmar. Linking of India's North-Eastern states with Southeast Asia may not be on the priority list of the Government of India because it is far away from the so-called mainland states. The region is linked with the rest through a small 'Chicken's Neck' corridor. So, India would prefer continuing to link these countries through the eastern coast namely Tamil Nadu, Odisha, Andhra Pradesh and West Bengal (Bezbaruah & Sarma, 2013, p. 60)

There are several draconian laws that impede growth in the region. It is often argued that the Indian Government's approach towards the North-East has been for strategy purposes and not for its development (Sarma, 2013, p. 44). In many ways, the North-East is kept as a buffer zone for mainland India. Even the actual intent of many developmental projects in the region is highly suspect. This can be exemplified from the fact that many of the big development projects taken up in the region are done by the Central Government or an external authority. There is always suspicion in the minds of the people of the region about the benefits of big projects (Chakraborty & Ray, p. 308). In fact, the simmering perspective is that it is the external big companies or the Central Government that is extracting resources from the region. For example, there are many hydro-electric projects and dams to harness power in the region. But how much benefit the people here are getting is still vague.

Apart from the challenges, there are also enormous benefits promised to be ushered in by the Look East Policy. The North-East has lengthy international boundaries. The region is borders China, Myanmar, Bangladesh, Bhutan, and naturally there is endless potential for international trade and commerce. Historically, the region had old-age trade ties with neighbouring countries like China, Tibet, and Myanmar. There was free movement of people in many areas. But after the British left India and when the region became part of the Indian Union, new artificial political boundaries were created. As the result, the North-East was completely cut off from the international scenario. Cross-border trade became restricted and for security purposes, people-to-people contact was snapped. And since the region suddenly happens to be located on the periphery of a new political India, all road connectivity and communications are backward and neglected. Even the inland river routes that were previously functioning have been frozen. The overall result is that the region became so landlocked that all avenues for economic activities were obstructed. However, the new prospect is that the North-Eastern region can revive old-age trade ties with its neighbours and more so with Southeast Asia. The Look East policy can be seen as a heralding force in that direction.

At the time of India's independence, the North-East was one of the most prosperous regions in the country and it became what it is today due to artificial geo-political changes in the subcontinent. There are boundless advantages that the Look East Policy can bring to the North-East. There will be tremendous connectivity between the North-East and Southeast and East Asia. Having racial affinities, the ease of doing business and opportunities for deeper intermingling will be widened. The North-Eastern states can have massive collaboration in tourism, health, education and other service sectors. If the advantages are properly tapped, the North-East can shine economically.[5] Its strategic location can attract foreign investment.

Geographically, many of the Southeast Asian markets are closer to the North-East than markets in so-called mainland India. If the Look East Policy is properly functional, there will be huge savings in terms of time and money spent on the distance. And as people of the North-East and Southeast Asia belong to the Mongoloid race, people-to-people engagement will be much easier. Without any doubt, the North-East can attract FDI, both from within and outside the country provided there is a conducive environment for business and industry. The region can be an international centre for trade. There is an enormous potential in the region to become a centre for business on a global scale. It is blessed with boundless natural resources and skills.

The North-Eastern region is rich in hydro power potential. Many states there have the capacity to generate surplus hydro power which can be sold in the neighbouring countries. There is a variety of agricultural products, floriculture products, handlooms and handicrafts, tea products, herbs and medicinal plants. These can be exported to the international market with huge returns. There are large reserves of oil, gas, coal, limestone and minerals in the region. Many of these raw materials are untapped and can be utilised in the future. As the region is blessed with a large number of biodiversity and heritage sites, the tourism industry can flourish. With its physical location, many tourists from Asia can be attracted. In addition, the region has a high literacy rate and the young generation is highly exposed to Western education. It is an asset to establish contacts with the people of Southeast Asia.

Even though the association of North-East India with the Look East Policy was never a part of the initial policy, there are a multitude of advantages that the region can capitalise.[6] According to NER Vision 2010, the people of the region aspire to be peaceful, strong, confident and engaging with the global economy in the near future. So, there is an urgent need for progress, good governance, eradication of poverty, literacy, freedom, et al. There is much more that the LEP can offer for thc North East region.

Concluding Remarks

With the constantly changing geo-politics in the globe, no country can ever remain isolated. This is perfectly true for India if it has to rise as a global player in the coming decades. As the 21st century is touted to be an Asian Age, India needs to collaborate with countries around the globe. It is in this direction that India took up its ambitious Look East Policy. As India is in Asia, its priority is to have cordial relations with the Southeast and East Asia countries through policies and diplomacy. India's focussed attempt to associate with the ASEAN is a very positive move. This will not only give India economic and strategic advantages; it will also open up the roads to develop the long isolated North-East region. The world is moving fast, and the North-Eastern region cannot remain dormant for long. Despite all the hardships ingrained with the Look East Policy, the region must brace up to seize the fruits that it can offer. Nevertheless, the ultimate touchstone of the success or failure of the Look East Policy in the North-East will be determined by the holistic ability to fine-tune the momentum between the earnest readiness of the region to meet the challenges ahead and the genuine ambitions of the Government of India in implementing it.

ENDNOTES

1 It is interesting to note that Communist-inclined countries like Vietnam, Cambodia and Laos were not initially part of the ASEAN. The Soviet bloc considered ASEAN as an ally of the Western bloc as it maintained cordial relations with the USA. In fact, it was assumed that ASEAN was made to counter Communist influence in the region.

2 When India suffered loss of prestige and status in the Chinese aggression of 1962, the Southeast Asia countries were not so optimistic about India's prospects. Moreover, India got entangled with its aggressive neighbour, Pakistan (Limaye, 2003, p. 41).

3 Apprehension of demographic change exists in the region. Special state laws, implementation of the Sixth Schedule and Inner Line Permits are in existence. The Inner Line regulation and Restricted Area permit is a complicated problem in the region (Upadhyay, 2013, p. 109).

4 Applying A.G. Frank's theory, (Frank, 1966, p. 5), the North-East region, in the post-independent era, has been subjected to depend economically on the Centre. The contemporary under-development of the region is the product of the asymmetric relation between the Centre and the region.

5 With huge potential, the North-East can be an economic powerhouse in the country (Ministry of Development of North Eastern Region, 2011, p. 2).

6 It is unequivocally true that the Government of India never takes genuine efforts to develop the region on par with other states. The region has been ignored and neglected, and so no major developmental programmes are implemented there. This can be exemplified from the recent failed policy taken wherein India had made investment to purchase gas from Myanmar, but which has been given to China. India's plan was to link the pipeline via Bangladesh, but not through the North-East which could have been a better strategic move. But the Indian Government followed a short-term accountant's perspective (Sikri, 2009, p. 4).

REFERENCES

Baru, Sanjaya. India and ASEAN: The Emerging Economic Relationship Towards A Bay of Bengal Community, *Working Paper*, No. 61, ICRIER, New Delhi, 2001.

Bezbaruah, M.P. & Amiya Sarma. 'India's Look East' Policy: An Opening to Asian Prosperity or a False Hope for the Northeast? In M. C. Behera (ed.) *Northeast and Globalisation Issues Betwixt and Between*, 2013.

Chakraborty, Gorky and Asok Kumar Ray. *The Look East and Northeast India*, Guwahati: Aakar Books, 2014.

Frank, A.G. 'The Development of Underdevelopment,' *Monthly Review*, September, 1966.

Goswami, H, 'Transport Connectivity and Border Trade of the North-Eastern Region,' in M. C. Behera (ed.) *Northeast and Globalisation Issues Betwixt and Between*, 2013.

Khanna, V. N., *Foreign Policy of India*, Noida: Vikas Publishing House Pvt. Ltd., 2007.

Limaye, Satu P. India's Relation with Southeast Asia Take a Wing, *Southeast Asian Affairs, Southeast Asian Affairs*, 2003.

Look East Policy and the North Eastern States, Govt. of India, Ministry of Development of North Eastern Region, 2011.

North Eastern Region Vision 2020, Ministry of Development of North Eastern Region, NEC, 2008.

Sarma, Atul. "The North East as Gateway to South East Asia: Big Dream and Home Truths,' in M. C. Behera (ed.) *Northeast and Globalisation Issues Betwixt and Between*, 2013.

Sikri, Rajiv. 'India's Look East Policy: A Critical Assessment,' Interview with Rajiv Sikri, *Southeast Asia Research Programme*, New Delhi, 2009.

Sikri, Rajiv. *Challenge and Strategy Rethinking India's Foreign Policy*, New Delhi: Sage Publications India Pvt. Ltd., 2016.

The ASEAN Declaration (Bangkok Declaration) Bangkok, 8 August, 1967.

Upadhyay, Vandana. 'Looking Beyond the Borders: Globalisation and the Development of Northeast India,' in M. C. Behera (ed.) *Northeast and Globalisation Issues Betwixt and Between*, 2013.

Wallerstein, Immanuel. 'The Rise and Future Demise of the World Capitalist System: Concepts for Comparative Analysis,' *Comparative Studies in Society and History*, Vol. 16, issue 4, 1974.

5

CLMV and Act East Policy: Exploring New Avenues

Pankaj Jha

ABSTRACT

In the India-ASEAN Action Plan for 2016-2020, special emphasis has been given to enhance trade, economic ties and investment with Cambodia, Laos, Myanmar, and Vietnam (CLMV). Given the fact that the CLMV is a relatively less-developed region in Southeast Asia and does have a good potential for development both in terms of trade and manufacturing, many growth possibilities exist. Low labour costs and relatively cheap land rates make it a promising region. However, in terms of development of infrastructure and sound fundamentals in terms of the banking and financial sectors it needs much concerted efforts. India has been engaging this region during the last decade and has even agreed on deferred timelines for reduction of trade and tariff barriers under India-ASEAN CECA. There are three basic initiatives that make this region one of the important vantage points for India's outreach towards the East Asia. This includes the reinvigoration of the BIMSTEC Organization. The high-level meeting between BIMSTEC-member countries and the BRICS nations point towards India's objectives. Secondly, the development of the Mekong India Economic Corridor (MIEC) and the completion of the trilateral highway would integrate this region with a 1.3 billion-people market and develop complementarities. Thirdly, the CLMV countries, in particular Myanmar, have attracted a lot of investment while Vietnam has been showing an impressive economic growth ranging from 5-7 per cent each year. Also, the increasing investment from Japan and other Asian countries shows that it can emerge as another hub in terms of low-cost manufacturing. Further, the CLMV countries have emerged as a bloc that can create political synergies and has seen relatively stable regimes. The region as a whole has been seen in a new light and, therefore, this paper would highlight the complementariness and development of synergies between the two sides.

Introduction

In the strategic and economic lexicon, partnerships happen between any two countries depending on the defence and security complementarities in the strategic domain while in the economic domain the mutual economic benefit in terms of division of labour and the developing of interdependence through complementary production, value chain and non-competitive products helps in forging links. However, in the contemporary international discourse, strategic and economic links have become so enmeshed with one another that every strategic link needs to develop more synergies in the economic sphere. In fact, many regional and international economic cooperation initiatives have merged the differentiation between strategic priorities and economic links. The issue which was deliberated about two decades ago does not hold fort when it comes to the marginal utility and the enlargement of partnerships spanning the political, economic, strategic and cultural domains. In the case of mainland Southeast Asia, while the major players in ASEAN who include Thailand, Singapore, Indonesia and Malaysia have earned their dividends with regard to greater interaction with the Indian sub-continent, mainland southeast Asia, particularly the CLMV countries, have not been able to convert the free trade agreement and other related services agreement to mutual benefit, given their low economic base as well as relatively poor developmental status. Among the developing economies such as CLMV there are four levels of engagement that have been the foundation of the interaction between the two regions.

If one analyses the historical interactions between the two civilizations, the imprints of Indic influence as well as Hindu and Buddhist culture are visible in different parts of mainland Southeast Asia. The one defining element in the relationship particularly is with regard to the limits of influence of Theravada Buddhism wherein Cambodia is seen as the outer limit of the Theravada influence while Laos and Vietnam have adopted strands of Tibetan Buddhism (Tantric and Shamanic) which is more amalgamation of Mahayana and Bonism. The reincarnating Lamas is another important aspect of differentiation between Indian and Tibetan Buddhism. The basic differences between the two have been in terms of rituals and norms as well as practices adopted by the two different strands of Buddhism. The interaction between the two practiced forms of Buddhism has at times led to synthesis of norms and rituals while at another level there has been a latent struggle for supremacy. The evolution of BIMSTEC and Mekong Ganga Cooperation addressed the issues such as culture and P2P interaction.

The second aspect of interaction between India and CLMV countries has been primarily focused on strategic and defence interactions. According to K. Subramanyam, India had a large stake in ensuring that Chinese pressure on Indochinese states is contained: 'We have a large stake in ensuring that the pressure in Indochina is contained. That has been our basic policy from the Fifties. The only country that can do this is Vietnam, the most capable nation of the region.

That is why where the strategic interests of India and Vietnam coincide"[1] Further, India-Myanmar military interactions have been regular but there have been jarring phases when Aung San Suu Kyi was given the Nehru Award for International Understanding in 1995 when the two armies were conducting counter-insurgency operations. Myanmar has now begun high-level defence interactions and their sailors and even naval aviation pilots are getting regular training in Indian establishments. The Myanmar army, especially the higher command, is keen to develop the army as a truly professional army with a larger role in defence and international peacekeeping operations. XCAMBODIA and Laos also do get defensive equipment and Indian defence forces conduct special training modules for the Cambodian armed forces. Among the four countries, only Myanmar does not have the political commissar system while two—Vietnam and Laos—have included it in their military training hierarchy. These institutional and structural differences have not created any major problems, However, because of a military equipment deficit, Cambodia and Laos have not yet been included in the bilateral military exercises and high-level interaction mode. The interactions have been substantial but sporadic. While Vietnam has emerged as an important strategic partner, the remaining three countries have not been accorded that special status.

The third important foundation for interaction has been the Mekong Ganga Cooperation and BIMSTEC. While the two institutions have been in the nascent stages but with increasing interests of the member countries, the sub-regional instrumentation is showing institutional promise.

The fourth level of interaction has been through the ASEAN institution in which most of the CLMV countries were given deferred timelines for implementing and ratifying most of the institutional arrangements regarding free trade and investment. However, while India–ASEAN have a 'Strategic Partnership,' the role of the vision regarding CLMV countries still needs better clarity. Besides, the low number of Indian Diaspora in most of these countries has debilitated interaction at the social and P2P level.

CLMV nations are relatively new members of the Association of Southeast Asian Nations (ASEAN) and share a number of similarities, although they differ in the size of their markets and economic priorities, among other things. While Vietnam, for example, has achieved high levels of economic development, per capita income and industrialization, the other members of the group still have low per capita income and limited human resources.[2] CLMV's similarities include their primarily agro-based, transition economies, high poverty incidence rate, insufficient infrastructure and institutions that are still too weak for a shift to a market economy. Although CLMV have enjoyed a certain degree of macroeconomic stability in recent years and are considered one of the fastest-growing economies in the region, unemployment and underemployment still persist. CLMV are still facing huge challenges in fighting poverty, narrowing gaps in wealth among the population, and addressing development gaps within the regions. Although each country in CLMV faces different development constraints, CLMV as a whole has a huge potential for future development that will depend on individual country efforts and support from development partners within and outside the region.[3]

Institutional Mechanisms

While launching the Look East Policy, India has prioritized its growth story of liberalization to replicate that of the new 'tiger economies' of Southeast Asia that had charmed international agencies with their export-led industrialization and better annual average growth. At the Fourth ASEAN Informal Summit held on 22-25 November 2000 in Singapore, the ASEAN leaders agreed to launch an Initiative for ASEAN Integration (IAI) that gave direction to and sharpened the focus of collective efforts in ASEAN to narrow the development gap within ASEAN as well as between ASEAN and other parts of the world.[4] The IAI Work Plan for CLMV focuses on the priority areas of Infrastructure Development (Transport and Energy), Human Resource Development (Public Sector Capacity Building, Labour & Employment and Higher Education), Information and Communications Technology, and Promoting Regional Economic Integration (Trade in Goods and Services, Customs, Standards and Investments) in the CLMV countries.[5]

Within this CLMV region, there has been concerns raised with regard to the deferred integration of the region into the larger East Asian regionalism. Under the various institutional processes most of these countries are found wanting in terms of economic development, infrastructure, trained manpower and regular power supply. However, the whole outlook changed with the inclusion of these countries in different institutional frameworks beginning with ASEAN. The four countries joined ASEAN in a staggered way. While Vietnam joined in 1995, followed by Myanmar and Laos in 1997 and Cambodia in 1999 paved the way for their inclusion in the booming regional economy, Cambodia's inclusion in ASEAN effectively paved the way for the end of its international isolation and facilitated its participation in Regional Comprehensive Economic Partnership (RCEP) and its inclusion in the ASEAN Free Trade Agreement (AFTA). Its accession to WTO in 2004 acted as a catalyst for its membership in the ASEAN Economic Community (AEC).

With regard to Vietnam, the *Doi Moi* economic reforms programme begun in 1986 with an objective of developing a "socialist-oriented market economy", made it an emerging economy with incremental liberalization of the equity markets, increased facilitation for FDI and structural reforms in terms of institutions and capacity building. Myanmar which has been ostracized in the international community got included in the regional value chain with the incremental lifting of sanctions in 2014, and the increasing Foreign Direct Investment which became more intense improved. At one point of time, Myanmar was getting a lot of FDI from European countries and the USA following the general elections that were held after nearly three decades of military rule. The rise of Aung San Suu Kyi and her party, the National League for Democracy, as well as negotiations and a conciliatory approach towards minorities and ethnic communities living in the peripheral regions of Myanmar created the necessary structure for further integration of the reclusive country into the ASEAN regional economic framework. Laos was also showing signs of revival with a demonstration of willingness to diversify its economy.

In the political sphere, with the exception of Vietnam, other economies enjoyed benefits owing to the increasing Chinese investment and expansion of the regional value chain. Vietnam being one of the claimant countries in the Spratly Islands dispute had to weather the Chinese assertive posture which to a large extent led to demonstrations and anti-Chinese protests within Vietnam. The loss of property and Chinese investment did create fissures between the two countries. Further, the increasing tensions between the two countries on China–Vietnam the border, despite the border agreement and the demarcation of fishing zones in South China Sea has aggravated problems.

Vietnam along with few other countries are increasingly seen as the next eligible members for the BIMSTEC. The sub regional organisation which have given birth to the BBIN transport corridor and with the negotiations likely to be concluded for Myanmar-India-Thailand Trilateral transport highway, CLMV countries might be the new entrants to the transport corridor network.

BIMSTEC

The Bay of Bengal Initiative for Multi-Sectoral Technical and Economic Cooperation (BIMSTEC) was envisaged as a regional organization through the Bangkok Declaration (6 June 1997) comprising seven member–states (India, Myanmar, Nepal, Bangladesh, Bhutan, Sri Lanka, and Thailand) lying in the littoral and adjacent areas of the Bay of Bengal constituting a contiguous regional unity. In the initial stages, the precursor to the BIMSTEC was 'BIST-EC' (Bangladesh, India, Sri Lanka and Thailand Economic Cooperation). With the admission of Nepal and Bhutan at the 6th Ministerial Meeting (February 2004, Thailand), the grouping was rechristened as 'Bay of Bengal Initiative for Multi-Sectoral Technical and Economic

Cooperation' (BIMSTEC).[6] The forum was aimed to develop trade and economic linkages while at the same time working on social, technical and economic aspects of cooperation. The inclusion of BIMSTEC ministers in the BRICS summit in 2015 by India clearly showed that India wanted to engage its periphery and also prioritize it in the larger scheme of things. It was particularly seen as a snub to the Chinese proposal of BCIM which even though endorsed by Prime Minister Modi during his China visit (May 2015) is yet to see tangible movement. The other organization that connects India with this region is the Mekong Ganga initiative which is now transformed into Mekong India Economic Corridor.

Mekong India Economic Corridor

With India increasing its economic clout and the urge to underplay the increasing Chinese dominance in the region, India worked out a strategy to engage these countries with the objective of sustaining cultural and historical interaction with a dose of trade and investment complementarities. The development of the Kaladaan Multi Modal Transport Project and the development of a trilateral highway were based on the premise that the two projects would enhance trade and investment between India's North-East and Southeast Asia. However, the two projects took more than 15 years to get completed with parts of the two projects still in limbo. Mekong-India connectivity has been envisaged as a constituent of India's obligations under the Asian Highway Network. Further, the possibility of United Nations Economic and Social Commission for Asia and the Pacific (UNESCAP) sponsored Trans-Asian railways might take shape in future once the Asian Highway is realized. MIEC would help in connecting Indian manufacturing with ancillary industries in the CLMV region as well as those in Thailand. This corridor also fits into the Indo-Pacific corridor envisaged by the US government.

Indo-Pacific Economic Corridor

Another important aspect of India's Act East policy and its stress on connectivity and trade has been US government interests in the Indo-Pacific Corridor and also look for the possibility to undercut the Chinese One Belt One Road project. The USA has indicated with regard to revival of the two connectivity and infrastructure projects in Southern Asia as a result of which India would become an indispensable player. This is aimed at particularly countering the OBOR project by China. The Trump Administration, drawing inspiration from Hillary Clinton's speech in July 2011 at Chennai has revived the New Silk Road (NSR) initiative, and further references have been made to bring legitimacy to the Indo-Pacific Construct through the Indo-Pacific Economic Corridor which will connect South with Southeast Asia.

This has also been endorsed by a specific project under US aid. It clearly states 'to support the United States' "vision of an Indo-Pacific Economic Corridor (IPEC), the U.S. government will undertake activities to promote greater regional economic connectivity in Asia. USAID, in collaboration with the U.S. State Department—which funded this activity with its centrally-managed funds for advancing regional cooperation in South Asia—will implement a two-year $1.86 million activity to: Foster economic growth and regional trade in South Asia; Increase private sector competitiveness in the region by enhancing the business environment ; Engage the private sector on economic issues, particularly regional trade, in South Asia and between South and Southeast Asia and Encourage stronger economic integration between South and Southeast Asia, engaging regional institutions and international financial institutions as appropriate".[7] Given the fact that multiple stakeholders are emerging in the CLMV region, it is likely that this region would see strategic manoeuvres as well as investment from different sources.

Developing Infrastructure and Growth Linkages

Even though China has been propagating that the "One Belt, One Road" does not pose any threat to any country, it is designed with China in the centre, aimed to facilitate its trade and also tacitly build its strategic periphery, thereby, using other countries as mere tools. Moreover, the maps that are being circulated among the international media and their own internal maps are starkly different. In the internal maps that are circulated, both Hambantota and Gwadar are listed as critical ports while listing the ports in Myanmar and Cambodia as Chinese ports. CCB reports from Shanghai and Beijing are of the view that the Silk Road Economic Belt and the Maritime Silk Route do have a strategic angle to them, but given the fact that China is increasingly being assailed as a revisionist power and criticised for taking an assertive stance in the East China Sea and South China Sea, the strategic angle has been kept on hold. However, within coastal and landlocked provinces, there are serious differences on the priorities of Beijing. The popular feeling in the landlocked provinces of China is that India and the Southern Asian region are very important for their growth and connectivity should be improved even at the cost of giving certain concessions. Complete details of implementation and trade under the "One Belt, One Road" initiative are yet to come out both in international discourse and Chinese documents. Nevertheless, China is still falling short of convincing the world community as to how the "One Belt, One Road" initiative would yield equitable dividends for all, and not just for China. Amid ambiguities, one thing is clear for China—the MSR and the "One Belt, One Road" initiatives would serve Chinese interests better in the long run. However, that should not deter the countries of the region from engaging China in deliberations on the proposed "One Belt, One Road" initiative.

In the Chinese aid documents (2011 and 2014), special reference has been made with regard to the development and infrastructure projects in the Indochina region. This includes the building of bridges, connecting roads and better infrastructure. However, most of the Chinese aid and assistance are meant to help its own exports to the region. While India and Japan are also looking towards this region and there has been an incremental influx of investment in the region, the problem is that of basic infrastructure, more particularly in Myanmar, Cambodia and Laos. The slow development of Sittwe port and Dawei port have left much to be desired as it was felt that with regard to environmental clearances and developing critical support infrastructure around ports, the response of the Myanmar government was tardy. However, with the development of these two ports, more connectivity and economic opportunities would emerge. Further, the blue economy is also gaining momentum and with the exception of Laos almost all the other three countries are looking for the possibilities in this regard. Further, the discourse in different forums such as BIMSTEC and MIEC need to also focus on developing the shipping and freight network which is much desired. The role of fisheries and increasing the localised yield would also serve the food security objectives of the region. Another element which is of importance is that the work along with the Mekong River Commission (MRC) might emerge as a joint voice with regard to China's dam building projects in the case of Mekong and Brahmaputra. Already, CLMV countries are part of the Mekong River Commission in which China is an observer but it would be appropriate if such a trilateral initiative between China, Bangladesh and India can coordinate with Mekong River Commission. While these are a few suggestions, it would be prudent to look into the possibilities that India envisages with regard to the CLMV countries; the India-ASEAN Action Plan makes a provision for it.

India–ASEAN Action Plan 2016-2020

In the India-ASEAN Action Plan, special mention is made with regard to the objectives and it states "support ASEAN's efforts in narrowing the development gap within and between ASEAN Member States through the implementation of IAI Work Plan II and its successor documents, as well as alleviating poverty and promoting sustainable development in order to realize the ASEAN Community and regional integration." The document adds—"Continue to support CLMV Countries, in the implementation of the IAI; continue to support the less developed countries of ASEAN, including CLMV countries, in wider areas, among others, human resources development, rural household electrification programmes, information technology curriculum and IT teacher training, and further increase the number of fellowships and scholarships; and explore cooperation on the establishment of a rural development research institute in Cambodia, Laos PDR, Myanmar and Vietnam by India".[8] This clearly amplifies India's objectives of capacity building and developing a congenial atmosphere for Indian investment. With regard to connectivity, the same action plan outlines: "work closely to promote physical connectivity in the region by completing the missing links between South and Southeast Asia, including, but not limited to, expediting the completion of India-Myanmar-Thailand trilateral highway and extension to Laos and Cambodia; developing a new India-Myanmar-Laos-Vietnam-Cambodia highway; and encouraging private sector participation in the development of roads and railways and relevant logistics networks."[9]

With regard to promoting tourism also, these four countries were among the first to grant e-visa schemes which was followed by Visa on Arrival schemes for tourists from these four countries. Further, as it is apparent, there is a need for bringing about synergies in the development of the North-East region of India and also support complementary economic projects across the CLMV region. This would help in building linkages and better understanding between the two regions.

Conclusion

If one looks at the engagement between India and the CLMV countries, there is a multilayered engagement. However, with regard to India, there is a distinct policy conundrum. India is willing to interact with the region through multilateral institutions but prefers bilateral interactions so as to meet its objectives and tailor-made complementarities. If one looks at the cooperation between the four countries, while a lot of noise has been made about connectivity and has been the main term in most of the Delhi Dialogues, the process of growth has been slow. This has also been reported by ERIA in its reports. With regard to manufacturing, China is miles ahead of India but India does have critical elements that make it stand out in competition to China. This includes health, education and the linkages through Buddhism. These latent but promising vistas might work wonders given the fact that in the long run, India aspires to emerge as a services hub and a promising knowledge economy. The interactions among the four countries show that they are keen on developing their primary sector and want to get out of the 'Dragon's clasp' that has muted their capacities. Training, education, renewable energy, medicines, agriculture and also building more understanding about international trade regulations and sustaining their potential through regular interaction is another aspect. India has felt that this region is its natural extension both in terms of defence and strategic aspects. However, the problem with institutional policy making is that the visionary approach has been replaced by the demand-and-supply attitude. While it is important that the CLMV countries develop, in order to have mutually beneficial ties India would have to cater to the developmental needs of its own states so that the potential which is harnessed abroad can meet the aspirations of the local people. There is a need for an outcome approach rather than a repeated action plan.

ENDNOTES

1 K. Subramanyam. "Indochina-Strategic Perspectives", in T.N. Kaul, Ed., *India and Indochina: Perspectives of Cooperation* (New Delhi: Patriot Publishers on behalf of the Indian Centre for Studies on Indochina, 1987), p..43

2 Chap Sotharith. Development Strategy for CLMV in the Age of Economic Integration, http://www.eria.org/research/images/pdf/PDF%20No.4/No.4-part0-Executive%20Summary.pdf

3 Chap Sotharith. Development Strategy for CLMV in the Age of Economic Integration, http://www.eria.org/research/images/pdf/PDF%20No.4/No.4-part0-Executive%20Summary.pdf

4 http://www.aseansec.org/pdf/IAI_doc1_6904.pdf

5 Initiative For ASEAN Integration (IAI) Work Plan For The CLMV Countries, http://www.aseansec.org/pdf/IAI_doc1_6904.pdf

6 BIMSTEC Background at http://bimstec.org/overview/

7 Indo-Pacific Economic Corridor, Phase II: Assessment of Non-Tariff Barriers in South Asia, Asia and the Middle East Economic Growth Best Practices (AMEG) Project Chemonics International, Inc. Task Order No. AID-OAA-12-00008, July 14, 2016, at http://pdf.usaid.gov/pdf_docs/PA00MBPK.pdf (Accessed 23.3.2018)

8 Plan of Action to Implement the ASEAN-India Partnership for Peace, Progress; and Shared Prosperity (2016-2020), http://asean.org/storage/images/2015/August/POA_India/ASEAN-India%20POA%20-%20FINAL.pdf (Accessed 23.3.2018)

9 Plan of Action to Implement the ASEAN-India Partnership for Peace, Progress; and Shared Prosperity (2016-2020), http://asean.org/storage/images/2015/August/POA_India/ASEAN-India%20POA%20-%20FINAL.pdf (Accessed 23.3.2018)

6

Trade Potential of North East India with ASEAN[1]

Sunetra Ghatak

ABSTRACT

India's economic partnership with ASEAN, which has completed 25 years recently, has been well-documented. The North-Eastern Region (NER) of India is the bridgehead of India's connectivity with Southeast and East Asia. In addition, the NER is central to India's Act East Policy (AEP). However, in relative terms, the NER is one of India's most economically laggard regions, contributing only 3 per cent to the country's gross domestic product (GDP); on the other, about 98 per cent of the NER's borders form India's international boundaries. At the same time, no other region in India can outperform the NER in terms of availability of natural resources. In this scenario, the NER has a great potential to be an important hub in shaping the future economic, political and security environment between ASEAN and India. In view of the above, this paper attempts to assess the trade potential of the North-eastern states of India with ASEAN with the help of secondary data. This study focuses on the following set of issues:

(i) It makes an assessment of the volume and composition of the trade pattern between India and ASEAN; (ii) the study tries to provide an enumeration of economic potential and facilitating factors for economic integration of the NER with ASEAN; and (iii) it discusses the issues that need to be addressed for realizing trade potentials.

1. Introduction

India's economic partnership with ASEAN,[2] which has completed 25 years recently, has been well-documented. India's journey as a dialogue partner with ASEAN began in the early 1990s with the initiation of the 'Look East Policy' (LEP), which was rechristened as the 'Act East Policy' (AEP) in 2014. Ever since India introduced the economic reform process in the early 1990s and transformed its 'Look East' to 'Act East', there have been continuous efforts to make this relationship result-oriented and practical, but India is still struggling to achieve bilateral trade of US$ 100 billion with ASEAN. Further, it has been realized that the South East Asian countries can play a pivotal role in developing the North-Eastern Region (NER),[3] which has fallen far behind the rest of the country in terms of economic growth as well as overall development since independence. The NER of India remains a land of unexplored potential and is the bridgehead of India's connectivity with Southeast and East Asia due to its critical geographic location. Although it is an industrial desert hence almost all immediate consumables are imported from outside the region that contributes only 3 per cent[4] to the country's Gross Domestic Product (GDP), but no other region in India can outperform the NER in terms of availability of natural resources.

The eight states of NER comprise 3.77 per cent of the national population,[5] occupy about 8 per cent of India's total geographical area and are the focal point of trade by sharing 98 per cent (over 5,300 km) of India's international boundaries. The region stands way below in terms of key economic indicators since the per capita GDP is far below the rest of the country—although the sex ratio and literacy rate are as good as the rest of the nation (see Table 2). In the recent past, a large number of projects have being undertaken in different sectors such as infrastructure (power, road, railways, air connectivity, inland waterways, telecommunication and information technology), plantations, irrigation and flood control, tourism, human resource development (education and health), handlooms and handicrafts, etc. for these regions.[6] Among the connectivity projects, a trilateral highway is committed to link India (Moreh in Manipur) with Mae Sot (Thailand) via Myanmar. Therefore, more movement of goods and economic activity along the route through Myanmar is anticipated which is expected to enhance the importance of the NER. Not only that, the recent signing of FTA[7] between India and ASEAN is expected to be beneficial for both the regions, especially for the NER. The region will get maximum benefit by utilising its geographical proximity with ASEAN and available resource potential. But before that, one should know the current economy, infrastructure and trade potential of the region. And, more importantly, research is needed to identify the commodities in which the region has a comparative advantage.

In view of the above, this paper attempts to assess the trade potential of the NER of India with ASEAN with the help of secondary data. The study focuses on the following set of issues: (i) it makes an assessment of the volume and composition of the trade pattern between India and ASEAN; (ii) the study tries to provide an enumeration of economic potential and facilitating factors for economic integration of the NER with ASEAN; and (iii) it discusses the issues that need to be addressed for realizing trade potential. The rest of the paper is organised as follows. Section 2 consists of three sub-sections. Sub-section 2.1 gives an overview of India and ASEAN merchandise trade while sub-section 2.2 provides a brief of NER economy. Finally sub-section 2.3 talks about the border trade scenario with Myanmar. Section 3 is divided into two parts. Part 3.1 is based on the data and methodology used in the study while 3.2 discusses the results. Section 4 concludes the study.

2. The Economy and Trading patterns of NER and ASEAN

Over the past decade, trade and investment relations between India and ASEAN have continued to improve. India's exports to ASEAN have increased from US$ 1.22 billion in 1992-93 to US$ 26.38 billion in 2016-17 and imports increased from US$ 1.54 billion to US$ 39.15 billion. In this section, we start with an analysis of the merchandise trade of India and ASEAN and then look into the socio-economic profile of the NER of India to identify the economic, industrial and production possibilities of the region. Finally, we analyse the activity of border trade with Myanmar.

2.1 Overview of India and ASEAN Trade

Bilateral trade between India and ASEAN has grown at a Compound Annual Growth Rate (CAGR) of 11.9 per cent between 1995 and 2016 in which the total trade reached nearly US$ 64.3 billion in 2016. The share in India's exports to ASEAN as a percentage of total world trade accounts for 10.97 per cent in 2016. The import share is 10.55 per cent of the total global trade. India's exports to and imports from ASEAN have been reported in Figure 1.

Figure 1: Trends in Indian Exports to and Imports from ASEAN countries, 1995-2016

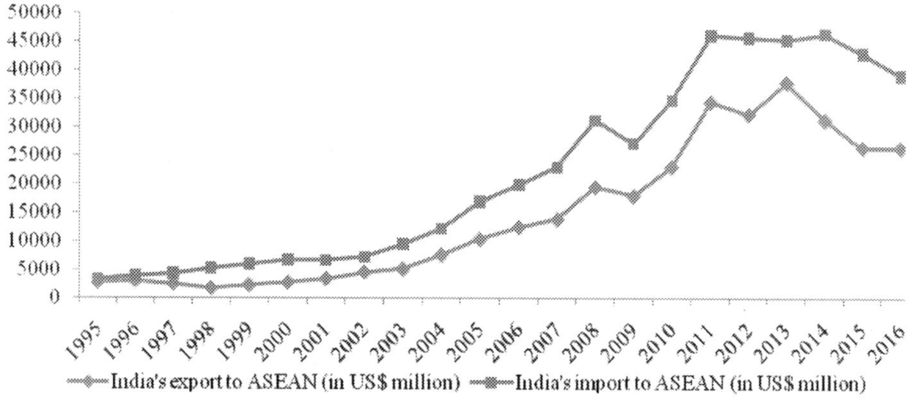

Source: UNCTAD Statistics.

Within the ASEAN countries, India's major bilateral trade happens with Thailand, Malaysia, and Singapore (see Table 1). In the year 2005-06, Singapore accounted for more than 50 per centshare in India's total exports to ASEAN followed by Indonesia, Malaysia and Thailand with a market share of 13 per cent, 11 per cent and 10 per cent, respectively. In 2016-17, export shares in the ASEAN market have undergone a major change where Singapore, Vietnam, Malaysia and Thailand stand with a share of respectively 31 per cent, 21 per cent, 15 per cent and 12 per cent in India's total exports to ASEAN. On the import side, the combined share of the four countries (namely, Singapore, Indonesia, Malaysia and Thailand) in the total imports from the ASEAN continues to be high (though it has fallen from 92 per cent in 2005-06 to 88 per cent in 2016-17). In 2005-06, Singapore was the largest source of imports with a share of 31 per cent of total imports which has been overtaken by Indonesia with a share of 34.1 per cent in total imports from the ASEAN in 2016-17.

Table 1: India's Bilateral Trade with ASEAN countries

(in US$ million)

Country	*2005-06*		*2016-17 (P)*		*CAGR (2005-06 to 2016-17)*	
	Exports	*Imports*	*Exports*	*Imports*	*Exports*	*Imports*
Brunei	43	1	38	571	-1.12	78.08
Cambodia	24	1	115	39	15.31	39.52
Indonesia	1380	3008	3306	13872	8.27	14.91
Lao PDR	5	0	29	172	17.33	0.00
Malaysia	1162	2416	5219	8716	14.63	12.37
Myanmar	111	526	1096	1001	23.14	6.02
Philippines	495	235	1524	573	10.76	8.44
Singapore	5425	3354	9105	7441	4.82	7.51
Thailand	1075	1212	3175	5613	10.35	14.95
Vietnam	691	131	6510	2693	22.62	31.63
Total ASEAN	10411	10884	30117	40691	10.14	12.74

P: Provisional; *Sources:* Export-Import Databank, Department of Commerce and DGCI&S, Kolkata.

2.2 Overview of NER Economy

This study focuses on the trade potential of NER states with ASEAN. Therefore, it is important to know the size of the NER economy, current industry profile and infrastructure of the region along with the border trade scenario. During the period from 2004 to 2015, Arunachal Pradesh, Mizoram and Sikkim have grown faster than the Indian economy. In the case of state-wise performance, not surprisingly, the difference in per capita incomes between the country and the region has steadily diverged, except for Sikkim. The services sector's contribution had increased during 2004 to 2015, which has witnessed a 53.88 per cent share in GDP, followed by

Table 2: Socio-Economic Profile of NER

States	*Arunachal Pradesh*	*Assam*	*Manipur*	*Meghalaya*	*Mizoram*	*Nagaland*	*Sikkim*	*Tripura*	*NER*	*NER share# (%)*
Population density (Per sq. km.)	17	397	122	132	52	119	86	350	176	368
Sex ratio (per 1000 males)	938	958	992	989	976	931	890	960	954	943
Literacy rate (percent)	65.38	72.19	79.21	74.43	91.33	79.55	81.42	87.22	78.84	74.04
Infant mortality rate (per 1000 live births)	30	47	9	42	32	12	18	20	30	37
NSDP growth (%) (Years 2005-2015)	18.52	14.07	12.9	13.34	17	15.74	24.65	15.21	16.43	16.79
PC NSDP growth (%) (Years 2005-2015)	13.67	11.42	8.41	11.66	11.93	10.89	20.79	11.07	13.67	15.23
Agriculture* (Year 2014-2015)	45.4	22.7	16.4	15.1	18.5	26.5	12.3	19.2	22.29	45.4
Industry* (Year 2014-2015)	24.4	21.8	22.9	30.7	22.7	13.9	55.8	25	23.83	24.4
Services* (Year 2014-2015)	30.2	55.6	60.7	54.3	58.8	59.6	32	55.8	53.88	30.2
Net Value added during 2014-2015 (Rs. Billion)	3.4	81.89	0.7	6.27	0	1.22	44.24	4.72	1.46$	9751.61

Note: # India average, *Sectoral Contribution in GSDP at current prices during 2004 to 2015 (%), $ Share of NER; # in percentage.
Sources: Census of India, 2011, Annual Survey of Industries 2014-15, CSO, Government of India.

23.83 per cent for industry and 22.29 per cent for agriculture. Table 2 briefly states the important socio-economic indicators by including population density, sex ratio, literacy rate, infant mortality rate, NSDP and PCNSDP. Interestingly, NER proves better in education and health despite its poor economic performance.

The size of the manufacturing sector of NER has been very negligible accounting for only 10 per cent of GDP in 2014-15, except for Sikkim. Industrialisation has failed to take off in the region and Assam is by far the largest industrialised state (nearly 74 per cent), while Arunachal Pradesh has no registered manufacturing industry.[8]

Not only do the people of the region not have access to basic social and infrastructure services[9] compared to the rest of India, the NER states suffer from inadequate infrastructure and inefficiency. Physical infrastructure such as electricity, communications, transportation and banking and finance are limited and unevenly distributed among urban and rural areas. Table 3 presents the basic infrastructure and logistics indicators of the NER for the year 2014. Roads are of particular importance in the region because they provide access to inland parts of the NER. The main constraint to development is high transportation cost, which has been negating NER's advantage of having a vast international border.

Table 3: Infrastructure Indicators of NER, 2014

States	*Road**	*Rail**	*IWT**	*Airport***	*Tele-density^*	*Electricity$*
Arunachal Pradesh	33.55	0.14	-	7.16	32.34	1.75
Assam	367.34	31.14	47.17	11.47	46.61	0.43
Manipur	93.33	0.06	-	4.48	37.77	0.68
Meghalaya	54.92	0.39	-	8.92	41.23	1.61
Mizoram	51.89	0.07	26.52	4.74	31.89	0.98
Nagaland	230.90	0.67	56.52	6.03	34.33	0.67
Sikkim	92.59	-	-	14.09	34.85	2.24
Tripura	295.83	18.36	-	28.61	40.45	1.82

Notes: *km per 1000 sq. km. of area. **Number per 100,000 sq. km. of area. ^Per 100 population. $ Installed electricity per 10,000 population.

Source: Calculated based on various items of Statistical Abstract, Government of India.

2.3 Border Trade of NER

The trade of goods and services across borders is highly dependent on effective transportation links. Myanmar is the only ASEAN country that shares a land border with India's North-East, thereby providing a bridge between India and Southeast Asian markets. Therefore, border trade has a special significance for the economies of the NER states. NER's informal trade volume with Myanmar at the border is growing fast and has been more than its formal trade.[10] From Table 4, it has can be seen that NER's exports to Myanmar through the land-border has increased from US$ 4.50 million in 2010-11 to US$ 18.62 million in 2015-16. In 2015-16, NER's imports from Myanmar increased to US$ 53.02 million from US$ 8.30 million in 2010-11. The total trade with Myanmar stands at US$ 71.64 million in 2015-16. Nevertheless, the border trade facilities at NER are still inadequate to support the rising trade volume and need drastic improvement in border infrastructure.

Table 4: Trends in NER's Trade with Myanmar

(*US$ million*)

Year	*NER's exports to Myanmar*	*NER's imports from Myanmar*	*NER's total trade with Myanmar*
2010-11	4.50	8.30	12.80
2011-12	6.54	8.87	15.41
2012-13	11.67	26.96	38.63
2013-14	17.71	30.92	48.63
2014-15	18.11	42.61	60.72
2015-16	18.62	53.02	71.64

Source: Department of Commerce; Ministry of Development of North East Region, Government of India.

3. Empirical Analysis

Trade data at the state level is not available. Therefore, we are unable to capture the trade participation of the NER states directly. However, following Marjit et al. (2007, 2010) we construct a Trade Openness Index which helps us to know the contribution of NER production in the nation's export and import to ASEAN countries. We discuss the methodology and sources of data to from the trade openness index in section 3.1.

3.1 Data and Methodology

The basic idea of the trade openness index of Marjit et al. (2007, 2010) is simple. The lower the value of the index, the more open the state takes part in the bilateral trade. This index has been constructed using weighting techniques to combine export and import intensities, ranks of correlation of state production share with national export and import shares of the states. The hypothesis is that if a state's production bundle closely matches the national export bundle, i.e., the state produces more of prominent exportables, the state is likely to be export-oriented and vice-versa. Therefore, for a specific state, the level of output (including industrial and agricultural) has been linked to all-India trade figures to get an approximate indicator of how open it is. Now, as a particular state progressively takes part in international trade, its factors of production will increasingly enter the export sector and that state tries to restructure its production structure to the demands to grow faster (Marjit et al., 2007; Maiti et al., 2010).

The construction of the openness index is a four-step method. In the first, we identify the gross value added (GVA) of each industry (at the 2-digit level of National Industrial Classification) for NER[11] from 1992-93 to 2014-15.[12] After tallying the NIC classification (see Annexure 1), we include manufacturing and agricultural commodities (NIC 10-30 as per NIC 2008) and then include the share of value added contributed by each industrial group for all the NER states for all the years calculated from the Annual Survey of Industries (ASI).[13] Therefore, the share of value added by an industrial group for a particular state is calculated by the following formula:

$$\underset{S_{it}}{\overset{k}{\Sigma}}= \frac{GVA_{it}^{k}\ (= NVA_{it}^{k} + DP_{it}^{k})}{TVA_{it}^{k}\ (=\Sigma_{i=10-12}^{3.1} GVA_{it}^{k}} \quad 1992\text{-}93, \ldots, 2014\text{-}15, \tag{1}$$

where S_{it}^{k} = production share of ith industry in k^{th} state at time period t; GVA_{it}^{k} = gross value added of ith industry in k^{th} state at time period t; NVA_{it}^{k} = net value added of industry producing in k^{th} state at time period t; DP_{it}^{k} = depreciation of industry producing in k^{th} state at time period t; TVA_{it}^{k} = total of all gross value added of all industries of the kth state at time period t.

The second step is to match the production commodities with the exportable commodities. For this, a comparison is made between the Harmonised System of trade classification (i.e., HS) data in the Directorate-General of Commercial Intelligence and Statistics (DGCI&S) publications with ASI data. After collecting trade data and classifying it in this way, the share of the products under consideration in total exports and imports of India is calculated thus:

$$x_{it} = \frac{X_{it}}{X_t} \text{ and } m_{it} = \frac{M_{it}}{M_t} \tag{2}$$

where x_{it} is share of ith industry in total exports in the tth period; X_{it} is the export value of the ith industry in the tth period; X_t is the total export value of India in the tth period; m_{it}, M_{it}, M_t are for imports, respectively.

The third step is to correlate x_{it} with $\underset{S_{it}}{\overset{k}{\Sigma}}$ and m_{it} with $\underset{S_{it}}{\overset{k}{\Sigma}}$. These correlation coefficients clarify how the production structure of the states is compatible with the export and import structures of the country. Further ranking of the correlation coefficients has been made in such a way that it provides rank 1 to the state with highest correlation and vice-versa. This rank can be seen as indicative of the export and import performance of the states over the years.

The final step is to calculate the trade openness index. Using the export performance rank and the import-competing performance rank (i.e., the inverse of import performance rank), equal weights to each of these ranks are assigned arbitrarily to calculate the overall openness index. Therefore, the Trade Openness Index is as follows:

$$O_t^k = \frac{1}{2} R_{xt}^k + \tilde{R}_{mt}^k \qquad (3)$$

where R_{xt}^k provides the rank correlation of the export share of kth state and $\tilde{R}_{mt}^k$ [Rtilde] is the inverse of the rank correlation of the import share of kth state. O_t^k is the value of the trade openness index.

In order to relate the trade openness index of the states with their respective per capita incomes, the states are ranked according to their PCNSDP. The PCNSDP data has been collected from the Central Statistical Organisation (CSO) with the base 2004-05. These ranks for selected[14] NER for the years 2009-10 to 2014-15 are ultimately correlated with the export performance rank and the import-competing performance rank to know the existing relationship of the states of having export-led or import-competing regional development. Finally, the scatter-plot with a trend line is presented for the rank of states PCNSDP and the trade openness index to find out the relationship of the regional income with the trade openness of that region.

3.2 Results and Discussion

The result of the trade openness index is presented in Table 7. The trade openness index has been calculated for the period 1992-93 to 2014-15 but the results presented are from 2009 onwards since the long run data for Sikkim and Tripura were not available. Among NER states, Sikkim has the second highest export performance in 2014-15 (see Table 5) and it has the lowest import competitiveness-ranking (see Table 6). Its openness index turned out to be 3 in 2014-15 (see Table 7). Since its export performance rank is high and inverse import-competing performance rank low, this implies it is involved with more exportable production and less import substitute production as per the hypothesis. This is also similar to Manipur. Hence Sikkim and Manipur are more open states in the NER. In contrast, Assam is the least open state in the NER.

Table 5: Export Performance Rank of NER

NER	*2009-10*	*2010-11*	*2011-12*	*2012-13*	*2013-14*	*2014-15*
Assam	1	2	1	1	1	2
Manipur	5	3	3	4	3	4
Meghalaya	4	5	5	3	4	3
Nagaland	6	6	6	6	6	6
Sikkim	3	4	4	5	5	5
Tripura	2	1	2	2	2	1

Source: Author's calculations.

Table 6: Import Competing Performance Rank of NER

NER	*2009-10*	*2010-11*	*2011-12*	*2012-13*	*2013-14*	*2014-15*
Assam	6	5	6	6	6	6
Manipur	3	4	4	2	3	2
Meghalaya	1	1	2	4	2	3
Nagaland	4	3	3	3	4	4
Sikkim	2	2	1	1	1	1
Tripura	5	6	5	5	5	5

Source: Author's calculations.

Table 7: Yearly Openness Index Values of NER States

NER	*2009-10*	*2010-11*	*2011-12*	*2012-13*	*2013-14*	*2014-15*
Assam	3.5	3.5	3.5	3.5	3.5	4
Manipur	4	3.5	3.5	3	3	3
Meghalaya	2.5	3	3.5	3.5	3	3
Nagaland	5	4.5	4.5	4.5	5	5
Sikkim	2.5	3	2.5	3	3	3
Tripura	3.5	3.5	3.5	3.5	3.5	3

Source: Author's calculations.

Now this openness index is linked with the state's income over the period to find out if there is any relationship between regional income and trade openness. Figure 2 presents the coefficient of variation of PCNSDP of the NER states from 2004-05 to 2014-15 which clearly reveals the income variation among NER states with an increasing trend over time. The coefficient of variation has increased 17.64 per cent in 2004-05 to 43.85 per cent in 2014-15.

Figure 2: Trend of Coefficient of Variation of PCNSDP across the NER States

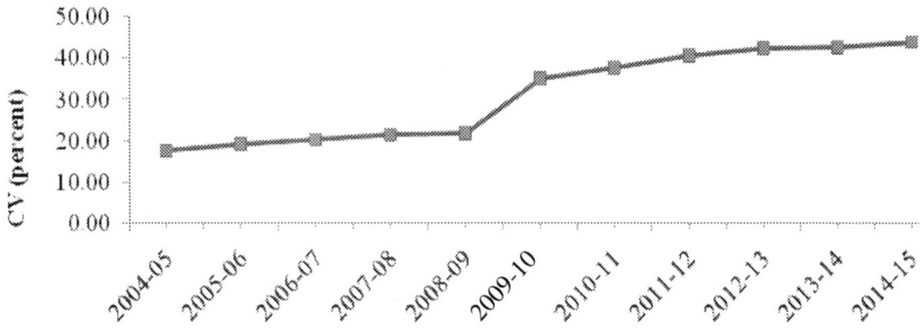

Source: Author's calculations based on CSO.

Figure 3 presents the scatter plot of the correlation coefficient between the ranks of PCNSDP and export performance of the NER states from 2009-10 to 2014-15. This figure clearly shows that the trend of the correlation coefficient increases over time, which directly implies that the inter-regional disparity as explained by the export performance of the states is on the rise.

Figure 3: Trend of Correlation Coefficient between PCNSDP Ranks and Export Performance Ranks across the NER States

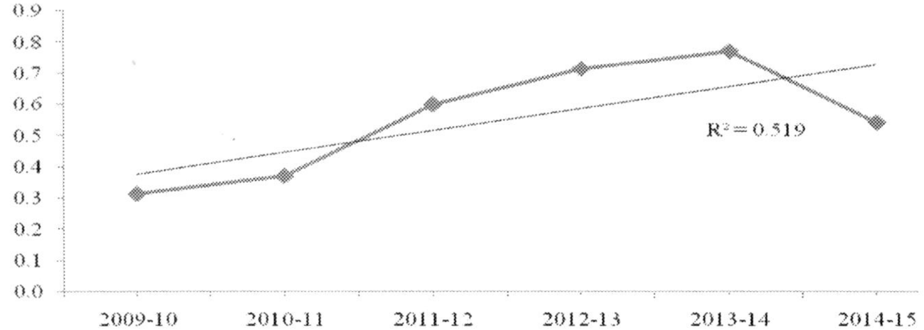

Source: Author's calculations based on CSO, ASI, DGCI&S.

Figure 4 shows the trend of correlation between PCNSDP ranks and import-competing performance ranks across NER states during the same period. The correlations are positive with a downward trend, i.e., over time the correlation becomes weaker.

Figure 4: Trend of Correlation Coefficient between PCNSDP Ranks and Import Competing Performance Ranks across the NER States

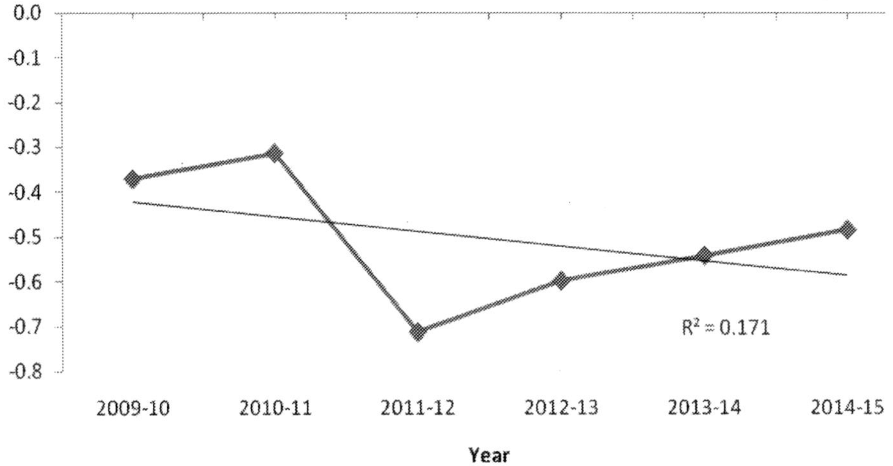

Source: Author's calculations based on CSO, ASI, DGCI&S.

Combining the ranks of export performance and import-competing performance with the rank of PCNSDP, it can be said that more export-oriented and less import-competing states gain in terms of per capita income over time. Lastly, the correlations are plotted in a scatter diagram (Figure 5) to link the openness of NER state trade with their PCNSDP. This shows a rising linear trend which implies that over time the extent of regional income has a gradually strong positive relationship with trade openness in that region.

Figure 5: Trend of Coefficient of Variation of PCNSDP Ranks and Openness Index Ranks across the NER States

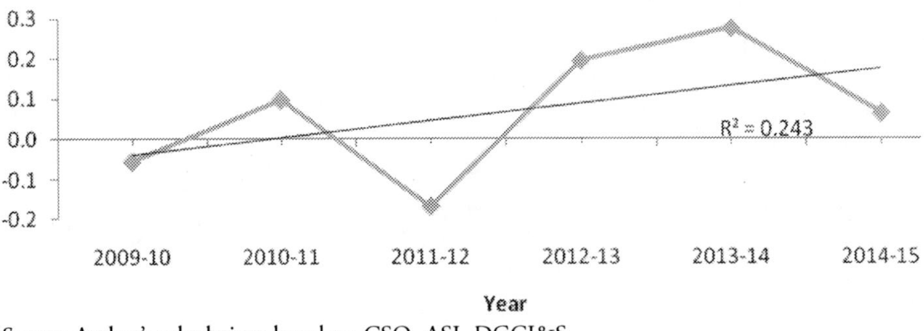

Source: Author's calculations based on CSO, ASI, DGCI&S.

Therefore, an assessment of the regional income disparity of states with export- and import-led development reveals that states become gradually more correlated with openness over the years. Nevertheless, the analysis provides ample support in favour of the initial hypothesis that states increasingly enter into the export sector and restructure their production to attain international demands.

Here it is important to mention that India's exports to ASEAN consist of mineral products and organic chemicals. In contrast, India's imports consist of electrical and non-electrical machinery, vegetable oils, fats and mineral products. NER states mainly produce and trade food, beverage, tobacco, textiles, wood, paper, leather, chemicals, rubber, plastics, petroleum, pharmaceutical, non-metals, base-metals, metal products, machinery, equipment and transport. Table 8 presents the commodity-wise export and import structure of India with ASEAN.

Table 8: Commodity-wise Export and Import of India with ASEAN

Product Category	*Share in Total Exports to ASEAN (in %)*			*Share in Total Imports to ASEAN (in %)*		
	2006	*2016*	*AGR (2006-2016)*	*2006*	*2016*	*AGR (2006-2016)*
Minerals Products	23.6	26.1	10.1	27.6	23.4	8.0
Chemical Products	14.3	15.1	9.5	9.7	9.6	10.0
Machinery & Electrical Goods	8.3	11.4	12.9	29.9	22.9	6.9
Base Metals	15.6	10.1	3.8	5.5	7.1	13.3
Vegetable Products	3.2	6.5	17.7	3.1	2.8	8.7
Live Animals	3.2	5.7	15.9	-	-	-
Transport Equipment	1.6	5.1	23.8	2.1	2.1	10.2
Textiles	4.1	4.9	11.2	1.7	1.4	7.6
Gems & Jewellery	14.3	4.6	-4.1	0.7	2.3	25.1
Processed Food	5.4	3.6	3.9	0.5	0.9	18.0
Rubber & Plastic	3.1	2.5	6.6	4.0	7.2	17.6
Instruments	1.0	1.3	11.3	2.1	2.0	9.9
Paper	0.5	0.5	9.3	2.0	1.1	2.8
Stone & Cement	0.4	0.5	12.8	0.4	0.4	8.9
Fats & Oil	0.3	0.5	15.0	7.3	14.2	18.5
Footwear	0.2	0.3	16.1	0.1	0.2	17.7
Wood	-	-	-	2.7	1.9	6.0
Raw hide & Skins	-	-	-	0.1	0.2	16.4
Miscellaneous Goods	0.3	0.3	11.9	0.6	0.4	6.9
Total	100	100	8.9	100	100	10.1

Source: WITS Database.

The prospects of NER reaping the benefits of increased trade and economic cooperation between India and ASEAN critically depend on complementarities between the availability of products in the NER and their demand in the ASEAN market. It is seen that even though the share of primary products like food and live animals in India's total exports to these countries is negligible, the growth of primary product exports to these countries provides an opportunity for the region to increase its share in India's export basket. There are a large number of products in the region which, with a little support from the different stakeholders, could become potential export products. Tea, handicrafts, bamboo and spices are some of the products from the region that could do well if allowed access into ASEAN markets.

4. Conclusion

The economic partnership with ASEAN has already begun looking towards the east. Bilateral trade with ASEAN has increased 25 times over the past 25 years and it is increasing. Current data shows that India-ASEAN trade contributes only 10 per cent of India's total trade and hence is expected to show high trade potential in the near future. Countries like Thailand, Malaysia and Singapore are the main trading partners of India while Myanmar shares a border with the NER and therefore it will be able to trade many items if NER is entitled with basic infrastructures and marketable commodities. Better transport connectivity and maritime connectivity between India and ASEAN, especially Myanmar, are fundamental to their mutual growth and development. So far, the projects that have been undertaken by India with Myanmar include the Kaladan Multimodal Transit Transport Project and the India-Myanmar-Thailand Trilateral Highway which are yet to set off. Hence, it has been argued that if cross-border corridors are developed, NER may show better performance in the medium to long run. Therefore, NER's integration with the mainland by providing infrastructure development and better connectivity is likely to offer enough opportunities for the development of the region.

The study has developed a ranking of the NER states according to their exposure to international trade to know the trade openness of the region. This is a proxy measure since trade data is not available at the regional level. The findings suggest that Sikkim and Manipur have a greater trade potential to grow in the future. Sikkim is involved in promoting trade and industry. Further findings establish that states with relatively high levels of income are also those with greater exposure to trade and such a relationship has grown stronger over time. Therefore, a state can create higher PCNSDP by switching its production from import-competing sectors to the export sectors. However, NER will not be able to obtain any benefit unless it transforms itself into a major production hub and matches its production with exportable commodities. An appropriate economic policy for the region as a whole and development of infrastructure only can help the region realise its economic growth and trade potential, especially in the context of the 'Act East Policy.'

Annexure 1: DGCI&S Trade Classifications Tallied with ASI Data

ASI Rs. lakh	*NIC Code 2008*	*NIC Code 1998*	*DGCIS&S Rs. lakh*
Food, beverages and tobacco	10,11,12	15,16	Chapters 1-24
Textiles	13,14	17,18	Chapters 50-63
Wood	16	20	Chapters 44-46
Paper	17, 18	21, 22	Chapters 47-49
Leather	15	19	Chapters 41-43
Chemicals	20	24	Chapters 28-38
Pharmaceuticals	21	-	Chapter 30
Rubber, Plastics and Petroleum	19,22	23,25	Chapters 39-40
Non-metals	23	26	Chapters 68-70
Base-metals	24	27	Chapters 72-81
Metal products	25	28	Chapters 82-83
Machinery and Equipment	27,28,31	29,30,31,32,33,36	Chapters 84-85 + Chapters 90-92
Transport	29,30	34,35	Chapters 86-89

Source: Author's compilation.

ENDNOTES

1 I am thankful to Prof. Prabir De, Coordinator, ASEAN India Centre, RIS, New Delhi, for his constant encouragement and valuable interaction for this research paper.

2 The Association of Southeast Asian Nations (ASEAN) consists of ten member–countries, viz., Indonesia, Malaysia, The Philippines, Singapore, Thailand, Brunei, Darussalam, Vietnam, Lao PDR, Myanmar and Cambodia.

3 The North-East consists of eight states, namely, Arunachal Pradesh, Assam, Manipur, Meghalaya, Mizoram, Nagaland, Sikkim and Tripura.

4 For details, kindly see Annual Reports of the Ministry for the Development of North-East Regions for various years.

5 Census of India, 2011

6 For details kindly see Annual Reports of the Ministry for the Development of North-East Regions for various years

7 India-ASEAN FTA was inked on August 13, 2009 in Bangkok after six long years of negotiations that began in 2003 as part of the Comprehensive Economic Cooperation Agreement (CECA) between India and the 10 Southeast Asian countries. The AIFTA, which at present only includes an agreement on trade in goods (TIG), has come into force from January 1, 2010

8 Summary Results for Factory Sector: ASI 2014-15, CSO, Government of India

9 The standard development indicators such as road length, access to healthcare and power consumption in the region are below the national average (NEC, 2012)

10 Refer, for example, RIS (2012)

11 In our study, we have taken Assam, Manipur, Meghalaya, Nagaland, Sikkim and Tripura

12 The reference period was taken after 1992 to capture the effect of LEP

13 Industry at 2-digit NIC 2008; Summary Results for Factory Sector: ASI 1992-93 to 2014-15, CSO, Government of India

14 Trade Openness Index has been calculated for six NER states due to data limitation.

REFERENCES

De, P. and Majumdar, M. (2014). *Developing Cross-Border Production Networks between North Eastern Region of India, Bangladesh and Myanmar: A Preliminary Assessment.* RIS, New Delhi

De, P. and Iyengar, K. (2014). *Developing Economic Corridors in South Asia.* Asian Development Bank, New Delhi.

Marjit, S., Kar, S. And Maiti. D. (2007). Regional Trade Openness Index and Income Disparity: A New Methodology and the Indian Experiment, *Economic and Political Weekly,* 24 (9): 757–69

Maiti, D. and Marjit, S. (2010). *Regional openness, income growth and disparity across major Indian states during* 1980–2008, IEG Working Paper No. 304, Institute of Economic Growth, University of Delhi

II. BORDER AND CONNECTIVITY

7

A Political Economy Analysis of Growth Episodes in the North-Eastern Region

Debajit Jha

1 Introduction

There is a large literature that deals with the dynamics of the economic growth of Indian states. While most of these studies (e.g., Marjit and Mitra, 1996; Kar, Jha, Kateja, 2011) excluded the North-Eastern states from their analysis based on the assumption that they are relatively small and the impact of their economic growth is negligible to the overall growth of the nation, the economic performance of these states has become important in recent years in the wake of the 'Act East Policy'. Moreover, while the growth performance of the region has remained dismal for a long period, the high per capita income growth of some of these states (e.g., Meghalaya, Sikkim) in recent times has caught the attention of policy makers and the media.

Although, the theories of economic growth focus on the long-run growth of economies, literature has emerged that argues that the economic growth of the developing countries go through different episodes of high and low growth. The major contribution of the literature is the identification that i) the growth path of the developing countries and within country regions are not monotonically increasing or decreasing, but they experience episodes of growth acceleration, maintenance and collapse (e.g., Housman, 2005, 2006; Jones and Olken, 2008; Kerekes, 2011), and ii) kick-starting an episode of high growth is different from sustaining it in the long-run (Rodrik, 1999). While the traditional empirical growth framework could not provide an explanation for this non-monotonic path of development, some recent political economy approaches have tried to shed light on these issues (see Kar and Sen, 2016; Pritchett, Sen and Werker, 2018).

In this context, this paper discusses the actual growth performance of the North-East (NER) during the post reforms period.[1] The paper specifically tries to answer the following questions:

i) Is the growth path of the region stable over time or are there episodes of growth acceleration or declaration?
ii) If we can identify episodes of growth acceleration or deceleration, what are the factors that determine the onset of these different episodes of growth?
iii) Whether the high per capita income growth of the region is sustainable?
iv) What are the possible implications of the "Act East Policy" on per capita income growth of the region?

In order to answer these questions, we divide the paper into two parts. In the first, we identify structural breaks of per capita NSDP of the entire region as well as the individual states to identify the episodes of high and low growth during the post-reform period using a modified Bai-Perron (1998, 2003) method (henceforth BP). In the second part, we explain the episodes of high and low growth of the NER economy in terms of a political economy approach. The rest of the paper is designed as follows:

We discuss the method of identification and the episodes of growth acceleration or deceleration in NER in Section 2. Section 2.1 discusses the method of identification of growth episodes of NER using a modified Bai-Perron method while Section 2.2 presents the episodes of growth acceleration of NER during the post-reform period. Section 3 provides a political economy explanation of the growth episodes identified in Section 2.2 and discusses whether the recent episode of growth acceleration will be sustainable in the long-run. Section 4 concludes the study.

2 Growth Episodes of NER

In this section, we discuss the evolution of growth episodes in NER. We divide this section into two parts. The first discusses the method to study growth episodes and the second discusses the evolution of growth episodes in the entire NER.

2.1 Method for Identification of Growth Episodes

In the literature, growth episodes have been identified using the BP structural break test. This is a two-step procedure. In the first, the test identifies the maximum number of possible breaks by minimizing the sum of squared residuals with respect to a minimum specified distance between the breaks in a regression of the annual growth rate on the average growth rate of NSDP per capita. Thus, the break dates in this method are the global minimizers of the sum of squared residuals of a linear regression derived using a dynamic programming algorithm. In the second step, the method uses a sequential test in order to identify statistically significant breaks.[2]

Although the BP method can statistically identify structural breaks in the NSDP per capita series, a significant deficiency of this test comes from its limited power. This implies that the test may be unable to detect all the genuine breaks in the time series, especially under high volatility of the time series (Kar et. al., 2013). Bai and Perron (2006) confirm this problem decisively by carrying out some simulation exercises. Other studies (e.g., Jones and Olken, 2008 and Kerekes, 2011) have also accepted this drawback of the BP method and pointed out that the structural breaks identified using this method are only a subset of the genuine breaks. Jones and Olken (2008) using a Monte Carlo exercise show that the BP method in small samples detects only large structural mean changes, the size of which depends on the variability of the underlying series. This implies that when the underlying series is highly volatile, the BP test requires a large change in the structural mean in order for the change to be detected as a significant structural break. Thus, the problem with the BP method is that the set of structural breaks identified by this method only be a proper subset of the complete set of actual structural breaks.

In this paper, we try to identify such structural breaks that have remained unidentified using the BP test. For this, we use the first step of the BP method to identify the candidate breaks while in the second step we use a different criterion along with the BP test following Kar et al., (2013). We call this as a modified BP test. We recognise that a non-linearity is present in growth dynamics. When a country has registered growth acceleration, it becomes difficult to increase growth rates further to register another growth acceleration of that magnitude. Similarly, when a country has registered a growth deceleration, it is difficult to achieve another of similar magnitude. Thus, a smaller increase in growth rates has been considered as growth acceleration when it follows another growth acceleration. We apply the same logic for growth declaration. Based on this, the second step of the modified BP test is as follows:

(1) For the first structural break, a change of more than two per cent (positive or negative) is considered as a growth break because it is not known whether it follows a past acceleration or deceleration. After the first break, the threshold depends on the past history.

(2) When acceleration follows a previous deceleration or a deceleration follows an acceleration, the change in the absolute magnitude of growth has to be three per cent to be considered as a true growth break.

(3) However, when acceleration follows a previous acceleration or a deceleration follows one of the same kind, a change of only one per cent in absolute magnitude is considered a genuine break.

2.2 Growth Episodes of NER

In this section we have presented the results of the identification of the episodes of growth acceleration or declaration in the North-East region. For this we have added NSDP data of all the North-Eastern states and divided it with the population of the entire region to calculate per capita NSDP of the region.[3] Then we apply the modified BP test on the growth rate of per capita income. The results of the BP test are presented in Figure 1.[4]

Figure 1: Growth episodes in the NE economy

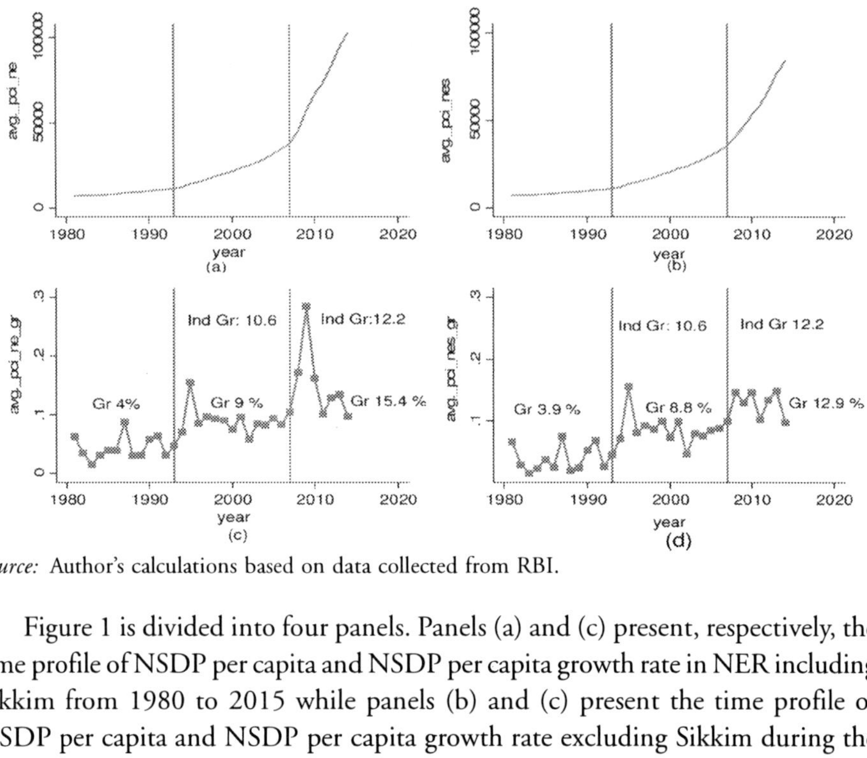

Source: Author's calculations based on data collected from RBI.

Figure 1 is divided into four panels. Panels (a) and (c) present, respectively, the time profile of NSDP per capita and NSDP per capita growth rate in NER including Sikkim from 1980 to 2015 while panels (b) and (c) present the time profile of NSDP per capita and NSDP per capita growth rate excluding Sikkim during the same period. In all the panels, the red vertical lines are placed on the year of the structural breaks identified using the modified BP test. In both the cases (including and excluding Sikkim) we found the presence of two structural breaks in the growth rate of per capita income of the region. Both the structural breaks are identified as up breaks (growth acceleration). Therefore, we identified two episodes of growth acceleration during the period from 1993 to 2015. The first episode of growth acceleration began as early as in 1993 and ended in 2007. The second growth acceleration began in 2007 and continued till the end of the period of our study.

While in the first episode of growth acceleration the NER was growing slower than the national economy (NER was growing at 9 per cent while the national average growth rate was 10.6), in the second episode of growth acceleration the NER has grown faster than the national average (NER was growing at 12.9 per cent while the national average growth rate was 12.2 per cent).[5] Therefore, in this section we derive two important results about the growth process of the NER. First, the growth dynamics in the region is not linear: there are two clear episodes of growth acceleration (1993 and 2007). Second, during the second growth episode the per capita income of the economy has grown faster than the national average per capita income. In the next section we provide a political economy explanation of the episodes' growth acceleration of the region and discuss the possibility of sustaining it in the long-run.

3 Explanation of the Growth Episodes in NER using a Political Economy Approach

In this section we present a political economy explanation of the growth episodes of the NER. In order to provide the political economy explanation of the growth episodes, we follow the framework developed by Kar and Sen (2016). This framework stands on three analytical tools—the rent space, the political space and the deals space. The interaction among them determines the episodes of growth acceleration and its sustainability in the NER. More specifically, the framework suggests that a movement from an environment of disordered deals to ordered deals brings growth acceleration. However, growth acceleration changes the nature of the rent space and the political space and consequently the deals space becomes either more open or more closed. While more open deals space produces a positive feedback effect which helps the growth of the region to sustain, a closed deals environment generates a negative feedback effect and subsequently growth collapses.

3.1 The Rent Space in the NER

The first analytical tool in our analysis is the rent space which describes the structure of economic opportunities available in the economy. The rent space characterizes the sectors of the economy along two dimensions so that the entire economy is divided into a 2 by 2 matrix. The first dimension divides the sectors according to whether the firms produce export-oriented commodities or for the domestic market. The second dimension on which the economy is divided is the source of profitability of the industries, i.e., whether the industries generate high-rent or competitive profits. This covers whether the firms produce profits using discretionary rents using the influence of politicians or bureaucrats, or by market competition. This division of the sectors of the economy is presented in Table 3.1. In it, the rentiers are the firms that produce export-oriented commodities in the high-rent sector. The export-oriented firms that lie in the competitive sectors are called magicians. In the case of the domestically-oriented sectors, the monopolistic or oligopolistic non-tradable sectors are called 'powerbrokers' and the competitive sectors are called 'workhorses'. In the present study we have included 'Mining and Quarrying' in the rentier sector while 'Registered manufacturing and business services (IT)' have been included in the magician sector. Powerbrokers in our analysis include 'utilities', 'construction', 'communications' and 'real estate', while 'agriculture', 'forestry', 'fishing', 'unregistered manufacturing', 'trade, hotels and restaurants', 'transport by other means', 'storage', 'dwellings and other services' are included in the workhorse sector.

Table 3.1: The Rent Space

	High-rent	*Competitive*
Export-oriented	Rentiers (Natural resource exporters)	Magicians (Manufacturing and service exporters, other agricultural exporters)
Domestic market	Powerbrokers (Legislative monopolies or oligopolies, natural monopolies or oligopolies, government services)	Workhorses (Importers, traders, retailers, subsistence farmers, local manufacturers, producers of non-tradables)

Source: Kar and Sen (2017)

In order to characterize the rent space in NER, we present the relative share of the rentier, powerbroker, magician and workhorse sectors in Figure 2 for the period 1993-94 to 2014-15. The figure shows that while the share of both the rentier and powerbroker sectors have increased in the first growth acceleration episode (1993 to 2007), the second growth acceleration episode (2007 to 2014) is marked by a sharp increase in the relative share of the powerbroker sector and a decline in the relative share of the rentier sector. Moreover, there is a clear decline in the share of the workhorse sector in both the growth episodes.

For robustness of the results, we have presented the relative share of the sectors in the rent space dropping (Sikkim known to have considerably industrialized during the second growth episode) from our analysis (see Figure 3). The relative share of the four sectors remains similar even after dropping Sikkim from the analysis. Therefore, in the rent space, there is an increase in the relative share of the rent-thick powerbroker sector during both the episodes of growth acceleration that are driven by the expansion of the less competitive high-rent sectors of the economy. To understand the reason for the changes in the rent space we have to understand what was happening in the political space.

Figure 2: Rent Space of the North-East Economy (including Sikkim)

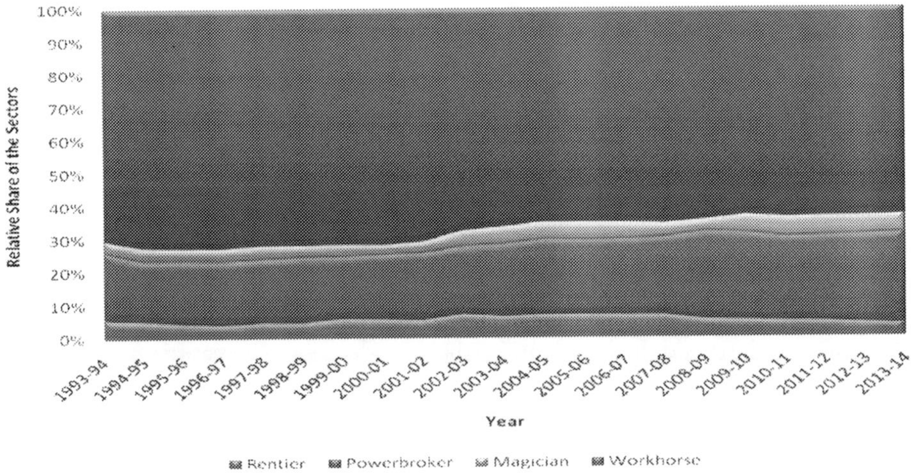

Source: Author's calculations based on data from RBI

Figure 3: Rent Space of the North-East Economy (excluding Sikkim)

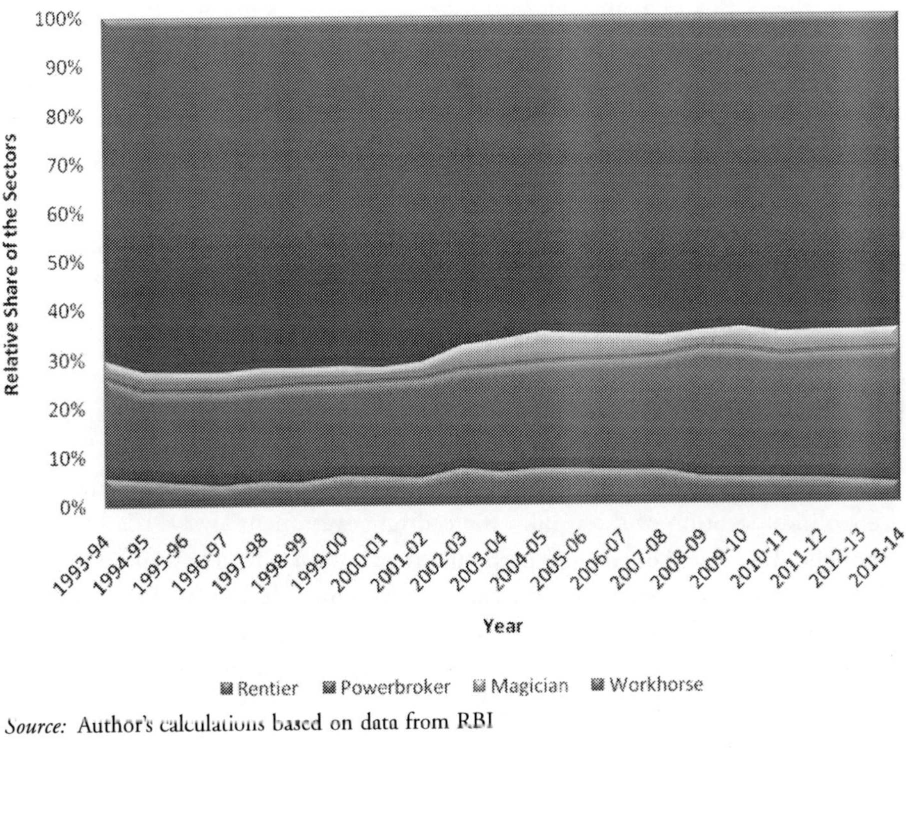

Source: Author's calculations based on data from RBI

3.2 The Political Space in the NER

The second analytical tool that has been used in this study is the political space. Two most significant elements of the political space for the analysis of growth episodes are: 1) horizontal distribution of power; and 2) vertical distribution of power. While horizontal distribution of power refers to the distribution of power between different political parties, vertical distribution of power refers to the distribution of power between elites and non-elites such as the judiciary, civil society and the middle class. When the horizontal distribution of power is high, i.e., concentration of horizontal power is weak, the settlement is more competitive. This is because in competitive political settlements many political parties compete for power with no certainty of winning the next election, whereas in uncompetitive political settlements, political power is concentrated in a leading party or individual. The competitiveness of the settlement decides the nature of rent sharing by elites (Kar and Sen, 2016). Rent sharing by the elites is more in competitive settlements. In the case of vertical distribution of power, the weaker the concentration of power, the higher is the strength of the non-elites to oppose the institutional arrangements that are perceived as corrupt or politically illegitimate (Khan, 2010).

In the NER, there are significant changes in the political space in the post-reform period. First, the political settlement becomes competitive over time. Figure 4 presents the number of major political parties that has contested in state assembly elections in the NER at different points in time. The figure shows that between 1991-94 and 2006-09 the number of registered political parties increased from 76 to 106 and has remained almost the same during 2013-2016. These numbers support the argument that the political settlement has become competitive over time. Thus, between 1991-94 and 2006-09 the concentration of horizontal political power has weakened which has resulted in an increase in rent sharing among political parties. None of the political parties or leaders was enjoying absolute political power. Second, elections became costly during the same period. This can be observed from the fact that all the political parties prefer candidates with deep pockets to contest elections. In order to finance costly elections, state political parties keep on demanding more funds from the centre in the form of development grants. Third, due to the geopolitical location of the region, the central government always tried to keep a stronghold over it. Fourth, the perpetual threat from China was increasing over time. Based on all these factors, the central government has released huge amounts of developmental grants to these states resulting in increasing the relative size of the powerbroker sector which has become the engine of growth in the region during the post reforms period.

Figure 4: Number of Political Parties that contested State Assembly Elections in different NE States

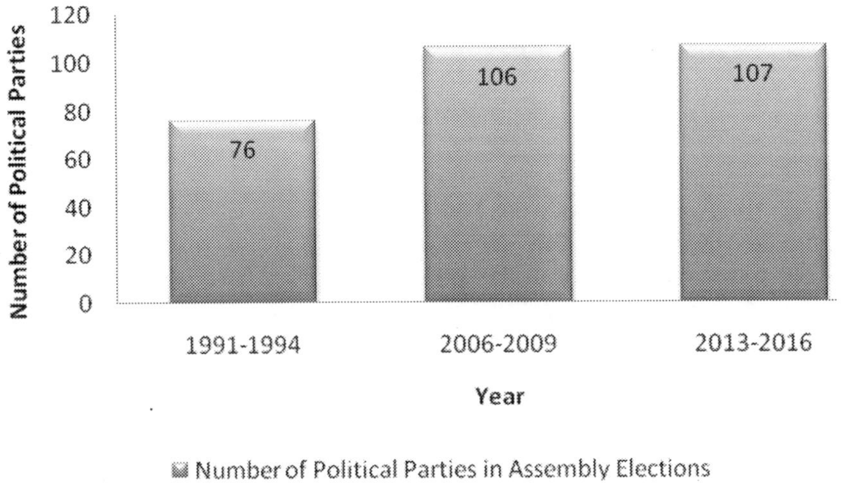

Source: Author's calculations based on data from the Election Commission of India

Although the changes in the political space can partially explain the reasons for the changes in the rent space, to understand the implications of the changes in it and the political space on the beginning and sustainability of the growth episodes, we have to analyze what was happening in the deals space induced by the changes in the rent and political space.

3.3 The Deals Space in the NER

The third analytical tool that has been used in this analysis is deals space. This captures the range of personalized and informal interactions between economic actors and the political elite. The deals environment is divided along two dimensions: 1) whether deals are honoured once they are negotiated (ordered vs disordered deals). Ordered deals are the one that once negotiated between investors and bureaucrats are delivered. In this case, investors are certain about the delivery of the deal. On the contrary, the deals that are negotiated between specific investors and political elite are called disordered deals. In this case, there is no certainty about the delivery of the deal; 2) The second dimension along which the deals environment is divided is its openness, i.e., whether deals are freely available to all investors or restricted to only a small number of elites ('open' vs 'closed'). While 'open deals' are freely available to all investors, small or large, 'closed deals' are provided by political leaders to specific investors with connections with political leaders or bureaucrats. The deals environment is presented in Table 3.2 by a 2-by-2 matrix.

Table 3.2: Typology of Deals Environment

	Closed (deals are available only to specific individuals/ organizations)	*Open (deals depend on actions of agents and not identities)*
Ordered (once negotiated, deals will be honoured)	Only those with political connections get to make the deals, but they can be confident that officials will deliver	Anyone can make a deal, and they can be certain that officials will deliver
Disordered (deals will be honoured so long as they are in the short-term interests of the political elite)	Only those with political connections get to make the deals, and even they cannot be certain that officials will deliver	Anyone can make a deal, but no one is certain that officials will deliver

Source: Pritchett and Werker (2012)

The analytical framework developed by Kar and Sen (2016) to analyze episodes of growth acceleration, maintenance and collapse suggest that economic growth is likely to accelerate when the deals space moves from disordered to ordered. The liberalization measures taken in the country in the early 1990s might have brought about the change in the deals space from a disordered to an ordered deals environment by abolishing licence raj in the industrial sector and opening up trade barriers in the international market, and consequently the first growth acceleration has taken place in the region in 1993. The second growth acceleration has taken place in 2007, which coincides with the year of the announcement of a significant change in the industrial policy for the NER (known as North-East Industrial and Investment Promotion Policy, 2007 (NEIIPP, 2007)) by simplifying the industrial permission process, introducing tax exemptions for different type of industries, etc. All these measures might have made the deals space more ordered and kick-started the episode of second growth acceleration.

3.4 Interaction between Analytical Tools: Will the Recent Growth Episode in NER be Sustainable?

While the changes in the rent space (relatively higher growth of the powerbroker sector) and the subsequent changes in the deals space discussed earlier are sufficient to start an episode of growth acceleration, they do not ensure that the growth rate of the NER will sustain in future. In order to sustain the growth momentum there needs to be a structural transformation that is expected to come "from a movement in the deals space from close ordered deals to open ordered deals, or from disordered deals to open ordered deals" (Kar and Sen, 2016). Moreover, these movements in the deals space may not be linear. As higher than national average growth started in

NER since 2007, there is expected to be two feedback effects. The first is economic in nature and depends on 'the rent space'. Since the growth process in the NER is driven by the rent-thick powerbroker sector, the deals environment is expected to become closed in the long run. This is because firms located in the powerbroker sector will push for closed deals and seek protection from competition to protect declining rent due to the entry of new firms or an open deals environment. Hence, firms located in these sectors are likely to maintain close personalized relationships with the political elite or bureaucrats to grab the process of licence allocation and erect artificial barriers to entry of new entrants. This is because in these sectors the government has a larger role to play in the allocation of operating and distribution licences and the control of entry over new firm. In contrast, if the growth process of the NER would have been driven by more competitive sectors like the magician or workhorse sectors, the deals environment would have been more open due to higher efficiency of these firms to cope up with the competitive environment. Thus, as the 2007 onwards growth acceleration episode in NER is biased towards the powerbroker sector, the economic feedback effect through rent space is likely to be negative on the deals space and the deals environment is expected to be closed in the long-run. The closure of the deals environment in turn is expected to bring a growth collapse of the region unless the growth of the powerbroker sector attracts competitive firms located in the magician and workhorse sectors.

The second feedback effect is political in nature and would depend on the political settlement and its evolution over time (Pritchett, Sen and Werker, 2018). The strength and direction of this feedback effect depends on how significant non-elite groups like civil society, the middle class, the judiciary and the media view the growth process, and how they mobilize themselves against what they think illegitimate in the growth process.

Since the growth episode in the NER is characterized by the growth of the powerbroker sector, the deals environment is expected to become closed. If the deals environment remains closed for a very long period, both political and economic feedback effect is expected to become negative which will lead to the closed ordered deals environment to be disordered. The growth episode will collapse. Therefore, the political economy analysis of the growth episodes in the NER suggests that the episode of high growth of the region will not sustain in the long-run unless the more competitive magician and workhorse sectors are growing due to high growth of the workhorse sector.[6]

3.5 What is the Expected Impact of "Act East Policy" on the Economic Growth in NER?

Now we will try to answer another related question, viz., the consequence of border trade on the economic growth of the region. In recent times, the central government has initiated the 'Act East Policy'. A major component of this policy is to engage in border trade with neighbouring countries. When the region will be involved in trade, the major product that can be supplied is natural resources because the region does not have manufacturing base. The consequence will be an increase in the share of the rentier sector of the economy. The deals environment will become more close and disordered if the competitive sectors like magician and workhorse do not grow simultaneously. Therefore, the impact of border trade on this region may be similar to many natural resource-rich countries in the world where high economic growth could not be sustained in the long-run (known as natural resource curse).

4 Conclusion

The nature of economic growth of developing countries or regions within them is different from the nature of growth of advanced countries. Although the growth path of today's advanced countries have followed a stable monotonically increasing path of growth for a very long-period, the developing countries often experience episodes of growth acceleration and declaration. The traditional neoclassical growth theories that assumed a stable monotonically increasing growth path for countries and within-country regions are insufficient to provide a true explanation of the nature of growth for the regions of a developing country. In this paper, we have tried to identify the nature of growth of the North-East region in the post-reform period. First, we tried to identify whether the growth path of the NER remained stable in the post-reform period or whether, by using a modified BP method, the region experienced episodes of growth acceleration or declaration. Then we tried to provide a political economy explanation of the nature of growth that has been experienced by the region. Finally, based on the political economy explanation of the nature of growth of the region in the post-reform period we tried to predict whether the recent high growth of the region will be sustainable.

We identified that the region has experienced two episodes of growth acceleration. The first growth acceleration began in 1993 and lasted until 2007. Although, the growth rate of the region during this period was accelerating, the region has grown slower than the national average. The second growth acceleration began in 2007 and lasted till the end of the period of our study. In contrast to the growth rate of the region during the first growth episode, the average growth of the region during the second episode of growth acceleration was faster, even faster than the national average. We argued that while the first growth acceleration episode in the NER might have started due to changes in the deals space from a disordered to a ordered deals environment brought about by the introduction of economic reform measures in the early 1990s, the second growth acceleration episode began due to the introduction of the industrial policy for the NER in 2007 (known as NEIIPP, 2007). Moreover, the growth in the region during the entire post-reform period has been driven by the high growth of the rent-thick powerbroker sector due to the changes in the political settlement, such as increase in political competition, increasing threat from China, etc. Since the competitive sectors like magician and workhorse sectors of the economy have grown very slowly during this period, the deals environment has become closed. Moreover, the high growth of the second growth acceleration episode might have generated a negative feedback effect through the rent and political space to the deals space which can bring a growth collapse in the region in the near future. We argued that all these factors may lead to a growth collapse unless the high growth of the powerbroker sector attracts more competitive and dynamic sectors of the economy to participate in the growth process which will make the deals space more open and all investors, small or large, will get equal opportunity to invest in the region.

ENDNOTES

1 The NER consists of eight states: Assam, Meghalaya, Manipur, Mizoram, Arunachal Pradesh, Tripura, Nagaland and Sikkim. Sikkim was included in the NER in 2002.

2 The sequential method first assumes a single structural break in the data series and tests for the equality of the regression parameters in the two segments. If the test rejects the null hypothesis of 'no break', then the sample is divided into two sub-samples and the same procedure is repeated for each sub-sample. This sequential method is repeated as long as the test rejects the null hypothesis and identifies another structural break.

3 NSDP data has been taken from *Statistical Handbook on Indian Economy*, RBI. The data has been taken at current prices due to non-availability of NSDP data at constant prices for some of the North-Eastern states.

4 To identify structural breaks, we have used the Stata module developed by Kerekes (2011).

5 NSDP per capita and NSDP per capita growth rates have been taken at current process due to the unavailability of constant price data for some of the NER states.

6 Although, the growth of the powerbroker sector is necessary for the growth of the magician sector (powerbroker sector provides the necessary infrastructure for the growth of the more competitive magician and workhorse sectors), a growth process driven only by the powerbroker sector may not be sustainable in future.

REFERENCES

Bai, J. and P. Perron (1998). "Estimating and Testing Linear Models with Multiple Structural Change," *Econometrica*, 66, pp. 47-78

Bai, J. and P. Perron (2003). "Computation and Analysis of Multiple Structural Change Models," *Journal of Applied Econometrics*, 6, pp 72–78

Bai, J. and P. Perron (2006). "Multiple Structural Change Models: A Simulation Analysis," In: Corbea, D., Durlauf, S. and Hansen, B. E. (Eds.). In *Econometric Theory and Practice: Frontiers of Analysis and Applied Research.* Cambridge University Press, Cambridge, UK, pp. 212-237

Berg, A., Ostry, J. and Zettelmeyer, J. (2012). "What Makes Growth Sustained?" *Journal of Development Economics,* Vol. 98, No. 2, pp. 149–166

Hausmann, R., F. Rodriguez and R. Wagner (2006). "Growth Collapses." *Kennedy School of Government Working Paper* RWP06-046

Hausmann, R., L. Pritchett and D. Rodrik (2005). "Growth Accelerations," *Journal of Economic Growth,"* Vol. 10, pp. 303-329

Jones, B. F. and B. A. Olken (2008). "The anatomy of start–stop growth," *Review of Economics and Statistics*, 90 (3), pp. 582–587

Kar, S., Jha, D. and A. Kateja (2011). "Club-convergence and polarization of states: A nonparametric analysis of post-reform India," *Indian Growth and Development Review*, Vol. 4, no 1, pp. 53-72

Kar, S., L. Pritchett, S. Raihan and K. Sen (2013). "Looking for a Break: Identifying transitions in growth regimes," *Institute of Economic Growth Working Paper, No.* 332.

Kar, S. and Sen, K. (2016) "*The Political Economy of India's Growth Episodes.*" London: Palgrave Macmillan.

Kerekes, M. (2011). "Analyzing Patterns of Economic Growth: A Production Frontier Approach," Mimeo

Khan, M. (2010). "Political Settlements and the Governance of Growth-Enhancing Institutions," Unpublished manuscript

Marjit, S. and S. Mitra (1996). "Convergence in Regional Growth Rates: Indian Research Agenda," *Economic and Political Weekly,* August, 1996

Pritchett, L., Sen, K. and Werker, E. (2018). "Deals and Development: An Introduction to the Conceptual Framework," in Pritchett, L., Sen, K. and Werker, E. (2018). (Eds.) In *"Deals and Development: The political dynamics of growth episodes."*

Rodrik, D. (1999). "Where Did All the Growth Go? External Shocks, Social Conflict and Growth Collapses," *Journal of Economic Growth,* Vol. 4, No. 4, pp. 385–412

8

India's Connectivity with ASEAN: A Micro-Level Study of Socio-Economic Connectivity and Its Impact on Border Trade at Zokhawthar (Mizoram)

Ruatdiki Hmar

The North-Eastern Region (NER) of India covers about 8 percent of the total geographical area of India and comprises the states of Assam, Arunachal Pradesh, Meghalaya, Manipur, Mizoram, Nagaland, Tripura and Sikkim. The region shares 98 percent of its border with the neighbouring countries of Bangladesh, Myanmar, China and Bhutan and 2 percent with the rest of mainland India. The NER was one of the areas where the changing economic environment taking place across the globe could not be harnessed or put to effective use prior to the 1990s. During the 1950s-1960s, the region had more or less nothing substantial to show in terms of economic development and economic achievement. With the ushering in of the era of globalization, the trend for establishment of closer border ties with other nations has gained vitality. Border trade across the NER is viewed with high expectations. While trade with Bangladesh and Bhutan had assumed certain significance in the wake of attempts made by India to establish South-Asian regional co-operation, trade with Myanmar has acquired added importance in the Indian context of the Look East Policy due to the geographical proximity of Myanmar. Traces of looking east have been traced since the colonial era with attempts made by the colonial rulers in raw material extraction and market expansion towards the South-East Asian nations. In the colonial and immediate post-colonial period, the NER was viewed as an anthropologist's paradise. In the 1960s, the region was viewed as a security prism in the context of the 1962 Indo-China War. In the 1970s, the region became a part of the political hotbed that was dominating the

Indian politics of this era. In the subsequent decades, the NER became a proposed hotbed for the development of India's Look East Policy. In the 1990s, the geographical proximity and South-East Asian continental linkage of the NER was made more relevant for India's attempts to attain better regional co-operation, promotion of cross-border trade and peacekeeping. Under the Look East Policy, the NER that was previously regarded merely as a sensitive border area was now viewed as a prospective economic zone. The Indo-Myanmar border is now perceived not merely in the context of a two-nation affair but as a via media for closer economic integration of India's relations with the East and South-East Asian nations.

I. Mizoram

The state of Mizoram is known for its political stability and high literacy rate. Based on the Statistical Handbook of Mizoram 2014, the total population of the state was 1,097,206 where 52 percent of the population was located in the urban areas. It has the second highest literacy rate in India and has a population density of 52 persons per sq km. The sex ratio is 976 and the state has the second highest per capita income in the NER. The tertiary sector has the largest contribution in the state income but absorbs only 33.60 percent of the total work force of the state. Fifty percent of the population is engaged in the agricultural sector that contributed only 20 percent of the state income. It has physical connectivity with two nations, Bangladesh and Myanmar. It shares a 722 km long border with these two nations. The state of Mizoram has witnessed a spike in the volume of informal trade. This may be due to the political and social stability found in the region, creating a conducive environment for economic and business activities. Due to the past political turmoil, hardships and authoritarian regime in Myanmar, a large number of people from Myanmar have migrated to India, especially in the state of Mizoram. The huge influx to Mizoram is due to the huge political, social, economic and cultural similarities between the people of Mizoram. A large proportion of the immigrants hail from the Chin state of Myanmar. Chins, being one of the ethnic Mizo tribes, prefer to settle and establish their economic base in Mizoram as compared to the other states of India. The immigrants from Myanmar and other neighbouring nations are also located in huge numbers in other parts of the NER.

In the Mizoram Peace Accord that was signed on 30 June 1986, the condition for border trade between Mizoram and its neighbouring nations, i.e., Myanmar and Bangladesh, was clearly envisaged. But even after the conclusion of the 1989 state assembly elections, nothing tangible was enacted for the development of Indo-Myanmar border trade. Even without any formal measures taken by the government for the development of the border trade, informal trade was flowing back and forth across the international border and foreign goods were coming in across the Indo-Myanmar border through the Zokhawthar-Rih sector. Even after the third state assembly elections, no concrete steps were taken to improve the border facilities through Myanmar. In 2003, progressive action plans for the development of the Indo-Myanmar border trade along with the establishment of the Zokhawthar Land Custom Station taken up.

II. Indo-Myanmar Trade (in the context of the NER)

Since the 1980s, prior to the collapse of the Soviet Union (the former USSR), the world economy has seen structural changes. Development strategies have been reoriented to improve performance and promote closer integration of economies around the world. The collapse of the socialist economies in the former Soviet Union and Eastern Europe had a profound impact on the participation of developing nations. Since the 1980s, there has been a rise in the adoption of open trade and regional cooperation in the international arena. In the context of India, during the first decade of economic planning (1950s to 1960s), there was little to show in terms of economic achievements. In the subsequent two decades, the fiscal inflow incurred in the region witnessed a rise that was generated due to the expansion-led growth initiated in the NER. Foreign trade and investment became an important component in the developmental programs of many developing nations. With the era of globalization and the ever-growing role of the World Trade Organization (WTO), the institutional framework for free multilateral movement of goods and services was strengthened and nations began scampering around, aiming to establish regional blocs. The policymakers retraced NER as an area of huge geo-economic potential and as a gateway for the promotion of trade and cooperation with India's immediate neighbours along with the South-East Asian nations. The Look East Policy, launched by P.V.N. Rao in 1991 drew the focus on the continental link of the NER with South-East Asia. The NER was viewed as a prospective economic zone; a gateway for promotion of trade and cooperation. With the launch of the NER Vision 2020 Document, there was a paradigm shift of the LEP to the NER. Under the Vision 2020 Document, Myanmar was considered as a key area for the promotion of trade and economic cooperation between India and the rest of South-East Asia. Under this Document, a two-fold structure for the development of the NER was laid down—short-term and long-term measures. For short-term measures, the development of border trade was given top priority.

The relevance of the NER gained dominance especially with the rolling out of the NE Vision 2020 document in 2008. The subsequent policies aimed to view the NE, especially Mizoram, as a trade corridor to Myanmar and the South-East nations.

NER became a prospective destination for both foreign and domestic investments. Under the wave of open trade policies, the impact was felt in India as well, especially in the NER. In the early 1990s, the growth of market-driven economies ushered in by liberalization and globalization did not have much of an impact on the NER due to issues of geographical remoteness, infrastructure deficiencies and recurring ethnic and militant incidents located in the region. The Indo-Myanmar Trade Agreement was signed in January 1994.

III. Border Trade Agreement

The Indo-Myanmar Border Trade Agreement was signed by the Government of India and the Union of Myanmar on 21 January 1994 which was operational from 12 April 1995. This Agreement aimed to find methods for the exchange of locally-produced goods among people living across the border and reduce the cost of goods by providing land route transportation. The Agreement initially permitted trade in 22 agricultural items but was later raised to 62 items, where even non-agricultural goods were permitted. The border trade was to be carried out from the Indian side through the establishment of Land Custom Stations (LCS) at Moreh in Manipur (corresponding to Tamu in Myanmar) and at Zokhawthar in Mizoram (corresponding to Rhi in Myanmar).

IV. Border Trade Mechanism

There was a three-stage mechanism with regard to border trade:

1) *Traditional/free exchange*: As per customary practice, trade was carried out among people living up to 40 km from the international border from either side. The value of exports was to be less than USD 1000 and exports were to be balanced through the import of goods of equivalent value within a few days. There was no custom duty imposed on these goods.
2) *Barter trade*: Under the barter trade mechanism, exporters and importers in possession of I.E.C. (Import Export Code) Certificates were allowed to carry out trade in the permitted 62 items. Customs clearance was a necessity and the exported goods were to be balanced by importing goods of equivalent value within a period of six months. The value of the bartered consignments was set at a maximum limit of USD 20,000 per transaction.
3) *Normal/Regular trade*: Under the normal/ regular trade mechanism, the export and import of goods were permissible under the EXIM policy in free-flowing currencies agreed upon by the two trading countries (i.e., India and Myanmar) through a system of advanced payment. Aside from the 62 listed items, all legal goods were tradable under the system of normal trade.

V. Land Custom Stations (LCS)

Land Custom Stations (LCS) are gateways for the transit of goods and services among nations and are platforms where formal trade between two trading nations takes place. In India, LCS are notified under section 7 of the Customs Act 1962 by the Department of Revenue, Ministry of Finance. The development of trading facilities in the LCS are undertaken by the respective state governments with funds provided under the scheme of 'Central Assistance to States for Developing Export Infrastructure and Other Allied Activities (ASIDE)' under the Department of Commerce, Government of India. India has 136 notified LCS out of which there are 11 functional LCS in the NER.

Analysis of Zokhawthar LCS (based on a field visit to Zokhawthar LCS on 7/03/2018)

Border trade is executed under the functional LCS at Zokhawthar. The task of promoting regular trade and collection of taxes at the border is undertaken by the Department of Trade and Commerce, Government of Mizoram. The LCS at Zokhawthar was inaugurated on 30 January 2004 and was deemed functional the very same day. The present-day composite buildings of the LCS were completed years after the inauguration by the BRO (Border Roads Organization) and the Government of Mizoram and upon completion were handed over to the Department of Trade and Commerce, Government of Mizoram on 14 September 2007. Prior to the construction of the composite buildings, the office for the LCS was a temporary Assam-type building. Currently, the Customs Check Point is located at the right-hand end of the iron bridge (the connecting physical infrastructure between India and Myanmar) and the immigration checkpoint of Mizoram Police is located directly opposite it. The immigration check post is guarded daily by 4-5 police officers to ensure that law and order is maintained at all times. The tradable working hours are from 8 a.m. to 6 p.m. (IST) and for normal non-trading passenger clearance, 6 a.m. to 6 p.m. (IST).

Infrastructural scenario at Zokhawthar LCS: Based on the field visit, the infrastructure-based conditions at Zokhawthar LCS are highlighted below:

1) *Weighbridge:* A weighbridge was set up but it has been non-functional since May 2013 and is in urgent need of repair.
2) *Warehouse:* There is a state-run warehouse which is run by the Department of Trade & Commerce, Govt. of Mizoram.
3) *Banking arrangement:* An SBI branch has been in operation since February 2016 which caters to the entire Zokhawthar village but is unable to accept

government challans/deposits and is also unable to cater to FOREX necessities for trading purposes.

4) *Telephone connectivity:* The Champhai BSNL station has provided landline connectivity to the LCS but does not provide its signal to Zokhawthar.
5) *Food Testing Mechanism*: Due to the unavailability of a laboratory to carry out food testing, food items are sent to the laboratory in Manipur, leading to a huge delay in transportation of goods.
6) *Status of composite buildings*: Customs officials, SBI branch, Trade and Commerce Department, staff of Agriculture Department and a plant quarantine officer occupy the composite buildings.
7) No cold storage, transit shed, LOC facilities and fax machine at the LCS site.

Import and Export particulars at Zokhawthar LCS: The following tables were obtained from the office of the Zokhawthar LCS on 7 March 2018:

Table 1: Import particulars during the last 9 (nine) years

Year (FY)	*Commodity*	*No. of Consignments*	*Quantity*	*Assessable Value (₹)*	*Revenue (₹) (Duty & Cess)*
2009-10	Reed Broom	01	15.00 MT	61,882	5,790
2010-11	Betel Nut	04	11.68 MT	4,33,548	40,564
2011-12	Betel Nut	07	60.00 MT	22,27,740	2,08,446
2012-13	NIL	00	00.00 MT	00	00
2013-14	Betel Nut	14	140.00 MT	1,61,56,394	15,11,594
2014-15	Betel Nut	66	584.00 MT	8,15,04,710	76,25,606
2015-16	Betel Nut	134	1132.50 MT	16,74,14,039	1,56,63,286
2016-17	Betel Nut	67	1500.00 MT	27,24,66,127	1,08,99,415
2017-18	Betel Nut	06	63.60 MT	1,59,83,152	75,04,444
(up-to-date)	Black Pepper	02	10.00 MT	9,70,295	11,98,749

Table 2: Revenue collection during the last 9 (nine) years

Year	*Personal Penalty*	*Auction Sale Proceeds*	*Customs Duty (₹)*	*Total (₹)*
2009-10	Nil	Nil	5,790	5,790
2010-11	Nil	Nil	40,564	40,564
2011-12	₹ 2,000	Nil	2,08,446	2,40,446**
2012-13	₹ 8,500	Nil	0	8,500
2013-14	Nil	Nil	15,11,594	15,11,594
2014-15	Nil	Nil	76,25,606	76,25,606
2015-16	Nil	Nil	1,56,63,286	1,56,63,286
2016-17	Nil	Nil	1,08,99,415	1,08,99,415
2017-18	Nil	Nil	87,03,193	87,03,193

VI. Cultural, Social, Economic Connectivity (voices from the field)

During a field study undertaken in the border areas, i.e., Zokhawthar village on the Indian side and Zokhawmawi village on the Myanmar side between 7 and 8 March, 2018 around 15-20 people were interviewed and observed accordingly in their surroundings.

Cultural Connectivity: The Chin tribes located in Myanmar in the Chin Hills are part of the Mizo tribes, i.e., are part of Mizo ethnic stock. They share common ancestral roots with their fellow Mizo counterparts in Mizoram and have a deep, entwined cultural linkage rooted in their values, lifestyle, language and societal set-up. Many residents of Zokhawthar and Zokhawmawi have relatives living across the border.

Based on the findings obtained from the respondents, the international border is not seen as a separation of people belonging to the same ethnic stock or as a blockage for promoting continued unity among the Mizo tribes living on both sides of the border. It is merely viewed as a state creation; a creation of geographical demarcation for political reasons to ensure peace and stability within and across nations.

Social Connectivity: The shared ancestral roots are also evident in the social connectivity that exists in both the villages.

a) *Societal set-up*: Both villages, as per the Mizo societal set–up, have influential and fully functional civil society organizations (CSOs), NGOs and local bodies. The Young Mizo Association (YMA) and the Village Council (VC) are among the most influential organisations. They have full allegiance from residents of the villages who in turn work towards their betterment and well-being. They play a key role in all areas ranging from governance to social sector initiatives. They have strong voices and are also accepted by the political powers due to their influence over the villagers. With regard to the YMAs and VCs of Zokhawthar and Zokhawmawi, they have a congenial relationship with their counterparts across the border. Many a time, joint meetings, consultations and joint action plans are initiated. Elected leaders from these bodies have both formal and informal consultation with each other on issues ranging from societal well-being, promotion of developmental initiatives, cross-border cultural events and in instances related to law and order.

b) *People-to-people contact*: The residents of Zokhawthar (Indian side) and Zokhawmawi (Myanmar side) have a deep-rooted people-to-people connectivity. The respondents from the field study share the same view.

They are all supportive of cross-border initiatives aimed at promoting greater unity. They have no issues with cross-border marriages and are supportive of them, Cross-border visits for both formal and informal purposes are rampant and the people do not face any hardship crossing the border from either side. The formal visits range from religious events and societal events like marriages, funerals and so forth. The informal events include meetings with relatives or friends, impromptu sports matches and other such gatherings. Many residents of these villages frequently visit the markets on the other side to purchase necessities.

Transitive Myanmar and its impact on people to-people-connectivity: The transitions taking place in Myanmar has had a huge impact on the nature and volume of people-to-people contact, especially in the context of these two villages. Based on the observations and experiences garnered from the respondents, it is evident that the transition towards a democratic Myanmar has physically and mentally given a positive boost for the development of greater people-to-people connectivity. Many initiatives in this regard have been undertaken. Citing some instances, during Independence Day 2017 and Republic Day 2018, there was a joint meeting of officials from the Indian side (represented by Mizo leaders) and the Myanmar side at Zokhawthar Tourist Lodge. In November 2017, a two-wheeler rally was organised by Assam Rifles (AR) from Aizawl (India) to Mandalay (Myanmar).

c) *At the non-governmental level*, special cases where joint cultural troupes to represent either village and joint sports events have been witnessed. In sports, the Zokhawthar Football League was established in 2017 which opened its doors to Mizo ethnic stock located at Myanmar, i.e., national citizenship was not taken into account. Educational trips/study tours, especially from Mizoram, have been on a steady rise. The Mizo clan from both sides are strongly rooted in Christianity and thus many religious denominations arrange visits by religious leaders and joint church programmes.

d) *Regarding education*: There is no institution for higher education in Zokhawthar. But at the primary and middle levels, schools have witnessed enrolment of students residing in Zokhawmawi (Myanmar side). But students from Zokhawthar are not enrolled in schools on either side.

e) *Impact of media*: The media has a huge impact, especially on the Mizo clan on the Myanmar side. Due to shared medium of communication technology, the Mizo channels and programmes aired in Mizoram are also viewed on the Myanmar side. Also, the serials/movies/soap operas dubbed in Mizo language telecast in Mizoram are also viewed with high anticipation by the Mizo clan located in Myanmar. Cross-border performance of local singers for numerous events are very much in demand.

f) *Tourism aspect:* Under the Government of Mizoram, many steps have been taken for the promotion of tourism in these areas. One particular initiative is the *Stay at Home* where, under this project, seven homes have been selected. Funds have been given to these homes to offer adequate facilities to tourists who may opt to stay in them to experience staying with a typical Mizo household. Many tourist agents recognized by the Government of Mizoram also include visits to these villages under their tourist packages.

g) *Regarding women*: There is a fully functional NGO for women, the MHIP (Mizo Hmeichhe Insuihkhawm Pawl) at Zokhawthar which ensures the well-being of women and children. Even though Zokhawmawi is yet to have such an organisation, the Zokhawthar MHIP has made a provision to ensure that membership is extended to the women of Zokhawmawi. Under the MHIP, SHGs (Self-Help Groups) for women entrepreneurs have been established since 2017. These SHGs offer loans at low rates of interest to their members.

Economic Connectivity: Social and cultural connectivity plays a key role for overall economic operations, especially in the context of these two villages. Due to the social and cultural linkage, petty traders hailing from either side are found in markets across the border. The economic transactions in the form of buying and selling of wares in determined by the prevailing rate of exchange, price factor and the variety of goods being offered. In many situations, goods arriving from Myanmar do not originate there. Myanmar is usually the middle agency for the export of goods originating from China and Thailand. Many residents of these villages depend on the border trade for their source of income. While some have a direct role in the export and import of goods, many are dependent on the indirect employment ranging from the loading and unloading of goods, cart or bike services needed for transportation of goods, etc.

a. Informal Trade

Even with many initiatives taken to promote formal trade across the two nations, the main cause of disagreement has been highlighted on the issue of the bridge which is the only legal route for trade-related activities. This bridge is unable to carry heavy loads and is deemed unfit to cater for a huge volume of goods. As such, illegal routes are utilised. The tables mentioned earlier in this paper have earmarked edible goods such as betel nuts/soyabari/black pepper as the main items imported from Myanmar. Most of the plasticware, footwear, blankets, cosmetics and a huge portion of electronic goods found in Mizoram owe their origin to Myanmar, China and Thailand. Goods from China and Thailand are also transported to Mizoram via Myanmar. Based on a report of the Indian Institute of Foreign Trade (IIFT), New Delhi the value of informal trade at Zokhawthar-Champhai was valued at INR 500 crore during the 1990s. There is thus a huge gap between formal and informal trade.

Based on the field study conducted at Zokhawthar and Zokhawmawi, the following obstacles or bottlenecks for the development of border trade between India and Myanmar via Zokhawthar-Rih were identified. For the success and full implementation of policy measures such as the Look East Policy and the subsequent Act East Policy; the Vision 2020 Document and other undertakings by both the central and state governments, the glaring issues highlighted below have to be deliberated at all levels and remedial measures taken accordingly.

b. Bottlenecks for Border Trade

1) Infrastructure-wise

- *Bridge*: The bridge is unable to meet the trade requirements as it is not able to carry heavy loads. Thus, for goods weighing more than ten tonnes, they are loaded and carted across the bridge using small vehicles or carts. This has reduced the volume of formal trade and has promoted the use of illegal routes and also diluted the appeal of trading between India and Myanmar via Zokhawthar LCS.
- *Lack of testing facilities*: The absence of adequate testing facilities for food products have been the root of hardship faced with regard to border trade. Edible goods entering Zokhawthar LCS are sent to the testing laboratory in Imphal, Manipur. The need to send food items to another state as well as the entire logistical requirement for the entire testing process has led to a massive delay in the mobility of goods.
- *Lack of advanced payment facilities at Zokhawthar:* Even with the establishment of an SBI branch at Zokhawthar LCS, it is unable to cater to foreign exchange requirements. In normal trade, there is a need for advance payment of goods in foreign currency. Due to the inability of the Zokhawthar SBI to carry out such transactions, the advance payments are being provided by HDFC Bank in Champhai town.

2) On Employment

The majority of employment avenues available around the border areas is temporary and based on many factors. Some are determined solely by the availability of seasonal food products in particular months of the year. The nature of the relationship between the governments of the two sides and the possibility of any disgruntled actions/policies may also lead to lack of employment avenues. In cases of tension between the two nations, situations may arise where traders may deem trade unfavourable leading to a fall in the volume of trade which may take a heavy toll on the livelihood of the villagers.

3) Human Aspect

- *Unskilled labour:* The majority of the labourers are unskilled, i.e., they lack proper skill to do specific tasks. This lack of skill is mainly due to the lack of skill-based programmes and initiatives for those living in the border areas. Skill development programmes may be recorded at a favourable percentage for the state as a whole but the border areas are highly neglected as they are concentrated in and around the state capital while the periphery of the state is highly neglected.
- *Lack of involvement of the people located in border areas:* Even with huge developmental initiatives being adopted for promotion of border trade, there is no involvement of people at the grassroots level. These villagers have no proper understanding or awareness policy measures, undertakings and lack the education needed to understand the policy implications and functioning of the LCS.
- *Role of community-based organizations:* There are many community-based organizations in Mizoram. Many of them have branches in different parts of the state. The ones located in Zokhawthar have a huge influence even with regard to border trade. There are instances when events that unfold in other parts of Mizoram may trigger these organizations to close the bridge for a day or even for a longer period. Other instances may call for the prohibition of movement of people across the border or impose restrictions. Such societal-based control hampers not only trade but also has a deep impact on social connectivity.

REFERENCES

A field study was conducted in Zokhawthar and Zokhawmawi on 7 and 8 March 2018. About 15-20 respondents were identified and interviewed. A detailed analysis of the Zokhawthar LCS was also undertaken.

Chakraborty, Gorky; Ray Ashok Kumar. 2014. *The Look East Policy and Northeast India*. Aakar Books, Delhi.

Chandran D. Suba; Sinha, Tuli and Kang, Harnit Kaur. 2011. *An Alternative Strategy towards Southeast Asia Looking through India's Northeast.* Samskriti, New Delhi.

Chakraborty, Gorky; Ray, Ashok Kumar. 2015. 'The Look East Policy From People's Perspective: A study on Mizoram,, in *NFI Report.* Institute of Developmental Studies, Kolkata.

April-October 2011-2012 Report by the Ministry of Finance and Industry, Government of India source: http://commerce.nic.in/publications/anualreport_chapter7-2011-12.asp accessed on 2/03/2018.

12th Five Year Plan by the Directorate of Commerce and Industries, Government of Mizoram, source: https://tradeandcommerce.mizoram.gov.in/page/12th-five-year-plan.html accessed on 4/03/2018.

http://www.mdoner.gov.in/node/1474accessed on 4/03/2018.

Trividesh Singh Maini. 8/11/2 014. "India's 'Look East' Policy Begins with Myanmar" in *The Diplomat,* source: https://the diplomat.com/2014/11/indias-look-east-policy-begins-with-myanmar/ accessed on 4/03/2018.

9

Importance of Myanmar in Act East Policy

Lalrinngheta

The location of Myanmar is strategically important as it lies in the threshold of the South-East Asian region. It borders Mizoram, Manipur, Nagaland and Arunachal Pradesh on the western side from where India plans to establish its mega policy, i.e., the Act East Policy through the continental route. On the eastern side, it was bordered by Laos PDR and Thailand. As a matter of fact, Myanmar is the starting point from where India tries to build up its relations with South-East Asian nations and beyond. Therefore, Myanmar holds a strategically significant position for the effective implementation of India's Act East Policy. India needs to maintain good relations with the Myanmar government first to reach further to South-East Asian countries. To play the game with Myanmar in India's favour in the midst of the counter-game played by China in its plan to befriend all countries neighbouring India is a very big challenge for India.

Besides, the internal political development of Myanmar, democratic set-up, peace and stability of the civilian government and the Rohingya crisis will be crucial factors in determining the credibility and suitability of Myanmar for India's Act East Policy successful result. Earlier, India's Look East Policy was mainly conducted through sea routes. Coastal states like Tamil Nadu, Andhra Pradesh and West Bengal mainly benefited from trade with ASEAN, East Asian and Asia-Pacific countries. The North-Eastern states of India, though being a corridor for land routes to the South-East Asian region, were long denied the benefits in terms of trade and infrastructure development. But with a renewed vigour of land and riverine routes to this region, the North-East states are now settling on the trade transfer corridor. But as already mentioned, land or riverine links with this region first need to pass through the immediate neighbour, i.e., Myanmar.

So, trade through land routes envisaged by the Act East Policy depends to a great extent on Myanmar. Once the India-ASEAN physical connectivity projects like the India-Myanmar-Thailand trilateral highway, which is expected to be extended to Laos and Cambodia, and the Kaladan Multi-Modal Transit Transport (KMTT) Project that envisages a direct trade corridor between Indian ports on the eastern seaboard and Sittwe port in Myanmar and then through riverine and road transport to Mizoram are completed, the geographical isolation of the North-Eastern Region (NER) will end and the region will be poised to play a meaningful role in integrating India with South East Asia. In 2013-14, five countries, i.e., Singapore, Malaysia, Thailand, Vietnam and Indonesia accounted for 93 per cent of India's total trade with ASEAN countries. Most of this trade was carried on shipping through the Bay of Bengal. The North-Eastern states got no benefit. So, Myanmar is very important for India and particularly for the North-Eastern states to successfully run trade relations with South-East Asia.

Gurudas Das in his article entitled 'India's Myanmar Policy: Implication for India's Northeast', argues that in spite of having a pragmatic approach India's Myanmar policy has failed to yield the desired result mainly because it has not made India's North-East as the fronthead of sub-regional cooperation. He identified the lack of economic development in the region as a potential factor hindering successful trade relations with Myanmar in comparison with Sino-Myanmar border trade. The Act East Policy through the continental route requires road and infrastructure development, regional security and peace, local participation in trade and improvement in local production both in agriculture and in industrial goods. That is why building good relations with the immediate neighbouring country is so vital. India needs to keep an eye on Myanmar's internal politics and economic situation to manage relations in good shape. Good road connections will provide an opportunity to boost the economy of the entire North-East which is landlocked and facing acute infrastructure and related problems.

The Indo-Myanmar border, stretching over 1,600 kilometres could play a crucial role for improving trade relations through land routes that would be beneficial for the adjoining North-Eastern states. One of the major setbacks in India's Look East Policy has been the absence of good trade relations with Myanmar which is not only India's immediate neighbour but also a gateway to ASEAN. Closer engagement with Myanmar will boost India's LEP.

Indo-Myanmar Relations

Indo-Myanmar relations had begun in ancient times. Buddhism, a religion founded in India, greatly influenced the people of Myanmar and even today 90 per cent of its population follows it. It was separated from British India in 1937. After India attained independence in 1947 from Britain, diplomatic relations began and it flourished for many years due to several factors like both were under British rule, cultural links, common interest in regional affairs, flourishing commerce and the presence of a significant number of Indians in Myanmar. Both countries used to work together in counter-insurgency measures. But bilateral relations went downwards when a military coup was launched in Myanmar in 1962 under General Ne Win. India condemned it. The military junta expelled the Burmese Indian community which further worsened relations and led to Myanmar's isolation from the rest of the world except China.

With the passage of time, there is a realization among intellectual and political think tanks in India that the growing Chinese influence on India's neighbour would have a detrimental effect on India's national interests in the long run. As a result, in 1987, Prime Minister Rajiv Gandhi visited Myanmar. Under prime ministers P.V. Narasimha Rao and Atal Bihari Vajpayee, Myanmar gained importance in India's foreign policy under its wider perspective of expanding trade and economic influence in South-East Asia. From the military standpoint it can be viewed as a counter strategy to the military influence in the South-East Asian region.

Land and maritime trade routes between Myanmar and India are improving gradually but slowly. Trade between India and Myanmar through the border trade points of Moreh and Zokhawthar in 2012-13 was only $6.5 million. However, the informal trade that takes place across the border is several times higher. Large, unregulated informal trade, fraught with security, health and safety risks have remained as challenges to border trade. Meanwhile, trade undertaken through shipping, i.e., the Kaladan Multi-Modal Transport Project (KMMTP) that connects Kolkata port with Sittwe port could ease the challenges to border trade. But if maritime trade flourished at the cost of the land route, North-Eastern states would be denied mega project benefits. India is the 12th on the list of investors in Myanmar with a cumulative investment of US$ 1.89 billion from 1989 to 2012. Foreign Direct Investment in Myanmar touched US$ 6 billion in the first nine months of the fiscal year 2014-15.

Myanmar under democratic reform is now openly playing a neutral role in its foreign policy. It is imperative to maintain close and cordial relations especially with her two giant neighbours.. After a democratic government was set up there, apprehensions have been growing over too much dependence on China. Even now, many of the big projects China has pursued in Myanmar were protested by the local people. For instance, China Power Investment Corporation investment in the $3.6 million Myitsone hydropower station on the Irrawaddy river hit a snag in early October 2011 as the Burmese Government suspended construction due to local residents concern about the human, environmental impact and perceived benefits. Most of the power generated will be exported to Yunnan province in China and local residents claimed lack of community feedback in the planning process. The Chinese government states that Burma will get $54 billion USD in tax revenues, share profits, free electricity. At stake is China's huge financial stake in the project and also the risk to the other big projects China has in the country. The China Power Investment Corporation states that only five villages with a population of 2,146 needed to relocate. The company has provided the affected villagers with two-storied houses, a 21-inch television and a 100,000 Burmese Kyat compensation which works out to about $140 USD.

The de facto leader of Myanmar, Aung San Suu Kyi, during house arrest used to criticize China. But after coming into power, she needed to follow pragmatic ideas. She chose China as the destination of her first foreign trip. Myanmar shares a 2,000km-plus long border with China and the existing economic and trade relations are needed to ensure economic prosperity and growth for the poor Myanmar economy. Moreover, various insurgent groups living along the border of China need to be handled with the help of China to maintain domestic peace.

On the bright side for India, Myanmar President U Htin Kyaw paid a landmark visit to India at the invitation of President Pranab Mukherjee from 27 to 30 August 2016. In the first meeting between the two top leaders, various issues in bilateral relations were discussed and Prime Minister Narendra Modi assured help to Myanmar both as a partner and as a friend. President Kyaw also assured that Myanmar's territory would not be allowed to be used for attack against India. India was receiving Myanmar's full cooperation on this issue even when the military junta was in control. With Suu Kyi's dispensation, this support is expected to continue with the same steadfastness and sincerity. Myanmar's commitment to India's security was reiterated during President Kyaw's visit. Both countries emphasized the importance of sound border management as an intrinsic element of maintaining border security, peace and stability along the entire length of their common border.

But in trade, the magnitude between India and Myanmar is not great in comparison to Myanmar with China. The Government of India undertakes some major infrastructure projects for connectivity with Myanmar as under:

1. *Indo-Myanmar Friendship Road:* A 250-km long Tamu-Kalewa-Kalemyo highway popularly called the Indo-Myanmar Friendship Road was inaugurated on 13 February 2001. It was mainly built by the Indian Army's Border Roads Organisation and aimed to provide a major strategic and

commercial transport route connecting North-East India and South-Asia as a whole to South-East Asia.

2. *India-Myanmar-Thailand Trilateral Highway:* The India-Myanmar-Thailand Trilateral Highway is under construction under India's Look East Policy that will connect Moreh (India) with Mae Sot (Thailand) via Myanmar. The Imphal-Mandalay-Bangkok 1,986-km route is expected to be completed by 2019. The road is expected to boost trade and commerce in the ASEAN-India Free Trade Area as well as with the rest of South-East Asia.
3. *Kaladan Multi-Modal Transport Project:* The Kaladan Multi-Modal Transport Project was the first major project undertaken by the Indian Government in Myanmar. India has finished constructing the Sittwe Port in the trouble-prone Rakhine state of Myanmar. Also, the extension of the Aizawl-Siaha National Highway by 90 kilometres to the international border at Zorinpui on the Indian side is nearing completion. In addition, four-laning of the 300-km Aizawl-Tuipang highway to ensure faster movement of goods between Sittwe and Aizawl is also nearing completion.

KMMTP is essentially a multi-modal transport project having three different stretches involving shipping, inland water and road transport stretches. The longest among them is the shipping segment from Kolkata to Sittwe Port in Myanmar. The Government of India is funding this project and it is considered an important investment for India in its neighbourhood. The cargo will set off from Kolkata and reach Sittwe in Myanmar by ship. The Sittwe Port would be linked to Lashio (also in Myanmar) via the Kaladan river transport route. Lashio would be connected to Mizoram via road transport (National Highway 54).

The completion of KMMTP will play a major role in the economic development of the North-East and will improve the bilateral relations between India and Myanmar. When completed, the KMMTP will shorten the current time taken to transport goods from Kolkata to Mizoram by three to four days, and the distance by around 950 kilometres. Other key projects that are being built by India are the Rih-Tiddim road, the project to build 69 bridges on the Tamu-Kyigone-Kalemo road, Yamethin Police Training Centre and a hospital.

On 20 December 2017, India and Myanmar signed an MoU aimed at developing Myanmar Rakhine state. This MoU comes in the backdrop of massive migration of Rohingya refugees from Rakhine to Bangladesh. The statement said that this MoU is intended to help the Government of Myanmar achieve its objective of restoration of normalcy in Rakhine and enable the return of the displaced people.

Advantages

India has advantages in dealing with border trade to facilitate effective and productive engagement with Myanmar.

Firstly, closely-related people living across the border can be a factor to bolster trade. For example, Mizos living in Mizoram and those living in the Chin hills of Myanmar have close cultural links from times immemorial. Besides, people living in the eastern districts of Nagaland like Konyak, Khiammugan and Yimchunger Nagas and those living in the areas of the Naga Self-Administered Zone (NSAZ) in Myanmar have close family ties and engage in cultural and economic exchanges. Some people on the Indian side own houses across the border along with cultivated land and forested areas and those from the Myanmar side used to buy basic essentials on the Indian side. Besides, a large number of students from NSAZ also study in schools in India. Such close affinity prevailing among the people across the border would facilitate trust building, people-to-people contact and cooperation in security-related matters.

Secondly, military and strategic cooperation with Myanmar along the border will facilitate in checking illegal drug trafficking across the border. In addition to this both countries would benefit in curbing insurgency activities frequently occurring in the border areas. Thus, there is potential for strategic military cooperation which enables the Myanmar Government to provide stability in its ethnic group regions like Shan state which in turn secures India's own north-eastern region. Thirdly, those regions in Myanmar bordering India were peaceful and less restive in comparison with those bordering China.

But when we talk about the advantages of border trade and connectivity with Myanmar, it is necessary to keep in mind that drug trafficking carried on by insurgent groups in Myanmar, especially by ethnic groups living on the border with China, need to be carefully checked. Yunnan province of China greatly suffered at the cost of close links with drug trafficking. As of now, most of the drugs and weapons trafficked illegally are taking the route of Mizoram and Manipur. Border police check-posts are needed to be strengthened and equipped with sophisticated materials and more men.

Myanmar Internal Politics

In October 2016 extremist group of ethnic Rohingya (Muslim) in the name of Arakan Rohingya Salvation Army (ARSA) attacked some military posts in Myanmar bordering Bangladesh. Combined military and police cooperation lasted from 9 October 2016 to 9 February 2017 in the Rakhine province. The United Human

Rights Commission had passed a resolution on 24 March 2017 and constituted a three-member commission to undertake a Fact-Finding Mission in Rakhine Province in connection with army atrocities and make a report to the UNHRC by March 2018. The Government of India abstained from taking part in the resolution keeping in mind the sensitivity of maintaining security and trade relations with Myanmar. This resolution was strongly criticized by Myanmar state councillor Aung San Suu Kyi.

Back in 2007, when anti-government protest in Myanmar had drawn international condemnation, India kept quiet. It argued that it respected the sovereignty of Myanmar and tried to refrain from indulging in Myanmar's internal affairs. This low-key response had been drawing criticism from the international community and from within as weakening India's credentials as a leading democratic nation. Then in the recent Rohingya crisis faced by Myanmar and the mounting international criticism of the brutal military activities, India still refrained from voicing condemnation against Myanmar. These kinds of unresponsive or pacifist policy towards Myanmar may be regarded as an important political strategy for winning its trust. But policy thinkers in India need to scale up pro-active engagement with the newly set up democratic government of Myanmar in other fields to diminish Chinese influence in Myanmar's internal affairs. The repatriation of Rohingya refugees from Bangladesh to Myanmar by following the recommendations of China clearly indicates the overwhelming influence of China on these two democratic countries.

How could China exert such pressure on the two neighbouring countries while Bangladesh itself failed to put pressure on Myanmar to repatriate Rohingya refugees camping in its temporary refugee camps. It was a big burden for the host country economically. India also fails notwithstanding the claim of India's Minister of State for Home Affairs that India is engaged in talks with Bangladesh and Myanmar to deport Rohingya refugees to Myanmar. India was in a dilemma whether to support Bangladesh in pressurizing Myanmar or support Myanmar in its fight against terrorism, a term used by Myanmar officials to describe the Rohingya extremist militant. When Prime Minister Narendra Modi visited Myanmar for talks with State Councillor Aung San Suu Kyi, a joint statement on the Rohingya crisis reflected only India's support to Myanmar in fighting terrorism. Later, the Indian Ministry of External Affairs issued another statement expressing concern about the refugees. Such a two-faced policy may not yield great dividends.

China, in its turn, stepped in with a three-point plan in the dilemma over a deal concerning repatriation between Myanmar and Bangladesh. In November 2017, Wang Yi, Chinese Foreign Minister, visited both Bangladesh and Myanmar and made a proposal. Under it, the two countries were to hold bilateral talks and reach a repatriation agreement which was later achieved. China, which has historically been wary of stepping into domestic conflicts in other countries, is being pro-active in this case. Its own interests are at stake. Beijing enjoys good relations with both Bangladesh and Myanmar; besides, Rakhine is an important link in its Belt and Road Initiative. China is building a $7.3-billion deepwater port in the province and has invested $2.45 billion to build an oil and gas pipeline connecting coastal Rakhine to Yunnan. China has put pressure on Myanmar because a protracted conflict in Rakhine will be decidedly against Beijing's economic interests. The signing of a repatriation deal suggests that this pressure tactic is working.

China Factor

Due to its strategic position as a corridor to the Indian Ocean, rich in oil and natural gas and as a buffer state between India and China, Myanmar holds great importance for China's foreign policy. Burma was the first non-communist country to recognize the Communist Peoples' Republic of China. Diplomatic relations between the two were set in 1950. China and Burma signed a treaty of friendship and mutual non-aggression and promulgated a joint declaration on 29 June 1954. When the military junta came to power, China was the only country that openly stood with Myanmar daring international condemnation. China is the most important supplier of military aid and extends extensive military and strategic cooperation. Since 1989, China has supplied Myanmar with jet fighters, armoured vehicles and naval vessels and has trained Burmese army, air force and naval personnel. Access to Burma's ports and naval installations provides China with a strategic influence in the Bay of Bengal, in the wider Indian Ocean region and in South-East Asia.

China exerts a great influence on Myanmar and pursued many projects in the field of oil and natural gas and in infrastructure development like building seaports, dams, bridges, roads and industrial projects. Many Chinese private firms have been involved in the construction of oil and gas pipelines from Burma's Arakan coast to China's Yunnan province. On many issues China blocked UN Security Council resolutions against Myanmar. There is a close link and cooperation between the two neighbouring countries. But bilateral relations between them are not flawless. Especially in the aftermath of democratic reforms in Myanmar in 2011, Myanmar tilted its foreign policy towards the Western countries, India and other South-East Asian countries provoking the Chinese government. It opens its foreign policy wider to avoid too much dependence on China. But China still remains the dominant player.

One of the most important factors behind the Sino-Myanmar relationship was the external pressures that pushed Myanmar into the embrace of China. This has not been seen as entirely positive in Myanmar and continued sanctions and refusal by the Western powers (the USA and EU), India and many other states to deal with Myanmar makes it possible for Chinese strategists to increase China's influence in Myanmar. In many areas, such as military and political, China is Myanmar's least preferred partner, not least due to the history China has had with Myanmar; but no alternative was available then. India and the world are now realizing the danger of unchecked Chinese influence in Myanmar and now extend a helping hand to them.

With regard to weapon supply also, China has emerged as the most important provider to Myanmar of military equipment and training but due to the poor quality of equipment, Myanmar finds alternative suppliers from India, Russia, Serbia and Ukraine.

There is a strong criticism of Chinese farms in Myanmar. Unfair and lack of proper environmental standards led to the exploitation of land and resources. Moreover, the absence of strict labour laws and fair distribution of benefits led to local dissatisfaction. The Chinese government has been critical of how different interest groups in China have behaved but has not taken any action against these unregulated business practices.

China is also concerned about the change in the direction of Myanmar's foreign policy and its tilt towards the West. The influence and strategic importance China will have in Myanmar is often exaggerated; China's rise is seen in a far too positive light, while the negative aspects of increased contacts are less apparent and often forgotten. The reality is that many dimensions of bilateral relations are tense and the Myanmar government is deliberately trying to balance different external actors against one another in order to minimize external pressure and maximize concessions—particularly from its weaker neighbour in a region where power is distributed unequally.

Thus, from the above statement, it is apparent that Myanmar is now playing a pragmatic foreign policy. Due to historic alignment and existing financial influence and commercial significance, it cannot ignore China in her foreign policy. Meanwhile, opportunities are opening wider for India after democratic reforms in Myanmar. India needs to speed up its strategic relationship with Myanmar in the fields of military, trade and commerce and people-to-people contact. It is indispensable to avail this opportunity to implement infrastructure development like road connectivity, seaport and river routes in Myanmar in the wider interest of trade with South-East Asia.

REFERENCES

Bhonsale. M.http://www.orfonline.org/research/myanmar-trade-with-india-rising-much-more-needs-to-be-done/

Bowman, V. (September 17, 2016). China Faces Tougher Laws in Myanmar. Retrieved from https://thediplomat.com/2016/09/china-faces-tougher-laws-in-myanmar/

Chhonkar, P. S. (February 6, 2017). Is a Border Fence an Absolute Essential along the India-Myanmar Border? Retrieved from https://idsa.in/idsacomments/border-fence-an-absolute-essential-india-myanmar-border_pschhonkar_060217

China-Myanmar Relations (n.d.) In *Wikipedia.* Retrieved 22 February, 2018, fromhttps://en.wikipedia.org/wiki/China%E2%80%93Myanmar_relations.

China-Myanmar Relations (n.d.). In *Wikipedia.* Retrieved 22 February, 2018, fromhttps://en.wikipedia.org/wiki/China%E2%80%93Myanmar_relations.

Goswami, N. (18 March 2014). China at your doorstep: Looking east from India's northeast.

Government awards contract for completion of Kaladan Project in Myanmar. (9 June 2017). Retrieved from https://currentaffairs.gktoday.in/tags/kaladan-multi-modal-transport-projects.

Gupta, A. (February 2, 2012). Myanmar's Critical Role in Bolstering India's Look East Policy. Retrieved from https://idsa.in/idsacomments/MyanmarsCriticalRoleinBolstering Indias LookEastPolicy_agupta_020212.

Han, E. (April 27, 2017). Border conflict no match for Sino–Myanmar relations. Retrieved from http://www.eastasiaforum.org/2017/04/27/border-conflict-no-match-for-sino-myanmar-relations/

India-Myanmar Relations (n.d.) In *Wikipedia.* Retrieved 23 February 2018, from https://en.wikipedia.org/wiki/India%E2%80%93Myanmar_relations

Joshua Thomas, C. & Das, Gurudas. (2016). Look East to Act East Policy: Implications for India's Northeast. Retrieved from https://www.google.co.in/search?q=Look+east+to+act+east+ policy +implication+for+India%27s+northeast.

Sachdeva, S. & Maini, T. S. (November 14, 2017). China Faces Increasing Competition in Myanmar. Retrieved from https://thediplomat.com/2017/11/china-faces-increasing-competition-in-myanmar/

Sajjanhar, Ashok. (2 September 2016). Visit of Myanmar President Upgrades Bilateral Ties. Retrieved fromhttps://idsa.in/idsacomments/visit-of-myanmar-president-upgrades-bilateral-ties_asajjanhar_020916

Sen, G. (December 15, 2016). A Joint India-Indonesia Intervention on the Rohingya Issue. Retrieved from https://idsa.in/idsacomments/joint-india-indonesia-intervention-rohingya-issue_ gsen_ 151216

Sun, Y. (December 9, 2015). A New Era for China-Myanmar Relations? Retrieved from https://thediplomat.com/2015/12/a-new-era-for-china-myanmar-relations/

Swanstrom, N. (June 2012). Sino-Myanmar Relations: Security and Beyond. Retrieved from http://isdp.eu/content/uploads/images/stories/isdp-main-pdf/2012_swanstrom_sino-myanmar-relations.pdf

Tao, X. (March 14, 2017). How Did Myanmar's Reforms Change Its Relations With China?. Retrieved from https://thediplomat.com/2017/03/how-did-myanmars-reforms-change-its-relations-with-china/

The China plan—On Myanmar-Bangladesh deal on Rohingya. (25 November 2017). Retrieved from http://www.thehindu.com/opinion/editorial/the-china-plan/article20798339.ece

10

Enhancing Indo-Myanmar Trade with Special Reference to Zokhawthar–Rih Border Sector

Lily Sangpui

ABSTRACT

The paper looks at the various aspects of the Zokhawthar-Rih trade sector situated along the Indo-Myanmar border. It examines the volume of trade and some observable impact it had on the bordering village of Zokhawthar located on the Indian side. In exploring the problems and challenges faced by different stakeholders who depend on border trade it discusses some pertinent prospects for increasing trade and ushering in development along the border region. Drawing from field observations, seminary discussion and secondary data, the paper concludes that trade across this sector facilitates mutual benefits across various stakeholders and that various socio-economic cooperation could be extended in order to change its transit nature which could substantiate to some extent India's imbalance of trade across the Indo-Myanmar trade zone.

Keywords: *Indo-Myanmar, Border Trade, Zokhawthar-Rih sector, Mizoram.*

Introduction

The opening of borders along the corridor of India's North-East has been dubbed as a paradigm shift toward placing the region on the policy radar to garner much needed market linkages and development. The North-East cannot overlook its advantage in sharing an enormous long stretch of international boundaries with its neighbouring countries when it is linked with the rest of India by just a 2-km narrow corridor at Siliguri. The once uncharted territory now holds an important geo-economic strategic location on its possibilities to integrate with the dynamics of South-East Asian economies and also as a strategic tool to further enhance regional cooperation with its neighbours. It is rightly subscribed that where the North-East ends, South-East Asia begins. With the onset of the Act East Policy, the erstwhile

Look East Policy, during the 1990s, India has opened up its border to facilitate trade across its North-Eastern frontiers. Sharing 98 per cent of its borders with countries such as Myanmar, Bangladesh, Bhutan, Nepal and China, the borders of the North-East which is often presumed to be liabilities is now viewed and deemed as a window of opportunities: opportunities to link with booming South-East Asia economics and as a means to usher in development along India's least developed North-East. The promotion of trade in a landlocked non-industrialised region of the North-East which has a natural advantage of trading is one aspect that could inevitably boost the region's much-needed growth and development. It becomes pertinent to replenish the much-needed development dreams through the opening of border trade zones. As trade signifies beyond just the exchange of items, it also encapsulates the inflow of people, culture, skills, knowledge and ideas taken together in absolute terms which affects people. It is in this light that this paper attempts to observe trade across the Zokhawthar–Rih trade zone and highlights some of the significant aspects it had on Zokhawthar, a bordering village in Mizoram on the Indian side. It also intends to point out some pertinent local problems and challenges faced by Indian traders. The paper concludes by drawing points on how this trade zone could be extended beyond its current transit nature, viz., as a channel to promote socio-cultural and economic ties between the Mizos and the Chins who share the same ethno-cultural and linguistic affinity.

India's Experience: Looking East and Trade

The mid-Eighties and Nineties were characterised by a phase of trade openness, globalisation and economic reforms. With the world being unified, regional groups were formed to bring economic and political ties closer and also to reap the benefits from being trading partners. Borders which were once seen as a liability are now seen as a geo-economic potential (Das, 2005). Opening up of borders and advocating a concept of shared borders began to take a forefront role in the policies of nations. The rise in regional cooperation and frameworks and with Myanmar joining the ASEAN, India felt the need to redirect its foreign policy. The Act East Policy, the erstwhile Look East Policy, was formulated towards garnering geo-economic potentials by linking with South-East Asia, countries via Myanmar (Bhaumik, 2014; Sikri, 2009). Another important dimension of the policy lies in its domestic considerations; to help transform the geographical handicap of the North-East region by taking advantage of its geo-strategic location. Using the 3Cs—Culture, Commerce and Connectivity—India's foreign policy towards South-East Asian regions began to take shape and develop.

Drawing on the potentials of border trade to leverage the economic as well as the much needed developmental aspect of the North-East region, in 2008 the Government of India broadened the conceptual contours of border trade (Das, 2016). To further the linkages between domestic economic imperatives and external economic environment, the number of exchangeable items was increased and normal trade (MFN) was permitted in Moreh and Zokhawthar (Das, 2016).

India has made significant strides through its Act East Policy in infrastructure development, especially in its supervisory and regulatory role (Sikri, 2009; Kalita, 2012). In a study conducted by Srinivasan (2012) on regional cooperation and infrastructure development in South Asia, it indicated an improvement in the level of households and income. It also shows a significant decline in poverty as the construction of rural roads resulted in substantially improved access to health and education services. The opening of a border and its linkages to development lie in promoting livelihood in border trade areas and in ushering in development (Das, 2006; Kabra & Singha, 2006). One finds support of this hypothesis from the data in Singh (2011) in his study of the Moreh-Tamu trade sector in Manipur where it is seen that there is a significant impact in the per capita income as depicted by the volume of trade and provides scope for employment generation. One also finds support of this hypothesis from the study by Romalsawma (2000) on Zokhawthar-Rih border trade where it indicated socio-economic development in Mizoram to the extent that 4.11 per cent of the total income of the state comes from this border trade and gave livelihood to at least 6 per cent of the total population of Mizoram. The border as such, acts not just as a transit point but also as a catalysing agent for regional development.

Despite the enormous geo-economic potential, India has not been able to derive the much-intended benefits. It has benefited some traders, industrialists and highly qualified professionals but has not met expectations in employment generation (Bhattacharjee, 2016). Considering the time frame of its formulation, the Act East policy has not shown much improvement in ushering in intended benefits. The problems persisted in the geopolitical contours of the North-East region and ASEAN countries coupled with slow infrastructure development (Bhaumik, 2014; Bhattacharjee, 2016). According to Taneja (1999), Thomas (2000) and Singh (2011), the domination of informal trade on account of problems in formalising trade and the dominance of high tariffs diverted much of the intended benefits. In the same study by Singh (2011), border trade does facilitate employment opportunities along the border regions in sectors like transport, small business enterprise and labour but it does not lead to much development as expected due to its transitory nature. In addition, the opening of border trade also brings in other non-security threats and ushers in social, political and economic dynamics especially among people residing in the border areas (Songate, 2010).

Indo-Myanmar Trade

Border trade refers to the transaction of goods and services across the border between those living near the international border (Das, 2016; Chutia, 2015). It is part of the trade that flows through the export and import (EXIM) framework of nations. Border trade facilitates the exchange of commodities in a bi-laterally agreed list overland by people living along both sides of the border (Chutia, 2015:10). India has opened up 42 Land Custom Services (LCS) in different border zones of the North-East states. With the signing of the Border Trade Agreement (BTA) between India and the Government of Myanmar in 1994, it was agreed to open up four border trade zones, viz., Moreh-Tamu, Zokhawthar-Rih and Longwa in Nagaland and Pangsau Pass in Arunachal Pradesh. Indo-Myanmar border trade is largely through Moreh, a small border town in Manipur and Namphalong in Sagaing division of Myanmar and through Zokhawthar, a border village in Mizoram. The Zokhawthar-Rih trade sector which is the second Indo-Myanmar Border Trade Point, the first being the Moreh-Tamu trade sector, was inaugurated in 2004.

Under the BTA, it the following three types of trade across the Indo-Myanmar border were agreed to, viz.

a) Barter trade of items not exceeding US$ 1,000 or its equivalent,
b) Barter trade of items up to a value of US$ 20,000 or its equivalent, and
c) Normal trade against payment for supplies.

The first two types of trade envisaged the exchange of goods without any monetary transaction. Providing clarity at the conceptual level, Das (2016) differentiates the barter system carried out as part of the subset under border trade with that of border trade under normal trade. Under the Indo-Myanmar Border Trade Agreement (BTA), it provides for barter trade of identified items under specific conditions as well as normal trade against payment. Under barter trade, India accrued a trade deficit as most of the items listed in the agreement were not found favourable for India as demand for Indian products was lower. This makes it difficult for Indian traders to exchange it for goods equivalent to imported goods (Bhattacharya, 2005; Das, 2005; Das, 2016). On account of this, the barter system was subsequently replaced by normal trade. Contemplating the difficulties and problems associated with the barter trade system, the Reserve Bank of India (RBI) on November 5, 2015 abolished it and laid down guidelines for the functioning of normal trade (Das, 2016).

Zokhawthar-Rih Trade Zone

Mizoram, which is located in the extreme east of North-Eastern India, has a border with Myanmar in the east and south, with Bangladesh in the west and in with

Assam and Manipur in the north. The state shares 450 kilometres of its international boundary mostly with the Chin Hills of Myanmar where the people from both sides share the same ethno-linguistic affinity. Prior to the opening of the border trade zone, there existed traditional trade across the border mainly among the Mizos and Chins. The existence of a porous border and make-up of the same ethnic composition along it accentuates natural trading ties and movement of people to and fro. In view of the import-driven economy of Mizoram and its backwardness in terms of infrastructure, slow growth of economy and various other socio-cultural and political factors, facilitating trade across the border could inject much-needed market linkages and development. It is widely recognised that the development of border trade was included in one of the clauses t enshrined in the Mizoram Peace Accord of 1986 between the MNF leaders and the Government of India (Songate, 2010).

Despite the signing of the Indo–Myanmar Trade Agreement on January 31, 1994, it took eight years to set up the infrastructure requirements and services to facilitate trade across the Zokhawthar-Rih sector. It was only after the construction of a Bailey bridge in 2002 over the Tiau river that runs between Mizoram and Myanmar that an impetus for the commencement of trade was seen. In 2004, the Zokhawthar-Rih border trade zone was officially inaugurated. This zone is marked by the Tiau river separating Zokhawthar village on the Indian side and Rih (also known as Rihkhawdar) village of Myanmar. In order to facilitate trade, the Government of Mizoram acquired 126.96 acres of land at Khawnuam in Melbuk village which is 8 kilometres from Zokhawthar for the establishment of a border trade township to accommodate Customs officers and staff. Twelve Assam-type residential quarters of Types 1, II, III and IV have been constructed along with a helipad and other basic amenities. In addition, a composite land customs building situated at zero point at a distance of 30 metres from the border was constructed to accommodate different trade-related departments and agencies.

Zokhawthar is a very small village with a population of around 2,025 people (Songate, 2010). It is located on the extreme east of Champhai district at a distance of 30 kilometres from the district headquarters. The state capital, Aizawl, is situated at a distance of 228 kilometres from zero point. Prior to the opening up of border trade, the main occupation of the people was jhumming (slash and burn) cultivation and people migrate to the nearby Champhai town for employment and education.[1] However, with the opening up of border trade, there is a shift in occupation. Cultivation is a secondary occupation and the majority of the people are now engaged in trade-related activities either in some way or the other as porters, traders, business persons and lorry drivers.

Border trade along the India-Myanmar border is carried out in three ways, viz., Traditional/Free Exchange Mechanism, Barter Trade System and Normal Trade. The barter system flourished in this sector until it was withdrawn in 2015 and replaced by normal trade. Unlike the limit of 62 tradable items under the barter system, in normal trade all goods and items are tradable provided they are not listed as restricted or prohibited as declared by the Directorate-General of Foreign Trade (DGFT). Unlike in the barter system, the onset of normal trade introduced a new mechanism by which export and import is permissible under the EXIM policy in freely convertible currencies or in currencies mutually agreed upon through a Letter of Credit (LoC) or advance payment. Besides, it made changes in the Customs aggregate duty of 4 per cent to 46.848 per cent (LCS Zokhawthar Report, 2017). This change in duty tariff posed a sense of reluctance among importers who feared losses. In addition, a lack of banking facilities creates problems for Indian traders that slow down the transfer of goods. In spite of the existence of a State Bank of India branch at zero point which was supposed to handle EXIM transactions, it is yet not equipped to handle trade-related transactions. Indian traders had to rely on HDFC Bank and IDBI Bank situated at Champhai to handle most of the advance payment for import transactions. In spite of the existence of infrastructure such as BSNL tower, office buildings and storage facilities, the bank is yet to function. Traders have to rely mostly on private storage facilities with no proper equipment to preserve goods.

Trade in Zokhawthar Sector

Trade at Zokhawthar presented an erratic trend with the total volume remaining extremely low though it pointed at times toward an increase. In 2009-10, the total trade was valued at only Rs 1.2 lakh, which increased to Rs. 1.85 lakh in 2012-13 but the next year it decreased to Rs. 1.79 crore. The decrease was on account of zero imports; the increase in volume of trade was because of a large import of betel nut. It again plunged to Rs. 8.15 crore in 2014-15 and reached the highest volume of trade in 2016-17 at Rs. 27.24 crore. The increase is on account of the high import of betel nut which has a huge market in Mizoram and in Assam (see Tables 1 & 2). As far as import items are concerned, betel nut constituted the largest item, followed by reed brooms and black pepper in a small quantity. Export is extremely limited to a single item. Soyabari is the main export item from India. The years 2010-11, 2011-12, 2014-15, 2015-16, 2016-2017 and 2017 until October 2018 saw zero export. Customs data on formal trade (see Table 2) shows lack of demand for Indian products; however, on further probing, the position is not as it seems to indicate. It is not the absence of demand but rather the inability of local traders from Mizoram to meet the demands for items required by their counterparts across the border because of technical hitches and structural and human capital inadequacies. There exists a large demand for fertilizers, pharmaceuticals, bicycles, auto parts and other agri-allied items. Mizoram being a non-industrial state and with an import-oriented economy makes it difficult for local traders to meet the demand. In most cases, they have to procure from other regions which, in the absence of good roads and other infrastructure, becomes unprofitable.[2] Also, the limited knowledge of trading mechanisms in trading across different regions and spectrums along with little enterprising skills often hold back local traders to explore the potential beyond the region. They feel unequipped to conduct vast trade involving huge financial transactions let alone taking into consideration financial constraints and lack of market information.[3] On the other hand, import of some items comes with curtailment, for instance, like fertilizers and pharmaceutical products. In such instances, the demand for these items is met through informal channels and traded mainly through unmanned routes.

Table 1: Import Particulars through LCS Zokhawthar

Year	*Commodity*	*No. of Consignments*	*Qty. (in metric tons)*	*Assessable Value (in INR)*	*Revenue (Duty & Cess) (In INR)*
2009-10	Reed Brooms	01	15.00	61,882	5,790
2010-11	Betel Nuts	04	11.68	4,33,548	40,564
2011-12	Betel Nuts	07	60.00	22,27,740	2,08,446
2012-13	Nil	Nil	Nil	Nil	Nil
2013-14	Betel Nuts	14	140.00	1,61,56,394	15,11,594
2014-15	Betel Nuts	66	584.00	8,15,04,710	75,25,606
2015-16	Betel Nuts	134	1132.00	16,74,14,039	1,56,63,286
2016-17	Betel Nuts	67	1500.00	27,24,66,127	1,08,99,415
2017-18	Betel Nuts	06	63.60	1,59,83,152	75,04,444
	Black Pepper	02	10.00	9,70,295	11,98,749

Source: Land Customs Station, Zokhawthar

Table 2: Export through LCS Zokhawthar

Year	*Commodity*	*No. of Consignments*	*Qty. (in Metric Tons)*	*Assessable Value*	*APEDA+AP*
2009-10	Soyabari	01	02.069	60,000	Duty-Free
2010-11	Nil	Nil	Nil	Nil	Nil
2011-12	Nil	Nil	Nil	Nil	Nil
2012-13	Soyabari	01	6.4000	1,85,600	Duty-Free
2013-14	Soyabari	02	29.000	18,12,500	Duty-Free
2014-15	Nil	Nil	Nil	Nil	Nil
2015-16	Nil	Nil	Nil	Nil	Nil
2016-17	Nil	Nil	Nil	Nil	Nil
2017-till date	Nil	Nil	Nil	Nil	Nil

Source: Land Customs Station, Zokhawthar

It is seen that on account of low formal trading Zokhawthar-Rih generates low revenue. In 2009-10, it collected just Rs. 5,790 which rose to Rs. 40,564 in 2010-11 and Rs. 2.08 lakh in 2011-12 but then decreased to Rs. 8,500 in 2012-2013. The decrease was due to zero import and also on account of duty-free items exported. From 2012-13 onwards, it showed a rise in revenue collection and 2015-16 indicated the highest revenue collected at Rs. 1.56 crore (see Table 3).

A comparison between revenue generated and seizure indicates that the worth of seizure exceeds revenue collected (see Tables 3 & 4). This sheds light on the prevalence and dominance of informal trade where it is estimated that more than 90 per cent of trade is carried out through informal trade. The existence of informal trade on account of problems in formalising trade has induced an enormous loss to the government. The desire to evade high tariff tax, the existence of porous borders, unmanned old routes and a free movement regime (FMR) contributes to the parallel running of informal trade. Import of cattle for meat, export items such as fertilizers and pharmaceuticals are carried out mainly through unmanned routes.

Table 3: Revenue through LCS Zokhawthar

Year	*Personal Penalty*	*Auction Sale Proceeds*	*Customs Duty*	*Total*
2009-10	Nil	Nil	5,790	5,790
2010-11	Nil	Nil	40,564	40,564
2011-12	2000	Nil	2,08,446	2,40,446 *
2012-13	8500	Nil	0	8,500
2013-14	Nil	Nil	15,11,594	15,11,594
2014-15	Nil	Nil	76,25,606	76,25,606
2015-16	Nil	Nil	1,56,63,286	1,56,63,286
2016-17	Nil	Nil	1,08,99,415	1,08,99,415
2017-till October 2017	Nil	Nil	87,03,193	87,03,193

* includes 30,000 (INR) realized against provisional release i/r of case No.06/CL/EXP/CUS/LCS-ZKT/11-12 dated 17/11/11

Source: Land Customs Station, Zokhawthar.

Table 4: Seizures at LCS Zokhawthar

Year	*No. of Cases*	*Seizure Value (Rs.)*
2009-10	31	25,38,200
2010-11	29	51,63,520
2011-12	18	69,47,700
2012-13	28	64,12,895
2013-14	08	40,90,240
2014-15	02	37,25,000
2015-16	Nil	Nil
2016-17	01	4,62,400
2017-18	02	6,01,75,000

Source: Land Customs Station, Zokhawthar

As one visits the markets of Aizawl and Champhai, one finds the market to be adorned with foreign-made goods which originate mainly in China and Thailand and small petty shops that sell edible food products from Myanmar. Close observation reveals that every household in Aizawl is adorned with at least one foreign-made product that originated from Third World countries in terms of electronic goods, food products, cosmetics, etc.[4] These products find are brought in mainly through informal channels unaccounted for in items traded resulting in an enormous loss to the government.

Problems and Prospects: The Way Forward

In assessing the volume of trade where India accrued a trade deficit along with the dominance of informal trade, a parallel line can be drawn whereby a large section of the population of Mizoram depends on this trade for their livelihood. The importance of trade in the lives of the Mizos cannot be underestimated. In a study conducted by Romalsawma (2000) on the implications of border trade in Mizoram, it is estimated that 4.11 per cent of the total income of the State comes from border trade and also provides a livelihood to 6 per cent of the total population of Mizoram. Many shops spring up selling food products of Myanmar, clothes and electronic goods which has a tag of 'Made in China' or Thailand. In Aizawl, one sees another livelihood activity carried out by street hawkers selling cheap apparel, electronic goods and cosmetic on the pavement and also going from door to door.

In the case of Zokhawthar, there exists a livelihood diversification; jhumming (slash and burn) which was the main occupation prior to border trade becomes a secondary occupation. Around 100 local traders, mainly from Champhai and surrounding areas, depend for their livelihood on this trade sector. For the bordering villages, trade escalates non-farm income generation and provides employment to a large number of people as porters earning between Rs. 500 and 1,000 per day depending on the consignments arriving at Zokhawthar.[5] The opening of trade has provided Zokhawthar with road linkage and other services such as bank, communication and transport. Drawing on the transformational nature of trade and potentials in place, the community set up the Zokhawthar Welfare Association (ZWA) to channelize resources and funds from trade for its progress and welfare. A major contribution came from the local traders' association of Mizoram and also from individual members. The Association sponsors a high school, looks into the requirement of teachers and contributes towards the salary of additional teachers. Besides, it caters to the welfare of the poor and needy through financial help and takes up numerous developmental initiatives for the locality. The population of Zokhawthar depends on this trade for their livelihood and lack of it would render most of the people jobless. Porters who depend on trade for their daily sustenance are worst affected. They have to rely on other sources of income when trade is closed.

The benefits of trade also percolate on the Rih side of the border. Retail and wholesale markets spring up and flourish there on the Myanmar border where visitors make purchases. On the other hand, in Zokhawthar, such development is yet to be observed. The opening of border trade at Zokhawthar is thus merely used as a transit point for the movement of goods. Zokhawthar alone as a hub of border trade could not attract much visitors/tourists from India. One could attribute this to distance from the state capital, difficult terrain and poor conditions of roads that increases transportation costs.

On another account, trade across the Zokhawthar border has its own rippling effects. Along with its benefits, it brought another dimension of non-security threats like increase in drug circulation and arms smuggling and other contraband substances and infiltration of Myanmar's migrants into Mizoram (Songate, 2010). Another pertinent problem is the nature of its terrain and topography. Being a hilly region with an incessant monsoon and prone to landslides, it levels out development work especially in road development. Apart from taxation, traders have to bear additional transportation costs on account of the terrain and bad roads. Transporting of goods cost one rupee per kilogram which adds to the cost of goods making the price vary for the same goods found at Moreh-Tamu Market (Manipur's Border Trade Zone).[6] The absence of laboratory testing facilities compounds the problems of traders across Zokhawthar LCS. They have to get samples tested either at Imphal or Assam where they have to shell out additional money for transportation and warehouse charges for their consignments. The inadequacies in terms of soft and hard infrastructure, banking services and telecommunication along with a with lack of awareness on trading regime, information, goods complementary and trade-related skills hinders the development of trade across the Zokhawthar-Rih zone.[7]

Given the spectrum of potentials, border trade could invigorate in terms of development of border regions and promote livelihoods. It is pertinent to endeavour and strengthen the trade zone and address those inadequacies. Some of the steps that could be taken to enhance this trade zone are:

1) The culture element enshrined under the three Cs of India's foreign policy towards South-East Asian regions needs to take shape to help expand beyond the designated transit point by taking advantage of the ethnic ties and historical significance the place has to offer. With a host of festivals and historical asymmetry exerted by the people of Mizo and Chin of Myanmar, a common platform to celebrate cultural commonalities and distinctiveness

could begin along the trade zone to facilitate greater visitation of people which could boost the local economy. This will eventually spiral affordable rooms that could be extended as hotels or homestead. The existence of many historical places in and around Champhai and Rikhawdar has to be explored, operationalised and promoted as a hub for socio-cultural meets and as a site for tourist destinations. Rih Dil (A lake situated on the Myanmar border) has a strong cultural connotation across the people of Zo as the passage of the death soul, and the existence of common cultural ties spells out for further collaboration. The existence of a Free Movement Regime should be taken advantage of for the promotion of cultural ties, tourists, etc.

2) Organise and promote border meets and haats to facilitate both bilateral and local trade.
3) Promote a spectrum of services in the areas of health and education. India can take advantage of a medical tourist destination. There exist potentials to promote medical tourism as lack of health care services often prompted people on the other side of the border to visit Mizoram and Manipur to avail health care services.
4) Revamp and promote local industries along with establishing forward and backward linkages for domestic as well as international trade. An entrepreneur development programme could be initiated for local youths and investors. In spite of the abundance of bamboo which could be processed in a variety of products, there is a dearth of bamboo processing units. Bamboo shoots, a delicacy in the North-East and South-East Asian countries has a huge market potential and bamboo food processing units can be set up in and around the border trade zone to augment development of the region and reduce costs in transportation.
5) Inject necessary soft and hard infrastructure such as all-weather roads, connectivity, laboratory testing facilities, health care facilities, broader banking services and institutions that will cater to human development resources such as entrepreneurship development.
6) Setting up of well-functioning communication towers/networks, information booths and upgradation of bank services in the border trade zone.
7) More studies on market-related research needs to be conducted to capture market demand, supply chain and networks and in other fields that could add knowledge to the existing literature on border trade and facilitate a better trading mechanism.
8) Promote and enhance traders' skills by organising exposure trips and interactive sessions from time to time.

Conclusion

The importance of trade in the demand-driven economy of Mizoram cannot be understated. It has generated employment opportunities, connectivity and promotes livelihood through the trade zone and the much-needed market linkages. It also opens up an enormous potential for revamping local industries and marketing domestic products. Despite its positive impacts and windows of opportunities, its growth is marred by structural constraints, and institutional inadequacy reducing it to only a transit point for the movement of goods and people. The dominance of informal trade needs to be addressed by injecting these inadequacies in formalising trade. The 3Cs of India's foreign policy towards South-East Asia need to be invigorated and take shape, especially the cultural components, considering the potentials of collaborating beyond trade as the Mizo and Chin tribes of Myanmar also share a close affinity and similar economic, socio and cultural structures.

ENDNOTES

1 Interview with an elder resident of Zokhawthar on 11 October 2017.
2 Interview with Customs officials at Aizwal, Champhai and Zokhawthar on October 2017.
3 Points highlighted during Interactive Meet among Mizoram and Myanmar Traders on 10 November 2017 at Champhai.
4 Observation during a visit to Aizawl and Champhai markets.
5 Interview with President of Zokhawthar Porter's Association and women porters at Zero Point.
6 Interview with Secretary, Mizoram EXIM Union.
7 Points deliberated during an interactive meet between Myanmar and Mizoram traders at Champhai on 10 November 2017.

REFERENCES

Bhattacharjee, D. (2016). India's Vision on Act East Policy. Paper presented at National Seminar on India's Act East Policy: Problems and Prospects in North East India, held at Imphal, 28-29 January 2016.

Bhattacharya, R. (2005). Trade Settlement Issues and Introduction of Letter of Credit for Promotion of Indo–Myanmar Border Trade. In Gurudas Das, N. Bijoy Singh, & C. J. Thomas (eds.) (2005). *Indo-Myanmar Border Trade: Status, Problems and Potentials*. New Delhi: Akansha Publications.

Bhaumik, S. (2014). Look East Through Northeast: Challenges and Prospects for India, ORA occasional paper No. 51, June. New Delhi: Observer Research Foundation.

Chutia, S. (2015). Prospects of Border Trade for North East Region of India with South Asian Countries. *International Journal of Research in Economics and Social Sciences*, Volume 5, Issue 10 (October).

Das, G., Singh, N. B. & Thomas, C. J. (eds.) (2005). *Indo-Myanmar Border Trade: Status, Problems and Potentials*. New Delhi: Akansha Publications.

Das, G. (2006). Border Trade in India's North-East Theory and Practice. In David R. Syiemlieh, Anuradha Dutta & Srinath Baruah (eds.) *Challenges of Development in North East India*. New Delhi: Regency Publications.

Das, R. U. (2016). *Enhancing India–Myanmar Border Trade: Policy and Implementation Measures*, Ministry of Commerce and Industry. New Delhi: Government of India.

Kabra, K.C. & Singha, R.K.P.G. (2006). Border Trade in Mizoram Emerging Trends and Future Prospects. In David R. Syiemlieh, Anuradha Dutta & Srinath Baruah (eds.) *Challenges of Development in North East India*. New Delhi: Regency Publications.

Kalika, H. (2012). India's Look East Policy: Challenges and Opportunities Ahead, *Global Journal of Human Social Science Arts & Humanities,* Vol. 12-13.

Singh, Ng. Dev-Karna (2011). *Indo-Myanmar Border Trade and Its Impact in the Economy of Manipur.* (Unpublished Doctoral Dissertation), Manipur University, Imphal.

Sikri, R. (2009). India's Look East Policy, *Asia-Pacific Review*, 16:1, 131-145.

Srinivasan, P.V. (2012). Regional Cooperation and Integration through Cross-Border Infrastructure Development in South Asia: Impact on Poverty. South Asia Working Paper Series, No. 14, November, Asian Development Bank.

Songate, P. (2010). *Indo-Myanmar Border Trade: The Study of Socio-Cultural and Political Dynamics in Mizoram.* (Unpublished Doctoral Dissertation), Mizoram University, Aizawl.

Taneja, N. (1999). Informal Trade in the SAARC Region.

Thomas. C.J. (2000). Indo-Myanmar Border Trade: An Assessment on the Moreh-Tamu Sector. In Gurudas Das & R.K. Purkayastha (eds.), *Border Trade North East India and Neighbouring Countries.* New Delhi: Akansha Publications.

Romalsawma, C. (2000). *Socio-Economic Implications of Border Trade in Mizoram: A Geographical Analysis.* (Unpublished Doctoral Dissertation), North Eastern Hills University, Shillong.

11

India-Myanmar Sub-regional Cooperation

Pradip Phanjoubam

An Indian Army colonel posted in Mizoram was arrested for complicity in a case of smuggling 52 gold bars estimated to be worth INR 14.5 crore from Myanmar in May 2016. This once again focussed attention on the illegal transport of goods and weapons across the border by insurgents, etc., especially in the Manipur sector of the international border along what was once National Highway 39, and now rechristened Asian Highway 1. These are some samples of the latest tales of the dark potential of these traditional trade routes between India and Myanmar. The good news is that these dark tales of illegal trafficking can with a single imaginative change of policy of the governments of the two countries transform into a thriving legal trade bringing in valuable income for either country other than the usual stories of general well-being that successful commercial activity brings to a wide spectrum of people.

The ground is indeed being prepared in earnest for this and according to a report, the 1400-km highway which will begin at Moreh and Tamu, the two neighbouring border townships along the Indo-Myanmar border in the Manipur sector and culminate at Tak in the Mae Sot district of Thailand is set to become operational in another two years. Announcing this, the Indian Ambassador to Thailand, Bhagwant Singh, who spoke to the press recently in Bangkok, said what remains to be completed are renovation works on 73 World War II era bridges in the Myanmar sector of this highway and once this is through, the highway will be ready for heavy traffic. This trans-Asian highway is planned to extend to more South-Eastern and even East Asian countries.

The Thailand-Myanmar-India highway is an existing infrastructure though not always in good condition and, apart from upgrading, a lot remains to be done in matters of standardisation. Issues of Customs gates, border visa office regime and the varying right and left side traffic systems in these countries too would have to be made uniform to the extent possible.

While Thailand and India follow the left-hand drive norm, Myanmar once had the same but now drives on the right hand side of the road. Quite peculiarly, a majority of the vehicles in the country are still right-hand drive meant for the old left-hand drive roads sometimes making it awkward for passengers of public transport vehicles for they are required to mount as well as dismount not on the edge but towards the middle of the roads. The government has in recent times issued a regulation to have citizens acquire only left-hand drive vehicles when buying new ones.

Since a political decision exists, the road should become a reality soon. However, there are cautions. India needs to take note of certain political and geographical realities in framing official policies as well as moderating expectations from its much hyped but long-delayed Look East Policy, now rechristened the Act East Policy by the new BJP government in New Delhi. In a nutshell, looking or acting east should not be just about commerce but also of strategic interest, and importantly, about the welfare of the people targeted. Unfortunately, these latter considerations have often been overlooked.

The reality is also that the former concern often overrides the latter. The tendency, therefore, has been to not look at Myanmar or the North-East as the primary targets of this policy. Instead, it is linking India with the vibrant economies of the more advanced ASEAN members that have been projected as the ultimate end of this policy. The North-East and Myanmar thus get reduced to merely a land corridor needed to establish this connection. Or else, the market-worthiness of the larger contiguous region of India's North-East and northern region of Myanmar, which has a few industries worth the name, gets calibrated in terms of their rich mineral deposits and other resources, including timber and hydroelectricity.

This approach, rather than resolving social-economic problems of this underdeveloped region has the potential of accentuating them as we have seen in recent times. The public opposition that led to the suspension of the Myintsone dam in Myanmar's Kachin State in September 2011 is an example. This dam, a joint venture between the China Power Investment Corporation, the Ministry of Electric Power of the then military junta in Myanmar and the Asia World Company, was at the time billed to be the 15th largest hydroelectric project in the world with a production capacity of 6,000 mw. Similarly, the Letpadaung copper mine at Monywa, operated by the Wanbao Mining Copper Ltd., a subsidiary of China North Industries Group Corp, a large arms manufacturer, in collaboration with the Union of Myanmar Economic Holdings Ltd., ran into trouble because of public protest in November 2012 and the terms of the project had to be renegotiated.

On the Indian side of the border, the continuing controversy over the more than 100 proposed dams over tributaries of the Brahmaputra in Arunachal Pradesh and the concerns raised by proposals for exploring and mining oil and natural gas in Nagaland and Manipur, are some more examples of social unrest and discontent this outlook can bring. In May 2016, two anti-dam protestors, including a Buddhist monk, were killed in police firing at the monastery township of Tawang on the India-China border in Arunachal Pradesh.

Again, when trade and commerce become the sole goal, the tendency has also been to opt for the easier maritime routes across the Bay of Bengal with the result again of pushing the North-East and northern Burma out of sight. In other words looking or acting east must not be allowed to bypass the North-East and northern Myanmar. This must not be treated as just a lament of those in the North-East, but a studied consideration of how important stability in this contiguous region is strategically wedged as it is between two emerging superpowers, India and China.

Mekong Sub-region Example

For the moment, China seems to be doing its homework better on this matter. It has used its bridgehead to South-East Asia, the Yunnan province, much more imaginatively and productively to connect with Myanmar and from there, the ASEAN. Yunnan adjoins northern Burma just as India's North-East does, but today China's integration with the region is far greater than that of India. China has been more proactively pursuing trans-border, sub-regional economic and cultural integration on other fronts too. Most pertinently, its role in the success story of the Greater Mekong Sub-region (GMS), almost vindicates the modern understanding of nation-state needs to transform to accommodate in a profitable way, the aspiration for integration of natural economic regions which were once undivided by national boundaries of the postcolonial world.

It is today acknowledged that the GMS project has greatly succeeded in bringing six nations that traditionally were bitter rivals to sublimate their antagonism through enhanced connectivity and economic interrelatedness. These nations along the basin of the mighty Mekong river, namely Vietnam, Laos, Cambodia, Thailand, Myanmar and Yunnan and Guangxi provinces of China have indeed managed to yoke past antagonisms into mutually beneficial channels of economic cooperation and reap the benefits of immense peace. The GMS initiative has in many ways forged a single economic unit out of these countries, strongly backed by the Asian

Development Bank as well as Japan and China for their own long-term economic and political benefits. It is relevant that the project's officially stated objectives are Connectivity, Competitiveness and Community.

The underlying logic behind the push for the evolution of economic regions and corridors is that the forces that led to the formation of the political reality of nation-states, with their hard, precise, zealously defended political boundaries, are seldom in congruence with natural economic regions that existed in pre-colonial days.

The outlook of India's Act East Policy too must seek to soften hard political boundaries without compromising its core sovereignty over territories within its boundaries at least in the economic spheres. Alongside the much vaunted and hyped objective of this project of connecting with ASEAN, it must also be equally about evolving an economic and cultural sub-region constituting of the North-East, Northern Myanmar, Northern Thailand, Northern Laos and Yunnan in China. Those who have travelled in this region will be amazed to find the cultural and ethnic affinities the populations here share. If this region overlaps a little with the GMS, so be it. It should be for the benefit of all. It would be a welcome miracle if the actualisation of such an economic region comes to supersede the obsession with political boundaries and closed ethnic identities that have been the roots of many deadly conflicts in the North-East.

There is no reason why such a miracle cannot happen. But this will entail a development agenda that empowers the people by opening up opportunities. This, coupled with administrative guarantees and safeguards against unfair trade practices and hegemonies should make a potent medicine. After all, what is freedom beyond the guarantees of these basic dignities?

Myanmar till very recently has been in the thick of political uncertainty and this too has been a big inhibition for India's Act East Policy. Now that this is no longer the case, with Myanmar embracing democracy, there are still some hiccups remaining as for instance in the country's dealings with its ethnic minorities, in particular the Rohingyas. But while the country sets its house in order, the liberalisation the country has undergone so far should be enough to begin work on the Act East Policy in earnest.

China's embrace of this outlook dates to much before India's own attempt. This is evident from the fact that in the GMS initiative, Yunnan has emerged as a prominent focal point of the entire project. The rest of the region wants access to this growing market as well as a little of the reflected halo from its increasing prosperity. China has since the 1980s been preparing to take the best advantage of these inevitable changes in regional outlook, and has been pushing its own well-known and publicised 'Kunming Initiative' whereby it sought to understand more comprehensively not just the economy but also the inner spirit of the region and the rest of South-East Asia through seminars, workshops and field studies.

The challenge and opportunity before India is that if China has used the geographical and ethnic affinities between Yunnan and the rest of South-East Asia to reach out to the latter without inspiring any sense of unease of being intruded upon, India too can do the same with a similar 'North-East Initiative'. The North-East can and would vibrate practically on the same wavelengths as any of these nations. But this should be no cause for insecurity that the North-East would prove disloyal to the nation. The Yunnan example should spell this out loud. Develop the place, unleash its natural potential by allowing it to follow the path of least resistance and a lot of the troubles should disappear.

The economic sub-region theory, although it came to be spelled out only in modern times, is not altogether a new understanding. The East India Company, arguably the first and most successful multi-national company, which at its peak controlled the trade and commerce of almost the entire world, intuitively and shrewdly saw this and calibrated their interrelated economic and strategic priorities accordingly on its map of concern. Relevant to this discussion are the three wars it fought with the Burmese kingdom, after each of which it annexed territories that formed an economic sub-region of this large country. In scholar Alastair Lamb's words in *Asian Frontiers: Studies in a Continuing Problem*, 'the British swallowed Burma in three gulps.'

Briefly, the chronology of the annexation of Burma would run in the following sequence. Various portions of Burmese territories adjoining East Bengal, including Arakan and Tenasserim were annexed by the British after their victory in the First Anglo-Burmese War; Lower Burma, including Pegu and Rangoon, was annexed in 1852 after the Second Anglo-Burmese War. In 1862, the annexed territories were designated as a minor province or British Burma of British India.

After the Third Anglo-Burmese War in 1885, Upper Burma was annexed and in 1897, the province of Burma in British India was created, thus becoming a major province (a Lieutenant-Governorship).

This arrangement was discontinued after 1937 when Burma began to be administered separately by a newly-formed Burma Office although it continued to share the same Secretary of State and the same building in London as the India Office.

Burma achieved independence from British rule on 4 January 1948. Lamb also notes that the only real war the British fought with Burma was the first. The next two were waged on a reluctant adversary on flimsy pretexts just so the British could annex territories that constituted economic sub-regions that it coveted.

India's Ties with Myanmar

Myanmar's relation with India thus has been historically close, politically as well as culturally. As noted, it was part of the same British India till as late as 1937. British India had administrative reasons for this and probably also wanted Burma (I am using 'Burma' for the colonial and pre-colonial period) not to come too much under the influence of the increasingly aggressive freedom struggle in the subcontinent at the time. But if the British had an explanation for their action, it was the response by Indians by and large, in particular the leadership of the Indian freedom struggle, which is confounding. This is particularly so because the separation happened at a time when the Indian freedom struggle was peaking. It is unimaginable there were no worthwhile protests even from the elite leadership of the struggle when a part of what was India was dismembered from it. In all probability, as a columnist of *The Telegraph*, Kolkata, Ashok Mitra, presumed in a column dated 18 May 2012, if the then British government had decided to also separate from India the region now known as the North-East, there would probably have been little protest as well. The Indian psyche has been always so obsessively fixated with its western borders and beyond that, this came to be at the cost of almost a complete neglect of its eastern region. The understandable outcome is the general shortfall in the nation's, as well as its citizens' understanding of the east. The price has also been dear. The endemic separatist problems in the North-East, and the almost complete lack of any intimately pursued South-East Asia policy until the dawning of a Look East Policy in the 1990s, is one. India's humiliating defeat at the hands of China in the brief 1962 border war over the McMahon Line is yet another.

As already stated, in colonial times, Burma suddenly came within the ambit of the British India government after the First Anglo-Burmese War that culminated in the signing of the Treaty of Yandaboo in 1826. This treaty is an important landmark in the history of the North-East as well. Indeed, with this event, a new chapter in the region's modern history came to be opened. Thereafter Assam was incorporated into British India and made a province of Bengal, unwittingly planting the seed for the uneasy relationship between Bengalis and Assamese to this day. Assam at the time meant almost the entire North-East with the exception of Manipur and Tripura, which were independent kingdoms, and the British chose to leave them as buffer protectorates for it suited their larger map of security.

Two more Anglo-Burmese Wars later, the last one in 1885, Burma came to be totally annexed into British India. Once Burma became a part of British India, there were efforts by the British to integrate the North-East with Burma. Quite interestingly, in 1895-96, to further their commercial interests, they even came up with the idea of railway links between Assam and Burma via the same routes the Indian Government is now considering similar railway links. The British plan was to "link the Burma railway system to Prome, in the centre from Lamding via Berima in the Naga Hills to Mayangkhong valley and so through Manipur to Tammoo and Monywa, in the north from Margherita over Patkoi range down the Hukong valley and on through Maiankwan to Mongoung on to the present Shwebo-Myinthkyina line." (L.W. Shakespear in *History of Assam Rifles*)

Pre-colonial Links

But the link between the North-East and Burma is much older than the arrival of the British in the region. Manipur, in particular, has had an engaging history of military as well as commercial relationship with its much larger neighbour, the Ava kingdom, seated at Ava/Mandalay. As for instance raids by Manipur's notorious cavalry, especially under their king Pameiba between 1725 and 1749, is said to have contributed to the fall of the Toungoo dynasty (D.G.E. Hall in *A History of South East Asia*), and in later years, revenge raids by the Konbaung dynasty which succeeded the Toungoo dynasty, devastated Manipur, causing dispersal of its population, many of them settling in the Cachar region of Assam, Tripura and Sylhet in East Bengal (Bangladesh). One of the first military expeditions of the founder of the Konbaung dynasty, King Alaumpaya, was a devastating raid on Manipur (Hall). Quite in the manner that Yale professor, James C. Scott predicted in his influential *Art of Not Being Governed: An Anarchist History Upland South East Asia*, these military expeditions often were to capture skilled populations from each other's kingdoms and resettle them in their own. There are many colonies of Burmese indigenised Manipuris skilled in various crafts settled in and around Mandalay even to this day. Likewise, the names of many settlements in the valley area of Manipur suggest these population pockets were originally of Burmese origin.

It will also be recalled that when the British entered Assam for the first time, it was after Burma under the seventh king of the Konbaung dynasty, King Bagidaw, had overrun and devastated Manipur and Assam and then threatened to make inroads into the British territory of East Bengal. The Burmese were then comprehensively defeated in Assam as well as in Manipur and the British annexed Assam but left Manipur as a protectorate state doing its bidding.

At the end of the First Anglo-Burmese War in 1826, the boundary between Manipur and Burma was considered to be the Chindwin river, thereby giving

Manipur custody of the Kabaw Valley. In 1834 however, following repeated complaints by the Burmese, the British gave away the Kabaw Valley to them, the logic being it would be easier to govern it from Mandalay. British officer Captain R. Boileau Pemberton then was given the task to delineate and demarcate a new boundary along the foot of the 'Murring Hills', which is roughly, where the present international boundary is. Not many are aware of it, but this 1834 boundary is one of the oldest demarcated international boundaries of India although in the coming decades it underwent some modifications. In 1882, the line was modified by the British Political Agent in Manipur, Colonel James Johnstone, to bring the restive Chassad Kukis within Manipur territory and in 1896, another Political Agent, Colonel HSP John Maxwell, re-demarcated the boundary introducing minor realignments and placed 38 boundary pillars along it.

Independent India's Myanmar policy has been rather tentative and noncommittal. It has been cordial sometimes and strained at other times. After Myanmar's independence in 1948, India assisted Myanmar's first civil government under Prime Minister U Nu financially as well as in terms of military hardware to overcome its birth pangs marked by an ethnic turmoil that severely threatened its very survival. After the military coup in 1962, Burma went into self-exile and isolation. Moreover, it piqued India when the new military junta nationalised all businesses and properties, discriminating against people of Indian origin, forcing over 300,000 of them to flee to India. In 1988, when there was a popular uprising against the military junta, India chose to side with pro-democracy leader Aung San Suu Kyi, but in the 1990s, when it had seemed the military was not buckling under even very tough sanctions by the USA and EU, thanks to the continued support of the Chinese and the refusal of ASEAN to abandon its neighbour, India began taking a U-turn to cosy up with the junta again. By then, however, Myanmar's partnership with China was already too secure to be dislodged.

With the return of democracy in Myanmar, India is now making a fresh approach and the North-East is eagerly and hopefully waiting to see this new approach take shape that would benefit the region. There will be hurdles, some historical and some of consequence to the new world economic order and geopolitics. When the British annexed Burma, they encouraged Indians who were much more acquainted with their administration to migrate to the country to fill the lower bureaucracy. Expectedly, Indians soon came to dominate not only the country's lower corridors of power but also trade and commerce. As many describe it, the Burmese capital of Rangoon was at one point virtually an Indian city. This was predicted to cause resentment amongst the local population, and in 1942 during WWII when Japanese forces entered Burma and swept the country, pushing back

British troops across the border into Manipur, there were anti-Indian riots in Burma forcing a wave of Indian refugees to head for India. There is a derogative Myanmar term for Indians 'Kala' or 'Kalar' which today is being used to describe the Rohingyas. This prejudice may however be older than the arrival of the British in 1885, though not as pronounced. In Amitav Ghosh's *Glass Palace*, when the first British cannons were heard in Mandalay, the first to feel the insecurity of the imminent breakdown of law were the 'Kalas'. Indeed, other than competition from China, ASEAN and the West, all of whom now take a keen interest in the new Myanmar, India would also have to work to neutralise this scar from the colonial past.

12

Act East Policy from Perspectives of Soft Power Engagements and Connectivity between Northeast India and ASEAN

Suwa Lal Jangu

ABSTRACT

The connectivity between India and ASEAN is one of focus areas of the Act East policy. The government and non-government actors are of the opinion that people-to-people contact and institutional connectivity between North-East India and ASEAN should be improved. People-to-people contact and institutional connectivity are being projected as 'soft-power' and 'soft-connectivity'. On the basis of soft-power and soft-connectivity, countries are being linked with neighbours and enter a system of regional cooperation. Cultural and historical links and modern soft-connectivity are termed as the 'soft-power' of a country, as geographical and demographic proximities and links between India's North-East and Myanmar are recognized as soft power. India's cultural and historical links via the North-East with South-East Asia are India's soft-power.

The contemporary shared political values and common interests of India and ASEAN play an important role in the building of soft-connectivity between them. Soft-power and soft-connectivity are the two important mechanisms in India's Act East policy. These two mechanisms are being used to address the gaps of people-to-people contact and institutional connectivity in India-Myanmar border areas. There are some big challenges in the way of soft power engagements and connectivity between India and Myanmar. First, building institutions and addressing coordination gaps. Second, improvement in cooperation-based planning and implementation process. Third, diverse geopolitical and socio-ethnic peculiarities in cross-border areas. And fourth, the presence of diverse political, social and legal systems in the two countries.

Introduction

Knowledge and technology are two inputs of globalization. Contact and connectivity are two outputs of globalization. Physical connectivity and military engagements compose hard-power but knowledge, peoples and institutional connectivity and engagements lead to soft-power. Institutions, culture and technology are the bridges to cover the gap in connectivity and contact between people and institutions in cross-border areas. Civil society organisations and institutions are sources of soft-power and soft-connectivity in the contemporary globalized world. As geographical and military links are known as 'hard connectivity' while economic, i.e., border *haat* market and social engagements are means of soft power.

Cross-border engagements and connectivity through knowledge, technology and machine shrink the gap and size of the time and space and resulted in globalised world. Twenty-first century diplomacy has moved from the drawing rooms of diplomats to the hands of the people. This is a positive trend that encourages people's participation and makes them stakeholders in the country's international relations. As the world order moves towards greater connectivity initiatives such as regional cooperation, it will foster greater people-to-people ties and at the same time help the country in the building of its position as a global leader in a new emerging multilateral world order (Garg, 2010). Soft-power engagements with neighbours is one of focus areas of India's Act East policy. These soft engagements are required prerequisites for establishing hard power and connectivity with neighbours. The North-East region was earlier more connected and engaged with its neighbours. The overwhelming approach of physical and economic connectivity should not be overshadowed by ethnic and cultural connectivity.

Soft Power and Soft Connectivity between ASEAN and India

As India continues to push for connectivity with ASEAN through the North-East under its Act East policy, soft connectivity is required in order to establish hard connectivity, i.e., road and rail links. As knowing the fact that soft connectivity is the key to all kinds of ties, India's North-East shares cultural and historical linkages with South-East Asian countries. These linkages can be utilized as software of soft power connectivity between India and ASEAN. Thai Ambassador to India, Chutintorn Gongsakdi, has said, "For Thailand, we will continue with ASEAN-India priorities. But we should also emphasis on hard connectivity because only one dimension is not enough. We need air, sea and land connectivity as well as soft connectivity is the key to India-ASEAN ties (Gongsakdi, 2018)."

Things like connectivity and other soft links between India and South-East Asia, both entities are moving in the right direction. Soft power and connectivity are the two keys of cooperation between the two. The ASEAN countries are committed to enhance the soft power engagements and connectivity with India. Building institutional connectivity and people-to-people contact between the India's

North-East region and the ASEAN region is an increasing development in both regions (Kurian 2014:134).

Nimmi Kurian argued that mere economic activity cannot ease tensions between the centre and North-Eastern states. There is a need for more institutional and people-to-people contact and connectivity between the North-East and ASEAN as felt by many politicians, academicians, media persons and activists of civil society organizations. It is imperative for India's soft-power reflection in ASEAN countries; the country needs to look and act in the North-East. For this, improvement in hard connectivity-related infrastructure in the northeast is required. The hard reality of inadequate hard-connectivity related infrastructure and facilities in the North-East should be realised. In this regard, more quick action is the need of the hour especially looking to connectivity as the main focus of the Act East policy (AEP). Acting in the name of AEP should be reflected on the ground of India's North-East region. India still could not have sufficiently utilized the soft-power of the North-East since the Look (Act) East policy was introduced.

India-ASEAN Soft-power Engagements

In the last one year, four events of soft power engagements between India and ASEAN were organized in India. First, India hosted the leaders of all the ASEAN countries as the chief guests on the 68th Republic Day celebrations and to mark the 25th anniversary of India-ASEAN partnership through a commemorative summit. Second, for the first-time an India-ASEAN artists' camp was held in Udaipur, Rajasthan. Third was the India-ASEAN music festival held in Delhi and fourth was the annual India-ASEAN Friendship Car Rally. These events not only brought the two more closer but also straightened the soft-power engagements between India and the ASEAN. Such events provide a platform for interaction, sharing and exchanging ideas, experience and skills.

The educated and technologically skilled young generation is always seeking opportunities to demonstrate their skill. Such opportunities are not available to the youth of the North-East. The lack of opportunity for youths is also felt by policy makers on both sides. The policy makers in India and ASEAN took an important initiative and organized bilateral events under the Act East Policy. Prabir De, the Chair of India-ASEAN Centre at think tank RIS run by the External Affairs Ministry says: "India's soft power in ASEAN is second to none. It is contrary to popular belief; younger generation in India and Southeast Asia are speaking more to each other through cultural space—music, arts, games and education. Social media has made positive impact on cultural ties (Chaudhury 2017)."

The soft power of India's North-East in ASEAN countries is the region's historical and cultural linkages. The soft power engagement is an engine of economic cooperation between India and Myanmar. As these soft powers are also the core areas of India's Act East policy like in the form of the 3Cs—Commerce, Connectivity and Culture. This policy is a sentimental instrument of soft power engagements between these two entities. Through this policy, India is establishing its soft power engagements with ASEAN countries. Not only India's future but also that of its North-East region's lies in the eastern world, i.e., South-East Asia.

The realization of India's prospects in ASEAN countries depends upon its outreaching approach like that of a similar approach in Africa. Sports activities, especially football, is an emerging prospect of soft power engagements between India's North-East states and Africa. African coaches, trainers and players are being engaged in the North-East through sports; similar opportunities can be explored by youths of ASEAN countries. Unlike China, India is not pursuing an aggressive foreign policy sidestepping local sentiments. The potential of India's soft power must be fully utilized to create bonds with the region, which is part of our extended neighbourhood.

In recent years, cultural diplomacy became one of the promotional tools of national interest in India's foreign policy. It is one of the soft powers through which India is reaching out to ASEAN countries. Cultural and religious diplomacy is helping to India in reviving its ancient linkages with ASEAN countries. Yoga as one of strategic instruments in India's cultural diplomacy is gaining popularity in East Asian countries. Through yoga, Buddhist links, Buddhist circuit in India, India-ASEAN youth summit, India-ASEAN music festival, etc., these countries are coming closer. These cultural activities and links play the role of bridges between the North-East and ASEAN. India's cultural diplomacy and soft power is reflected in Buddhism, revival of Nalanda University, chairs of Indian studies in ASEAN's universities, yoga, Indian cultural centres and joint restoration of monuments in Cambodia, Vietnam and Laos. Institutional connectivity and peoples leads to gains from soft power in ASEAN countries. By nature and history, India and ASEAN endowed a great heritage that can be utilized for soft power engagements (Ibid.).

Track-II Engagements: A Successful Road Ahead

Institutional and people-to-people connectivity is an important instrument of India's Track-II engagement with South-East Asian countries. The value of flexibility and the possibility of taking off of any track diplomacy between India and ASEAN s only when government officials are involved. Therefore, governments have a role to play at all stages. Track-II engagements can have an important place in the role of India's NER in the Act East policy (Haokip 2015).

A delegation of Members of Myanmar Parliament visited India in February 2017. It visited Mizoram University on 22 February. In an interaction with university teachers, the head of the delegation expressed his team's interest to visit India to learns federalism, autonomy and local governance. He said, 'we want to know more about the structure and functioning of federalism, autonomy and local-self-governance as currently our country is going through political transformation. Kindly treat us as students and do not expect much from us. Mizoram University is a neighbourhood school for us. We want to learn the structure and functioning of federalism and autonomy (Mizoram University 2017).

India's North-Eastern universities can become neighbourhood schools of learning federalism and autonomy for Myanmar's legislators and administrators. In this way, India's North-East can play a very important role in the fostering of soft power-based relations with Myanmar. In the North-East, a few institutions and platforms are in the fore of engaging with ASEAN countries. Therefore, the potential role of the North-East in India's ties with Myanmar is not properly tapped. In this region, except Guwahati, no other hub or urban platform is suitable for organizing mega or large events like India-ASEAN youth summit and cultural festival.

Recently, two such mega events were held in Udaipur in Rajasthan and New Delhi. It means the mainland is benefiting at the cost of the North-East's soft power links and connectivity with ASEAN countries. In other words, the Act East Policy is acting in the mainland and passing over the North-Eastern region. The North-East's Youth Forum for Foreign Policy (NEYFFP), is trying to bring to the fore the role of the NER in the Act East Policy by organizing Track-II engagements with ASEAN countries. The NER is not only a geographic but also an economic junction where South-Asia and South-East Asia meet. The Track-II-based connectivity between India's North-East and ASEAN is a win-win arrangement. Educational and civil society institutions can lead the Track-II based engagements between India and ASEAN. India's future lies with the eastern world that begins from the North-East region.

Soft Connectivity: the Key of India-ASEAN Relations

Connectivity is a major area of convergence for ASEAN and India. India is currently working with ASEAN on multiple connectivity projects. Physical and economic connectivity significantly improved between the two in recent years. The Ganga-Mekong Cooperation was the first project of cultural and emotional connectivity between the two. Many connectivity projects are in their completion stage and some new projects are proposed and have been approved by both sides. On 19 December 2017, India hosted the ASEAN-India Connectivity Summit (AICS). The purpose was to explore possibilities and means of connectivity between ASEAN and India, to support the Master Plan on ASEAN Connectivity (MPAC) and improve physical connect with India.

Soft connectivity is the mother of all kinds of connectivity. This area is now in the top priority in India's Act East Policy. Without soft power and connectivity, the benefits of physical and economic connectivity cannot be tapped. Soft power engagements between the North-East and ASEAN are required for hard power building. India and ASEAN are moving towards bilateral and trilateral motor vehicles agreement and realization of allowing free movement of cargo, passenger and personal vehicles along the roads linking India, Myanmar and Thailand. But there is neither an agreement nor realization of the need for institutional and people-to-people connectivity on both sides. However, giving substance to India-ASEAN relations through multi-sectoral connectivity will gradually change the geopolitical landscape of North-East India (Desai 2017).

Domestic Politics and India-ASEAN Engagements

A peaceful and stable political atmosphere is a pre-requisite for establishing any kind of connectivity between two border areas. The political atmosphere in a country includes democratic polity, political mainstream and leadership. Political reforms have been unfolding since 2010 under the nationalist government in Myanmar. Economic engagement with India is the top priority for ASEAN countries. The collective will of the ASEAN political community is pro-India. After economic power, India is now recognized as a political power in South-East Asia. The ASEAN countries came close to India on the issue of the South China Sea. This is not because India's energy interests are at stake there but an indication of the growing influence of India's hard power in this region. Similarly, ASEAN countries are also important for India's national maritime, trade and energy security.

But there are other aspects of a country's hard power as in nationalism and populism. Both cannot be used as the soft power of a country in international politics. Nationalistic agenda and populism-based foreign policy always tend to be negative. But soft power and connectivity always tilts towards peace stability and cooperation in bilateral relationships. Prime Minister Modi's foreign policy is wrapped in nationalism and populism. Through his nationalistic ordure and populistic appeal, he comes closer to NRIs abroad. Thailand's Ambassador to India has expressed his concern in these words: "Connectivity is important, but we are also at a point across the region when nationalism and populism are on the rise. To have connectivity work to its full potential, it is necessary to dial down the nationalistic rhetoric", Ambassador Chuntintorn Sam Gongsaki told *The Hindu* in an interview ahead of the India-ASEAN summit which had seen the presence of all the ten leaders of ASEAN in Delhi to commemorate twenty-five years of ASEAN and to be chief guests at the Republic Day Parade (Haidar 2018).

By virtue of its geopolitical location between South Asia and South-East Asia, the recent democratic reforms of Myanmar present a significant new opportunity for enhancing connectivity and soft power engagements. These engagements offer the promise of substantial gains for both India's North-East and Myanmar. Both the North-East and Myanmar have several sources of comparative advantage including rich natural resource endowments; shared culture, geographical proximities and historical cultural linkages. As mentioned above, these potential gains include contributing to economic integration, social networking and institutional connectivity and contributing to the processes of political reconciliation in Myanmar and India's North-East (Asian Development Bank 2013).

In recent years, Mizoram and Arunachal Pradesh ranked among the top ten states of tourist-destinations in India. Both states are also among the most peaceful in India. But the tourism sector could not become a major source of income in the North-Eastern states. It faces a lot of problems from lack of an international airport to lack of an integrated tourism circuit. Apart from the problem of connectivity with neighbours, several other problems are also associated with this region. Among them, some are lack of awareness and publicity about tourism, tourist visit prohibition, cross-border insurgency activities, lack of tourism infrastructure, weather-related factors and lack of a cohesive tourism policy for this region. Still the North-East region is not fully opened for foreign tourists and some areas are closed for all tourists.

Today's world is globalized where physical and digital connectivity is changing the definition of geography. Therefore, connectivity with the neighbourhood can be improved through use of soft-power engagements like tourism, education and health specially. There is a need to generate awareness about India-ASEAN shared culture, values and historical links in ASEAN countries. Tribal culture, rural culture and natural ecology are the key advantages. On the basis of these, the region has a huge potential for tourism promotion. Tourism may be used as a source of soft-power building in this region. The tourism-based soft power would help in boosting ties between India's North-East region and ASEAN countries.

Soft Power and Connectivity in North-East India

India's land connection with South-East Asia is through its North-Eastern region. This region has been neglected for long mainly due to its relatively poor representation in Parliament. A concrete policy is needed that allows the NER to be a key stakeholder in all stages of policy from making to implementation. In doing so, states will feel integrated with mainland India and benefit from better relations with its ASEAN neighbours. The North-East states do not act as smooth conduits linking India with its eastern neighbours. There is a lack of local stakeholders who are the engine of the region's development growth. Ethnic communities are socially organized and politically mobilized but economically they are poor. Identity is the *de facto* reality of the North-East. Connectivity-related infrastructural development marks the Chinese province of Yunnan which shares a border with Myanmar. It is an example of how China has moved toward establishing better ties with its neighbours, via its border region's based soft power. Boosting the local economy along with infrastructural development of the border region leads to soft power-based connectivity and relations with neighbours.

The cooperation between the region's states and the Union Government is mostly centralized. The cooperative federalism cannot be materialized here because the region has no political and demographic weightage. The lack of inter-state cooperation affects the interest of the region's development and the promotion of soft power-based connectivity. The soft power of the region includes tourism, education, sports, health, etc. These have value with ASEAN countries. The government should focus on developing its soft-power regionally. For example, there should be greater investment in sports, education and health infrastructures.

The Union Government is emphasising on soft connectivity and organising soft power engagements like sports, music and health between the NER and ASEAN countries. This would enhance people-to-people contract and has the potential to increase the influence of India's soft power. The greater role of the region's states is required in the connectivity projects with eastern neighbours (Maini 2013). In order to increase connectivity with ASEAN, it is important to focus more on the border areas and their infrastructure development in the North-East region. Connectivity with the neighbourhood and South-East Asia is India's priority. It is a commitment of the Union Government to act in the North-East.

Look East to Act East Policy: Name and Contents

India's Look (Act) East policy which aims to foster closer ties with South-East Asian nations has become one of the most important cornerstones of its foreign policy. In the third phase of the Look East Policy (LEP), three major changes were introduced. The first change related to the change in its nomenclature from Look to Act East. The second change related to its geopolitical area and extension beyond Southeast Asia so that it now covers Australia, South Korea and Japan. The third change relates to its key goal on connectivity alongwith cooperation. The key role of India's North-East is to accelerate connectivity with South-East Asia in India's Act East Policy (AEP). In the second phase of LEP during 2004-2014, there was greater urgency for India to accelerate economic and security cooperation with South-East Asia (Jangu 2016:183).

In the literal sense, India's LEP has shifted from looking to acting and from cooperation to connectivity in recent years. Will this literal change in the policy generate a good perception about the Act East policy among the people? Is this policy better after having added a smart word to its name? India's lead role in the building of institutional infrastructure with a futuristic goal yet realistic connectivity program is the key focus of the Look East policy. It has been known by the new name 'Act East Policy' since July 2014; the AEP has been pursued in a multifaceted manner by promoting connectivity and soft power-based relations with ASEAN. India has been trying to bridge its North-East region's isolation through the Act East Policy. Track-II diplomacy could not be effective in the LEP. In Myanmar, the provincial governments were weak and depended upon the national government for everything.

Guwahati, the hub of Northeast India, is an example of connectivity-driven integration. Organisations such as the World Bank have been entrusted to create a Vision Report and a new think tank will be supporting the Assam Government's 'Act East Department'. The Assam Chief Minister has been monitoring 'AEP' projects personally. The Imphal-Mandalay passenger bus service is expected to be operational by 2018. The linkages of soft power engagements enable the NER and Myanmar to emerge as a thriving area that promotes social development of communities along the border. To date, India's North-East and ASEAN have not come close to enjoying the same social success that the European community has reaped. India's North-East and Myanmar can be drivers of India-ASEAN relations and cooperation (Sahoo & Bhunia 2013).

The Northeast and Southeast Asia

Northeast India is less connected with its neighbourhood in the globalised world. Over emphasis upon wider economic connectivity through a narrow physical space is the true face of the connectivity approach between the NEI (North East India) and ASEAN. On the India-Myanmar border, people from both sides used to dry their wet clothes on the border fence-line. This is an indicator of people's psychological and social contact and connectivity. During a crisis, people in border areas make contact and connection with affected people. Civil society organizations, i.e., Young Mizo Association in Mizoram, provide fuel, candles, clothes, rice and first-aid kits to calamity-affected people in Myanmar.

There is not only geographical proximity but historical and cultural affinity also between North-East India (NEI) and Myanmar. Cultural orientation and ethnical roots bind northeast communities. Ecology, environment, forests and rivers and lakes are natural means of contact and connectivity. Education, traditional and ethnic knowledge and tourism are yet to become part of soft-power engagements between the NEI and ASEAN. People in the North-East feel that the Act East policy seems to overlooking and bypassing the NEI. Prime Minister Narendra Modi said the North-East would be made a gateway of South-East Asia. He also said that an economic corridor would be established using North-East India, Myanmar and the adjoining regions. North-East India would be a gateway of South-East Asia in the future (Business Standard 2014*)*.

India shares the ASEAN vision for rule-based societies and values of peace. These shared values lead India towards Southeast Asia as it is our future. India is closer to the East due to its shared values and historical links. India's future lies with the East, not with the West. During the Cold War, India's interests were associated with the West, but India's future is in the East. India's strength is the shared cultural, social, religious and historical links with ASEAN countries. However, these bonds and links do not help much in economic and strategic relations but these serve our soft power-based engagements.

New Areas of Soft Power Engagements and Connectivity

Human resources are used as 'soft power' for people-to-people and institutional connectivity. Experts are of the view that Indian civil society and the media can play an effective role in promoting bilateral ties with an important and strategic neighbour. Civil society could not play its important role in soft power engagements with neighbours during the military rule in Myanmar. But since 2010, when political reforms began, the social and political roles of civil society organisations have flowing to the ground level. Walter Fernandes, a senior Fellow in the North Eastern Social Research Centre, Guwahati, says:

> *"Civil society in Myanmar has been hounded by the government so far. Indian civil society can teach the Myanmarese civil society on how to deal with the government and the media can play an important role in this context. Northeast India should*

> *become a learning centre about India's immediate eastern neighbours. Media, strategic community, academic and civil society have to come together and collaborate (*The Northeast Today 2016*)."*

There is a need to lay more emphasis on improvement of cooperation between Indian journalists and the Myanmar media and better representation on all the important agendas of India-Myanmar relations, particularly focusing on the border regions of Myanmar with India. There the media has a very important role to play in shaping India-Myanmar relationships. "A meaningful interaction will lead to capacity development and partnership. We are happy to forge a relationship with like-minded agencies," she said. Mizoram is one state which can play an important role in India-Myanmar people-to-people ties. Mizoram has been a stage for disputes over the Chin refugees from Myanmar but now things are changing. According to Khin Zaw Win, director of the Tampadipa Institute in Myanmar, India's Act East policy, if implemented fully, can bring a lot of progress to the ASEAN region (Ibid).

Through the Act East policy, the North-East region (NER) could also become a hub for education the way it has become one for health. Patients from Myanmar are frequently being treated in Imphal; 90 per cent of patients in Shija Hospital are from Myanmar. An educational boom would bring huge returns for the region's economy if the education sector follows suit. Presently there is no student exchange program between India and Myanmar in higher education in the NER (De 2017).

Rivers and Border for Soft Connectivity and Engagements

Rivers serve as a means of multi-connectivity in the border areas of India and her neighbours. They connect and provide a source of transport, resources and people. Rivers have been using as a connectivity source by people and animals since ancient times. There are connective narratives among people. Management of shared-rivers by joint initiatives is the best way of soft-power engagements. There is a lack of a periphery and people-centric plans, especially management of shared-river and border areas. In many countries, shared-rivers are being managed not only for exploiting riverine resources but also to solve the issues of displaced inhabitants and maintaining the river's resources and ecosystem. The Kaladan Multi-model Transit Transport project is an example of shared-river based mode of connectivity and engagement between India and Myanmar. The shared-rivers and border communities are being used in promotion of soft power engagements in border areas. There is a huge scope and potential to capitalize shared-rivers as the source of transportation and economic opportunity.

North-East India is a completely land-locked region connected with the rest of the country by a thin "chicken's neck" land corridor. By virtue of nature, the North-East region of India is well connected by rivers with its neighbours. Therefore, it is necessary to utilize the shared-rivers in this region for improvement of connectivity with neighbours. The inland waterways are not only for improving transportation but also great sources of economic engagements. Therefore, border should be used as a river as the border community is like a river resource that not only links upstream and downstream inhabitants and cross-border communities. A theme of riverine connectivity is a pro-people approach of connectivity and boosting the relationship among countries. Border *haats* (markets) emphasis is an important form of cross border connectivity of commodities and communities. Rivers are the most comfortable, cheap and sustainable mode of transportation (Jangu 2017).

Key Imperative Areas for Soft Power Engagements

Security, strategy and national interests are the predominating issues in periphery-neighbourhood connectivity, i.e., connectivity between the North-East region and Myanmar. The border areas and communities are used like 'bridges' of physical and economic connectivity. Every day, more than five thousand people used to travel between China and Vietnam in the border areas. The inland waterway is the biggest mode of transportation among ASEAN countries. Annual intra-regional trade in ASEAN is 35 per cent of the total trade of ASEAN in relation to the world (News Asia TV Channel, 18 June 2018).

Such good data about the level of trade, connectivity and transportation in ASEAN countries are the result of soft power engagements among the South-East Asian countries. Trade cooperation, security and strategic partnership are deepening day by day without impacting the border area residents and their needs. The Ganga-Mekong cultural cooperation is an example of soft power and connectivity but the North-East region is yet to become a part of this. Economic and physical connectivity is overemphasized over soft power engagements and connectivity in this region.

1. *Civil Society Organisations and Media*: Border, shared rivers and other inland water sources are hard power areas and security strategic but these can be converted into soft power and engagement through civil society organizations and media.
2. *Border Haat Markets and Community Services*: The level and trend of relations between the two neighbours can be seen from the cross-border economic activities, i.e., *haat* (market) in border areas.
3. *Tourism and Hospitality:* A Buddhist circuit should be developed in the North-East region that would undoubtedly foster soft power based relations between India and Myanmar.

4. *Social-Cultural Show Parks*: Youth programmes and community social and cultural events should be organized in border areas. Social-cultural programmes and events and other such initiatives of discussion and exchanges would provide a great boost to confidence-building among India and neighbours.
5. *Games and Sports Activities*: The North-East region is an emerging jewel of the Indian sports crown. Its youths are endowed with talent of sports and athletic abilities. Establishment of a Sports University and games training centres in this region can promote soft power and engagement. The North-East region has the potential of promotion of India-ASEAN relations and engagement through sports.
6. *Festival and Music Events*: Organizing India-ASEAN youth festivals, music, dance, fashion, etc., in the North-Eastern states. These soft engagements among youths would provide a great boost to confidence building measures between India and its neighbours.
7. *Literature and Art:* Both are great depositories of shared history, values and experience. And both are sources of soft power. The North-East region has the tremendous potential to capitalize on literature and art for soft engagements between India and ASEAN countries.
8. *Health Education and Medical Services:* The NER could also become a hub of health education and medical services for its neighbours. The region has the potential of becoming a platform of joint research and education in medicinal plants and indigenous health methods. The health service boom would bring huge returns for the region's economy if the health sector follows suit.
9. *Educational and Training Institutions:* Opening of South Asian University and ASEAN University campuses in the North-East. India's North-East shares cultural and historical ties with ASEAN countries. A common university in the North-East would doubtlessly be attractive for students from South Asia and ASEAN. Education and academic institutions are always engines of soft power engagements.
10. *Religious Institutional Connectivity:* Religious bodies of the North-East and Myanmar can lead the peace process in Myanmar and also in the North-East region where some pockets are affected by insurgency. The visits, teaching and preaching programmes of religious bodies and community organizations of both sides could promote soft power engagements between India and ASEAN.
11. *Democratic Reforms in Myanmar:* Learning schools on federalism, autonomy and local governance can be established in the North-East region's

universities for Myanmar. Parliamentary representatives and administrators of Myanmar need to learn the functioning of the federal system, provincial autonomy and local governance. The country has been going through historical political reforms since 2010.

12. *Social and Environmental Activists and Institutions*: As rivers and forests are symbols of shared nature and history between North-East India and Myanmar they not only connect different geographical territories but also connect peoples of politically divided states. Social and environmental activists and institutions can help in re-establishing historical links. The role of social and environment activists of both sides is the key of success of joint projects of development of dam and transportation facilities on rivers.

The soft power engagement between ASEAN and China is the key of inter-regional cooperation and economic prosperity. Even China and ASEAN, especially the countries of South China Sea, face the issue of maritime rights in the South China Sea. China's hard power influence on its security and economic dominance in the ASEAN community is also a growing concern. But there may be differences between ASEAN and China on the issue of hard power but the soft power relations between the two will never be affected.

Challenges

There are many challenges in the efforts of soft power engagements and connectivity between India and South-East Asian countries. First, building institutions and addressing coordination gaps. Second, improvement in cooperative planning and implementation process. The third, diverse geopolitical and socio-ethnic peculiarities in the North-East region and ASEAN. And the fourth, diverse political and governance systems between the two countries. Apart from these, there is a lack of sufficient, efficient and effective local stakeholders to promote and lead the initiatives of soft-power engagements and connectivity between India's North-East and Myanmar. Market shutdowns, road blockades and protests for autonomy, separate statehood and regional power sharing are daily news in the North-East region. Even Myanmar is also crippled by ethnic, minority atrocities and communal insurgency especially in the border areas. Recently, Myanmar's security forces launched strikes against Chin state-based minority revolutionary army; thousands of Christians rushed to the India-Myanmar border (Manipur) and sought shelter in India. Temporary entry (for some days) was given to around 1400 people of the same ethnic minority in Mizoram.

On the issue of the Rohingyas, a minority, India's stand is more strategic and less an act of responsibility. There is a lack of an exclusive, explicit and extensive soft-power approach and soft-connectivity policy on both sides. There is also lack of social capital, human resources and institutional infrastructure that are much required in promotion and building of soft-power bases and soft-connectivity channels. Illegal cross-border immigration and infiltration is one of the dominant issues at least in the border areas of the North-East region. Interstate-border conflicts and interstate-ethnic insurgency harm the soft power engagement between India and Myanmar. The conflicts of interstate roads, rail connectivity and shared natural resources like rivers and forests affect the efforts of peace-building and cooperation within the region and with the neighbours.

The biggest challenging task before Myanmar's national unity government is to settle the national reconciliation process and assimilation of border area dissidents, ethnic and minority groups in the national process of political reforms. Myanmar has been passing through a transition stage from military rule to democratic governance since 2010. There is a lack of soft-power infrastructure and activities in the border areas of North-East India and Myanmar. Investors hesitate to come to the Autonomous District Council and Inner Line Permit states. Similar provisions in the border states of Myanmar also regulate the entry of outsiders. There is insufficient physical connectivity between India and Myanmar. There is no direct flight between the North-East northeast states and ASEAN countries. There is one common consensus among people across the North-East region and that is that the people are interested in the soft power engagements and connectivity with neighbours. But there is a lack of presence of local stakeholders to take up soft power engagements in this region. One of the major problems in soft connectivity is financial cost as ASEAN countries are not in favour of taking the responsibility of financial expenditure that would occur in the opening and running of offices in India's North-East region.

Conclusion

India needs a concrete policy—one that focuses on greater and comprehensive connectivity related infrastructure development especially in the border areas of North-East states. In the Act East policy, it is important to make people hope and believe that the North-East region (NER) will not be bypassed and that it will not benefit other economic hubs at the behest of the North-East. This sentiment is increasingly visible in the North-East, and it is not only of intellectual people but also among local politicians. Only then will the literal change in the Act East Policy be meaningful and successful in people's perceptions. The linkages of institutions, civil society organizations, academicians and activist networks will enable the NER and Myanmar to emerge as a thriving area that will promote social development of communities along the border areas. There should be a time-line of completion of projects of physical connectivity.

The entire region endorses the soft power approach and means of soft engagements. People-to-people contact and mobility, exchange and sharing programmes should be increased. There is also a need to improve educational and administrative institutes, academic and research collaboration, and exchange programmes and training between the North-East region and ASEAN as the North-East is being projected as a 'Knowledge Hub', 'Gateway of the ASEAN', 'Bridge' between South Asia and Southeast Asia and transit port and conduit like situation between the main-land India and the Southeast Asia.

The use of soft power to restore historical connections between the NER and Myanmar appear to be bearing fruit. Both India and ASEAN countries can take other initiatives to create a bridge between their youth by organizing India-ASEAN youth festivals. Mizoram and Arunachal have improved their respective rank in the list of the top ten tourist-destination states. These two states can be role models for other states in the region. Without a reasonable level of economic development and stability in India's North-Eastern states, as well as better infrastructure in its border areas. India's Act East policy cannot become a reality. Both India and ASEAN should mobilise soft power engagements looking at the democratic reforms in Myanmar and economic prospectus of the North-East. India's future is with the East and that begins from the North-East. The North-East and Myanmar are at a juncture of soft power engagements between India and South-East Asian countries.

REFERENCES

Asian Development Bank. 2013. Interim Report: Connecting South Asia and Southeast Asia, ADB Institute. pp. 12 & 13.

Business Standard. 2014. Palatine (Tripura). December 01.

Chaudhury, Dipnoan Roy. 2017. *The Economic Times.* 12 October.

De, Prabir. 2017. Can 'Act East' address Northeast India's isolation? *East Asia Forum.* 27 October. Accessed from http://www.eastasiaforum.org/?p=93423

Desai, Suyash. 2017. ASEAN and India Converge on Connectivity. *The Diplomat.* December 19.

Garg, Ibu Sanjeeb. NADI 2016: Connecting With India's Northeast. *The Diplomat.* July 20, 2016.

Gongsakdi, Chutintorn. 2018. Soft connectivity key to India-ASEAN ties. 21 January, *Financial Express.*

Haidar, Suhasini. 2018. Less nationalism, more connectivity: ASEAN leader. *The Hindu,* January 22. Accessed from http://www.thehindu.com/news/national/more-connectivity-needs-lessnationalism-and-populism-asean-coordinator/article22491820.ece

Haokip, Tongkholal. 2015. India's Look East Policy: Prospects and Challenges for Northeast India. Studies in Indian Politics, 3(2):198-211.

Jangu, Suwa Lal. 2017. 'The Implications of Kaladan Multi-model Transit Transport project for India's Northeast region and ASEAN,' in '*ASEAN calling: Sub-regional Cooperation and Northeast India* (ed.) Ujjwal K. Paul *et al.* Pentagon Press, New Delhi. pp. 71-93.

_____, 2016. 'India's Look East Policy: the Energy Security Perspective', in *Look East to Act East Policy: Implications for India's Northeast* (eds.) Gurudas Das and C. J. Thomas. Routledge: London, pp. 181-190.

Kurian Neemi, 2014. 'India-China Borderlands: conversations beyond the centre'. p. 134.

Maini, Tridivesh Singh. 2013. India's Northeastern states essential to India's Southeast Asia Policy. *East Asia Forum*. 13 August. Accessed from www.eastasiaforum.org/2013/08/13/indias-northeastern-states-essential-to-indias-south-east-asia-policy/

_____, 2015.North-East and India's Act East Policy. *RajyaSabha TV*. 25 October. Accessed from http://rstv.nic/north-east-indias-acteast-policy.html

Mizoram University. 2017. A visiting delegation of Members of Parliament from Myanmar. 22 February. *Mizoram University Newsletter*, June 2017, Aizawl.

News Asia. 2018. SME business review in ASEAN. News Now program. *News Asia TV Channel*. IST 9:30. 18 June 2018.

Sahoo, Pravakar and Bhunia, Abhirup. 2013. India's Engagement with Myanmar: India's Northeastern states essential to India's Southeast Asia Policy. *The East Asia Forum*. 13 August. Accessed from http://www.eastasiaforum.org/2013/08/13/indias-northeastern-states-essential-to-indias-south-east-asia-policy/

The Northeast Today, 2016. Media, Civil Society should Boost India-Myanmar Ties. 25 April.

13

Prospects of India-ASEAN Relations in the Light of Myanmar's Political Reforms

Jonathan Zodintluanga

ABSTRACT

India's relationship with ASEAN has been one of the key pillars of its foreign policy and the core foundation of its Look East/Act East Policy. Myanmar, on the other hand, being an immediate neighbour of India, has an important role to play in the actual implementation of India's Look East/Act East Policy. Owing to the recent political reforms in Myanmar, India-ASEAN relations in one way or the other is expected to reach the next level through greater enhancement of India's Look East/Act East Policy. The prospects of India-ASEAN relations from the perspective of Myanmar's recent reforms seem to be promising, positive as well as challenging.

Keywords: *India, Look East/Act East Policy, ASEAN, Myanmar, Relations*

Introduction

India's focus on a strengthened and multi-faceted relationship with the Association of South-East Asian Nations (ASEAN) is an outcome of the significant changes in the world's political and economic scenario since the early 1990s. India's own march towards economic liberalization and its search for economic space resulted in the Look East Policy, now known as Act East Policy. Hence, India's relationship with ASEAN is a key pillar of its foreign policy and the foundation of its Look East/Act East Policy. Myanmar, on the other hand, is a close and immediate neighbour of India. In fact, Myanmar is the only ASEAN member-country which shares an international boundary with India. Accordingly, Myanmar, in one way or the other, acts as a gateway for India's Look East/Act East Policy and also for its relations with ASEAN.

India and Myanmar share a close history with regard to kinship, culture, language, religion, historical perception and political experiences. Myanmar was a province of British India during British colonial rule. Moreover, they share an international boundary of 1,643 kilometres[1] passing through four north-eastern states in India. The Look East/Act East Policy of India has been more or less based on the consenting co-operation from Myanmar's government. A flagship project for India known as the Kaladan Multi-Modal Transit Transport Project (KMMTTP) was initiated in December 2010. It aims to enhance the Look East/Act East Policy of India. This project aims to link Kolkata and other East Indian ports through coastal shipping to Sittwe on the Arakan coast in Myanmar thereby enhancing connection through the Kaladan River and the route to Mizoram on the Indian side.

Meanwhile, a series of reforms has been under way in Myanmar since 2008, when the military regime adopted the new Constitution for Myanmar. The adoption of the new Constitution was followed by the General Elections in 2010 that clearly marked the beginning of political reforms in Myanmar. The Union Solidarity and Development Party (USDP), backed by the military, claimed a resounding victory. These were followed by the first open General Elections since 1990 in 2015 in which the National League for Democracy (NLD) won with an overwhelming majority. Hence, it marked the beginning of a civilian government in Myanmar since the military coup in 1962. The election marks a new stage in Myanmar's relationship, both within and without its borders.

Hence, a significant reform of recent times has been taking place in Myanmar. These political reforms and transitions in Myanmar will definitely have implications on India-ASEAN relations in one way or the other. As Myanmar is the gateway to India's Look East/Act East Policy, the recent reforms in Myanmar will have certain implications on the relations between India and ASEAN. Thus, this paper will attempt to highlight the implications of Myanmar's political reforms on India-ASEAN relations. It will further discuss the prospects and challenges of India-ASEAN relations in the light of recent reforms in Myanmar.

India-ASEAN Relations in Brief

As India progressed towards a more open and liberal trade-investment regime in the early 1990s, its interest in collaborating with its eastern and south-eastern neighbours deepened. India and the member-nations of the Association of Southeast Asian Nations (ASEAN) share colonial and cultural linkages that have evolved since their independence. During the Nehru era in India, various efforts were made by the country to build closer partnerships with the countries of Southeast Asia. The Conference on Indonesia organized in New Delhi in 1949 and the Bandung Conference in 1955 were only some of the various initiatives undertaken during that period. However, these efforts failed to reinforce the economic, political or strategic partnership between India and ASEAN. This was mainly due to the dominance of China-born communities in many Southeast Asian countries which encouraged these nations to engage more actively with China and, as a corollary, side-lining Indian interests in the region.[2]

India and Southeast Asia share deep historic trade and cultural ties. The Indian influence in Southeast Asia can be traced back to around 200 BC.[3] The region was also under the influence of the South Indian Chola and Pandyan dynasties. Trade between India and Southeast Asia was conducted via a land route through Assam and Manipur, reaching Burma (now Myanmar) and a maritime route across the Bay of Bengal. Goods that were traded included silk, gold and spices. Besides, among the major Indian exports were its religion, language and literature which was heavily syncretised into local cultures. South Indian scripts have heavily influenced the native scripts of the Thai and Khmer languages and the languages of Malay and Bahasa Indonesia. Indian architectural and religious influences can be seen in ancient structures like Angkor Wat and the stupas of Borobudur. Indian epics like the *Ramayana* and the *Mahabharata* have been expressed and interpreted in local culture like the Khmer Lkhaon and Balinese Kecek dances. Fast forward to the modern era, and India is still a strong partner of this region—via its relations with ASEAN.

The launch of India's 'Look East Policy' in 1992, which was later rechristened the 'Act East Policy', was a watershed event; it ushered in an era of reinvigorated partnership between India and Southeast Asia. Indian policymakers had long ago realized the strategic importance of the ASEAN region. The Act East Policy was a push in the right direction, focused on strengthening relations through greater economic and cultural exchanges. India-ASEAN relations have evolved over time, with India graduating from the Southeast Asian grouping's Sectoral Dialogue Partner[4] in 1992 to a Summit-level Partner in 2002. Since then, both sides have been actively engaged in fostering economic, security, political, and cultural cooperation. In 2012, during the first ever Commemorative Summit of India and ASEAN, the leaders of all the countries involved decided to elevate their engagement to one of a strategic partnership. The year 2017 marked 25 years of dialogue partnership between India and ASEAN, and five years of the strategic partnership.

India has a long history of people-to-people connectivity with Southeast Asian countries, particularly with Singapore, Malaysia and Indonesia, which are home to large populations of the Indian Diaspora. Indians comprise nine per cent of Singapore's population and seven per cent of Malaysia's. India and the member-countries of ASEAN jointly organize regular exchange programmes for students, farming communities, diplomats and business and media personnel, among others. However, there are certain restrictions on the movement of professionals and labour between India and Southeast Asia. Under the agreement on trade in services signed in 2015, India and ASEAN have agreed to liberalize trade in a few areas such as telecommunications and financial and insurance services, while regulating the movement of naturalised persons.

Between 1995 and 2016, trade between India and ASEAN grew at a compound average growth rate (CAGR) of about 11.9 per cent. Of the total trade of nearly US$ 64.3 billion in 2016, Indian imports from ASEAN countries accounted for a dominant share of 59 per cent, with exports to ASEAN economies accounting for the remaining share. Indian imports from ASEAN witnessed a robust growth of 12.3 per cent during this period while Indian exports to ASEAN recorded a CAGR of 11.4 per cent.[5] This indicates that the balance of trade has been in favour of ASEAN member-countries throughout the reference period. There are a few Southeast Asian countries such as Singapore, Malaysia and Thailand that have emerged as major export destinations for India. Since there are trade complementarities between India and Southeast Asian countries in areas such as agriculture, machinery and minerals, among others, trade relations have continued to expand, barring a few periods of East Asian crisis such as 1997-98 and the global financial crisis of 2008-09.

Meanwhile, in investments, India received nearly US$ 13.8 billion as foreign direct investment (FDI) from ASEAN economies in 2015-16. The major Southeast Asian economies investing in India are Singapore, Malaysia and Thailand. Over 99 per cent of total FDI inflows into India are from Singapore, with other Southeast Asian countries accounting for less than one per cent. The India-Singapore Comprehensive Economic Cooperation Agreement has provided an impetus to a growing partnership between the two countries. Conversely, Indian outflows to ASEAN economies were recorded at US$ 1.2 billion in 2015, up from US$ 0.6 billion recorded in the previous year. However, outward investments from India have followed a downward trajectory after 2012. Even earlier, in 2011, Indian investment in these countries dropped by US$ 1.9 billion.

In 2015, India accounted for only 1.3 percent of total net inflows into ASEAN.[6] India invested largely in the financial and insurance industries across Southeast Asia (60 per cent), followed by wholesale and retail trade (9 per cent), and real estate activities (8 per cent). Many Indian banks such as Bank of Baroda, Indian Overseas Bank and Andhra Bank have established branches in the ASEAN region. This is essential to integrate banking and financial services between the two regions. There is a range of policy measures including trade facilitation, liberalization of goods, services and capital, competition policy and infrastructure quality that promotes value chain integration. FDI flow is one of the major factors that enable integration of economies by linking them to regional and global value chains. At a business conclave in Jaipur in February 2017, the then Indian Commerce and Industry Minister, Nirmala Sitharaman, highlighted how textile manufacturers in India could benefit by engaging with less-developed countries such as Cambodia, Laos, Myanmar and Vietnam. There is also a potential to create value chains in textiles between India and a few ASEAN economies.

India-Myanmar Relations in a Nutshell

India and Myanmar have traditionally had much in common with cultural, historical, ethnic and religious ties, in addition to sharing a long geographical land border and maritime boundary in the Bay of Bengal. The India-Myanmar relationship officially got underway after the Treaty of Friendship was signed in 1951 after which the foundation for a more meaningful relationship was established during Prime Minister Rajiv Gandhi's visit in 1987. Bilateral ties received another significant boost when the two countries signed a trade agreement in 1994. For many years India did not open up to the authoritarian regime and it was only over a period of time that India started engaging with the military junta of Myanmar.

The importance of Myanmar to India lies in its naturally advantageous geographical positioning of belonging to South Asia, East Asia as well as to South East Asia. Myanmar is also an ASEAN country that shares a land border with India. Its position on the Bay of Bengal makes it a country of significance that the world's powerful nations want to be friendly with. Cordial relations with Myanmar have both security and economic implications for India. India has adopted a pragmatic and practical approach when it comes to its relationship with the Myanmar government and all stakeholders, involved in the safeguarding of peace and continuing progress in Myanmar.

Bilateral trade between India and Myanmar has grown from $12.4 million in 1980-81 to $2.18 billion in 2013-14.[7] Agricultural items like beans and pulses and forest-based products make up nearly 90 per cent of India's imports. Myanmar is also the beneficiary of a duty-free tariff preference scheme for least developed countries (LDCs). Both countries also signed a border trade agreement in 1994 and have two trade points along their 1,643-km border. The two countries have occasionally shared cultural exchanges through various cultural troupes and programmes initiated by both of them.

Political Reforms in Myanmar

Political reforms in Myanmar have been underway since 2008 when the military regime adopted a new Constitution. The adoption of the new Constitution was followed by the General Elections in 2010 that clearly marked the beginning of political reforms in Myanmar. The Union Solidarity and Development Party (USDP) backed by the military claimed a resounding victory in the first election for 20 years in the country. A week after the elections, Aung San Suu Kyi, a democratic symbol and leader of the pro-democratic movement was freed from house arrest. The nominal civilian government was formally established on 30 March 2011 with Thein Sein as the President thereby formally dissolving the military government.

With the establishment of a new government in Myanmar, general amnesty was granted to more than 200 political prisoners. New labour laws were initiated permitting the formation of labour unions and granting the people the right to strike. President Thein Sein also signed a law permitting the expression of the people's basic right such as the right to peacefully demonstrate their grievances. The National Human Rights Commission was established on 5 September 2011. For the by-elections to Parliament in 2012, the National League for Democracy (NLD) was re-registered as a political party after having been earlier declared an illegal party. The April 2012 parliamentary by-elections marked a landmark victory for the NLD which won with an absolute majority, winning 43 out of 45 seats.

The new government agreed to relax press censorship with the announcement of permitting the establishment of privately-owned newspapers from April 2013. In early 2014, the government of Myanmar finally abolished the 25-year-ban on public gathering of more than five people in the country. It also finalized a landmark agreement to open its telecom network, opening up its door to foreign investments. In July 2015, the date for the first open general election in the country since 1990 was announced. The general elections were held on 8 November 2015. In these general elections, the NLD won by an overwhelming victory by securing more than 85 per cent of the seats resulting in the formation of the civilian government under its leadership. The elected members to parliament convened their first meeting on 1 February 2016. Htin Kyaw, the nominated member of the NLD, was elected President of Myanmar on 15 March 2016.

The victory of the NLD followed by the election of Htin Kyaw as President affirmed civilian rule in the country. Myint Swe, the military-appointed member to Parliament was also elected as the First Vice-President. Henry Van Thio, the nominated member of the NLD was elected as the Second Vice-President. NLD leader Aung San Suu Kyi assumed the newly-created role of a state counsellor on 6

April 2016. The role of the state counsellor was similar to that of the Prime Minister. Accordingly, a civilian government was set up in coalition with the military-nominated members under the leadership of the NLD. This was a significant landmark in the history of Myanmar since the military coup in 1962.

However, the recent political reforms in Myanmar may not necessarily lead the country to a full-fledged democracy. There exists a stumbling block in the transition of the system, the main reason being the military-adopted Constitution of 2008. The military government at that time adopted the new Constitution to ensure the creation of a 'discipline-flourishing democracy' in the country. Provisions for the country to become a full-fledged democracy were never incorporated. In fact, the military, through the provisions of the Constitution, 'prevents and restricts' the country from becoming a full-fledged democracy. Under the 2008 Constitution, the official name of the country 'Union of Myanmar' was changed to the 'Republic Union of Myanmar'. The key provisions of the 2008 Constitution which directly or indirectly can hinder the democratic process of Myanmar; which in turn, could pose restrictions for the further development of India-Myanmar/ASEAN relations can be highlighted as follows:

i) It assigned the military 25 per cent of all seats in both houses of the legislature.
ii) It contained a provision that required a majority of more than 75 per cent to approve any constitutional amendment. Thus, a constitutional amendment was not possible without the consent of the military.
iii) The military had been granted responsibility for the preservation of the sovereignty and integrity of the country. It was also responsible for safeguarding the Constitution.
iv) It also continued to give the military control of three key ministries in the government—1. Border affairs, 2. Defence and 3. Home affairs.
v) It further granted the Commander-in-Chief of the Defence Services the right to take over and exercise sovereign power in case of a state emergency when the life and property of the people were endangered. Thus, the Commander-in-Chief could override the role of the President and the executives of the State in case of a threat to the integrity of the Union, national solidarity and loss of sovereign power.
vi) It also enabled the defence services, i.e., military personnel, to participate in the national political leadership role of the State.
vii) It prohibited anyone with a foreign spouse or child from becoming the President of the country.

Prospects and Challenges of India-ASEAN Relations in the light of Myanmar's Reforms

The transition to democracy in Myanmar is a development of great significance for India-Myanmar relations as well as for India-ASEAN relations. Thus, it will also impact the region as a whole. Since March 2011, when a nominal civilian government came to power and political and economic reforms were subsequently initiated by President Thein Sein, Myanmar's isolation is gradually receding. Given its geo-strategic location and natural resources, Myanmar is on the verge of a major take-off. President Thein Sein visited India in October 2011 and the Myanmar Foreign Minister, Wanna Maung Lwin, paid a visit in January 2012. India's External Affairs Minister, S.M. Krishna, visited Myanmar in 2011. Thus, there is a mutual interest in taking bilateral ties forward. As for India, fast-tracking its relations with Myanmar is a key challenge as it will boost its Look East/Act East initiative.

Accordingly, India took the initiative to develop its relations with Myanmar through high-level visits. The last prime minister of India to visit Myanmar was Rajiv Gandhi back in 1987. Then Indian Prime Minister Manmohan Singh finally visited Myanmar on May 27-29 in 2012. His visit projected India as a serious partner for Myanmar. It also helped recognize that Myanmar could become an effective partner for India. The current Prime Minister of India, Narendra Modi, also visited Myanmar from November 11-13 in 2014 to attend the 12th ASEAN-India Summit and 9th East Asia Summit.

India's External Affairs Minister, Sushama Swaraj visited Myanmar in August 2016. Meanwhile, Htin Kyaw, the newly-elected President of Myanmar, visited India in August 2016. Myanmar's State Counsellor and Foreign Minister, Aung San Suu Kyi, also visited India in October 2016 to attend the BIMSTEC Retreat and BRICS summit. Recently, India's Petroleum Minister Dharmendra Pradhan visited Myanmar in February 2017 with the intention of strengthening hydrocarbon relations between India and Myanmar. Recently, Aung San Suu Kyi visited India to attend the 69th Republic Day Parade in India as she was invited as one of the chief guests along with all the other ASEAN leaders.

Increasing connectivity, trade and infrastructure investment and greater security cooperation with South-East Asia are the core aims of India's 'Act East' policy. Central to the policy is increased engagement with Myanmar. The changed political structure in Myanmar, post the 2015 election, is the most important determinant of the future trajectory of India-Myanmar relations. Myanmar's biggest challenge in the coming years will be to control, consolidate and protect its borders and its sovereignty. Moving forward on a comprehensive peace agreement with the ethnic nations and containing insurgencies will be its primary goal. It will also want to focus on rebuilding its economy.

India, in turn, needs a stable neighbour in the east to control, consolidate and cater better to the north-eastern region. It also needs consistent, long-term policies, along with diversity in its engagements with Myanmar to ensure better reach in the subcontinent and the greater Indian Ocean region. India's interest in Myanmar within this context can be narrowed down to two factors: one, containing insurgency in the north-east and better integration of these regions with India. Second, a broader engagement which will include institutional and capacity building, economic investments and greater cross-border connections which in turn will boost India's Look East/Act East Policy.

The current state of India-Myanmar relations appears healthy. India has offered assistance to Myanmar for road development projects to build physical connectivity with Myanmar. These include upgrading of the Tamu-Kalewa-Kalemyoa road (about 160 km) in Myanmar across the border from Manipur; Kaladan Multi-Modal Transit Transport Project, which envisages development of road and inland waterways from Sittwe port in Myanmar to Mizoram; upgrading of Rhi-Tiddim Road (about 60 km) in Myanmar adjoining Mizoram; and some segments of Trilateral Highway Project (about 1,360 km) connecting Moreh (Manipur, India) with Mae Sot (Thailand) through Myanmar. The Kaladan Multimodal Transit Transport project and the Rhi-Tiddim project, once completed, is expected to transform India's North-East and the bordering Myanmar regions.

The India-ASEAN engagement has made impressive strides over the past 25 years, starting with a modest sectoral dialogue partnership in 1992, a full dialogue partnership in 1995, a summit partnership in 2002 and a strategic partnership in 2012. The invitation to all 10 ASEAN heads of state/government as chief guests for India's 68th Republic Day in the 2018 celebrations marked yet another and even more significant upgrade of the relationship. All 10 ASEAN leaders' presence reflected the importance they attached to the relationship. The unprecedented nature of the collective invitation extended to leaders of a regional grouping, in turn, reflects the Indian intent to highlight the priority it attaches to its South East Asian neighbourhood. Despite this record, it must be acknowledged that India-ASEAN relations have not measured up to expectations. There continue to be significant asymmetries in this expanding engagement.

There are a few challenges—in terms of physical, institutional and people-to-people connectivity—that could jeopardize the economic growth of these two regions. These barriers need immediate consideration by policymakers. Creating a value chain in fibres is another area of possible collaboration between India and ASEAN. Myanmar, for instance, is open to FDI in sectors such as garments, textiles and agriculture, which are conducive to creating a value chain between India and Southeast Asia. However, there remain certain challenges to establishing a supply chain, such as non-tariff barriers, poor connectivity and quality of infrastructure, among others.

Better transport connectivity is critical to India-ASEAN relations. After all, the seamless movement of goods and services across borders is highly dependent on effective transportation links. The reality is that transport and infrastructure barriers exist between India and Southeast Asia—including poor quality of roads, missing railway links, inadequate maritime and port facilities and lack of Customs cooperation. All these have implications for any potential integration between India and Southeast Asia. India's northeast is fundamental to efforts towards regional connectivity with ASEAN countries, given its strategic location. Myanmar, for one, shares a land border with India's northeast, thereby providing a bridge between Indian and Southeast Asian markets. Similarly, improving maritime connectivity between India and Myanmar is fundamental to their mutual growth and development. So far, the projects that have been undertaken by India with Myanmar include the Kaladan Multimodal Transit Transport Project and the India-Myanmar-Thailand Trilateral Highway.

The Kaladan Multimodal Transit Transport Project is the first major project undertaken by India in Southeast Asia. When completed, this project will connect Kolkata with Sittwe port in Myanmar, facilitating the movement of cargo across the India-Myanmar border through the sea route. This project will also provide an alternative transit route between India's north-eastern region and Myanmar by establishing new road and inland water connectivity links between them. The multimodal transit project includes various segments, starting with linking Kolkata to Sittwe across the Bay of Bengal, and going on to connect Sittwe with Paletwa town in Myanmar along the Kaladan River. There are also plans to connect Paletwa with the India-Myanmar border by road, which will further be extended to Lawngtlai town in Mizoram. Work on this project is expected to be completed by 2020. It is expected to revolutionize the transit system for goods and tradable services between India and Myanmar, later extending to other Southeast Asian nations such as Laos, Cambodia and Vietnam.

To deepen connectivity between India and ASEAN nations, it is essential to build effective institutional connectivity by harmonizing trade, investments and financial policies. Physical connectivity (transportation and soft infrastructure requirements such as telecommunications) has to be built in tandem with proper institutional arrangements to achieve improved cross-regional connectivity. According to a 2015 report by the Asian Development Bank, there are ample opportunities for energy trading between India and Myanmar. Given the vast natural resources and hydropower reserves of Myanmar, it becomes a potential source of energy for India. However, due to lack of adequate physical and institutional infrastructure between India and Southeast Asia, energy trading remains underutilized. Moreover, the presence of non-tariff barriers and restrictive institutional arrangements hinder the movement of goods and services. Trade facilitation measures to reduce the volume of documentation required—and thereby the time of transit—are necessary to improve economic exchanges between India and Southeast Asian countries. It is known that for the growth of the less-developed ASEAN countries (Laos, Cambodia and Myanmar), skilled labour and professionals are required. This is one area where India can play an important role.

Notwithstanding the massive promise carried by stronger connectivity between India and Southeast Asia, there are various barriers that hobble such integration. For one, the delay in completing infrastructure projects—including road, rail, seaports and highways—due to various political and financial constraints, has impeded the progress of economic cooperation. It can be suggested that India and ASEAN should identify their common challenges and shared interests as it will help them promote cooperation. Trade in services remains largely protected in ASEAN member countries. As India has a comparative advantage in the services sector, especially information technology services, domestic regulations in ASEAN economies need to be liberalized to promote cross-regional cooperation. The challenges of inadequate physical connectivity (road and rail linkages), along with infrastructural bottlenecks (non-tariff barriers) need to be addressed to strengthen India-ASEAN partnership. Further, ASEAN member countries and India have been working towards ratifying the Regional Comprehensive Economic Partnership Agreement, which is expected to improve trade and investment among all member countries. This process needs to be expedited. Greater progress is envisioned in India-ASEAN relations upon liberalization of the services trade, particularly in movement of natural persons and other areas of common interest and potential.

Conclusion

In the post Myanmar reforms, it can be said that India-ASEAN relations have quite a positive prospect owing to the civilian government established in Myanmar. The Look East/Act East Policy of India needs to be fully implemented by India in order to develop its relations with ASEAN as Myanmar is the gateway for India in its relations to ASEAN. India needs to focus on increasing its economic investments, cultural and traditional exchanges in Myanmar. A direct trade route, effective security and calculated investments can help in increasing trade. Encouraging private companies to invest in Myanmar, support for rebuilding institutions and continued involvement with the NLD and the military as it negotiates a new peace agreement are critical ways in which the bilateral relationship can develop. India's national security and growth in the region depend on it taking greater initiative and committing itself to consistent growth and development in the north-east region. Better protection of borders, long-term involvement with key projects (like the Kaladan Project), diversity in investments and a non-condescending approach to its nearby countries, especially ASEAN member countries ought to be the main focus of India's Look East/Act East policy.

ENDNOTES

1 Ministry of DONER, Government of India, Act East Policy vis-à-vis NER, International Border. Stable URL: http://www.mdoner.gov.in/node/202 Accessed on: 4th April, 2017.

2 I. Rao. (July-Dec 2012). 'Emerging India's Policy towards Southeast Asia during the Post-Cold War Era'. *Area Studies*, Vol. 6, No. 2, pp. 90-109.

3 Gnanasagaran, Angaindrankumar. (13 January, 2018). ASEAN and India, a future rooted in the past. *The ASEAN Post.* Retrieved on 3 March, 2018 from https://theaseanpost.com/article/asean-and-india-future-rooted-past-0. Accessed on: 3 March, 2018.

4 Sen et al., (July 17-23, 2004), 'ASEAN-India Economic Relations: Current Status and Future Prospects', *Economic and Political Weekly*, Vol. 39, No. 29, pp. 3297-3308.

5 ASEAN Investment Report 2017, UNCTAD. Stable URL: http://unctad.org/en/pages/PublicationWebflyer.aspx?publicationid=1901. Accessed on 3 March, 2018.

6 Ibid.

7 Ramaswamy, Shridhar and Tridivesh Singh Maini. (12 August, 2014). The Strategic Importance of Myanmar for India. *The Diplomat.* Retrieved on 9 March, 2018 from https://thediplomat.com/2014/08/the-strategic-importance-of-myanmar-for-india/

REFERENCES

Bhatia, R. (2014). *Change in Myanmar.* New Delhi: Shipra Publications.

Bhatia, R. (2015). *India-Myanmar Relations: Changing Contours.* New Delhi: Routledge India.

Bhogal, Preety. (5th January, 2018). India-ASEAN economic relations: Examining future possibilities. *Observer Research Foundation.* Retrieved on 7th March, 2018 from http://www.orfonline.org/research/india-asean-economic-relations-examining-future-possibilities/

Deeparghya, Mukherjee. (10th March, 2016). India-ASEAN economic linkages: Challenges and way forward. *Ideas For India.* Retrieved on 5th March, 2018 from http://www.ideasforindia.in/article.aspx?article_id=1593

Egreteau, R. (2016). *Caretaking Democratization: The Military and Political Change in Myanmar.* Oxford: Oxford University Press.

Gnanasagaran, Angaindrankumar. (13th January, 2018). ASEAN and India, a future rooted in the past. *The ASEAN Post.* Retrieved on 3rd March, 2018 from https://theaseanpost.com/article/asean-and-india-future-rooted-past-0

Gupta, Arvind. (2nd February, 2012). Myanmar's Critical Role in Bolstering India's Look East Policy. *Institute for Defence Studies and Analyses.* Retrieved on 5th March, 2018 from https://idsa.in/idsacomments/MyanmarsCriticalRoleinBolsteringIndiasLookEastPolicy_agupta_020212

Hlaing, K. Y. (2012). Understanding Recent Pollitical Changes in Myanmar. *Contemporary Southeast Asia,* 34(2), 197-216. Retrieved October 10, 2016, from http://www.jstor.org/stable/41756341

Kipgen, N. (2016). *Myanmar: A Political History.* Oxford: Oxford University Press.

Kyi, A.S. (1991). *Freedom From Fear: And Other Writings.* London: Penguin Books Ltd.

Kyi, A.S. (1997). *Letters From Burma.* London: Penguins Books Ltd.

Lall, M. (2016). *Understanding Reform in Myanmar: People and Society in the Wake of Military Rule.* London: Hurst Publishers.

Malik, P. (2016). *My Myanmar Years: A Diplomat's Account of India's Relations with the Region.* New Delhi: Sage Publications India Pvt. Ltd.

Mitra, Devirupa. (16th February, 2018). Expert Gyan: India's Engagement with ASEAN and Asian Geopolitics. *The Wire.* Retrieved on 4th March, 2018 from https://thewire.in/external-affairs/india-asean-relations-asia-geopolitics

Mukhipadhyaya, Gautam. (5th July, 2016). India-Myanmar Relations: Frontiers of a New Relationship. India Foundation. Retrieved on 8th March, 2018 from http://www.indiafoundation.in/india-myanmar-relations-frontiers-of-a-new-relationship/

Pillai, M. (1993). India and Myanmar: Tangle Ties. *Economic and Political Weekly,* 28(6), 213. Retrieved October 10, 2016, from http://www.jstor.org/stable/4399366

Ramaswamy, Shridhar and Tridivesh Singh Maini. (12th August, 2014). The Strategic Importance of Myanmar for India. *The Diplomat.* Retrieved on 9th March, 2018 from https://thediplomat.com/2014/08/the-strategic-importance-of-myanmar-for-india/

Ravichandran, Priya and Guru Aiyar. (14th March, 2016). India's prospects with Myanmar. *Livemint.* Retrieved on 4th March, 2018 from http://www.livemint.com/Opinion/fEorPG593mfp6uwi•ZHOu0L/Indias-prospects-with-Myanmar.html

Sharan, Shyam. (24th January, 2018). India-Asean ties: A cup half full?. *Hindustan Times.* Retrieved on 4th March, 2018 from https://www.hindustantimes.com/analysis/india-asean-ties-a-cup-half-full/story-CetCGMx6nXmIPC8BHGwAJL.html

South, A. (2004). Political Transition in Myanmar: A New Model for Democratization. *Contemporary Southeast Asia,* 26(2), 233-255. Retrieved October 10, 2016, from http://www.jstor.org/stable/257986

Steinberg, D.I. (2013). *Burma/Myanmar: What Everyone Needs to Know.* Oxford: Oxford University Press.

Toh, Elgin. (6th January, 2018). Asean, India celebrate 25 years of relations. *The Straits Times.* Retrieved on 5th March, 2018 from http://www.straitstimes.com/asia/asean-india-celebrate-25-years-of-relation

14

Connecting Lives on India-Myanmar Border: Issues in Migration and Public Health Hazards

Anasua Basu Ray Chaudhury

The porous international boundary of around 4,500 km[1] between Northeast India and its neighbours like China, Bhutan, Bangladesh and Myanmar has resulted in the easy flow of arms, drugs, illegal migrants and easy access by insurgents from bases in these countries. The Golden Triangle comprising Myanmar, Laos and Thailand results in the drug trade spilling over into Northeast India. It creates a high degree of drug addiction, especially among the youth of this region. India shares a 1,643-km-long border with Myanmar along the Indian states of Arunachal Pradesh (520 km), Nagaland (215 km), Manipur (398 km) and Mizoram (510 km). Thus, the bordering areas of both the countries face similar public health problems, especially in terms of the threat posed by infectious border diseases like malaria, human immunodeficiency virus infection and acquired immune deficiency syndrome (HIV AIDS) and tuberculosis (TB). While malaria on both sides could be triggered by similar climatic and ecological conditions, others like HIV and TB are more likely to be caused by the free movement of people across the border and other factors such as unregulated drug trafficking and involvement of refugee/ migrant Chin/Kuki women in the sex industry. Against this backdrop, this article seeks to identify the correlation between migration and the spread of border diseases, if any. It also evaluates the existing status of diseases among the bordering states of Northeast India and Myanmar. Lastly, it attempts to address the collaborative efforts by both the nations for an effective border health infrastructure, management and disease control strategy.

I. Public Health and Migration

As per the WHO, 'public health' is defined as the science of protecting safety and improving the health of communities through education, policymaking and research for disease and injury prevention. Activities to strengthen public health capacities and services aim to provide conditions under which people can be healthy, improve their health and wellbeing or prevent the deterioration of their health. Public health focuses on the entire spectrum of health and wellbeing and not only the eradication of specific diseases. Many activities such as health campaigns are targeted at populations. Public health services also include the provision of personal services to individuals such as vaccination, behavioural counselling or health advice.

For almost a decade, the predominant trend among existing scholars has been to emphasize the link between health hazards and international migration. Increased population mobility and opening up of multiple channels of international trade and communication heighten the risk of the transmission of infectious and non-infectious diseases across borders.[2] A pioneering study conducted by UNESCO and UNAIDS in 2000 sought to demonstrate the impact of the migrant population on the spread of HIV AIDS. The study pointed out that the migrant population is exposed to greater risks of health hazards owing to three factors, namely, economic transition and legal disabilities experienced by them; inability of the host or destination country's health services to respond to the practices of the migrant population and reduced access of the migrants to availability and accessibility of health and other social welfare services. Recent researches have reinforced this argument in a more nuanced manner. It is now being argued that migration in itself may not cause public health hazards but may contribute to the vulnerability of the migrants by exposing them to discrimination, gender inequality, sexual violence and exploitation, poor living conditions and lack of access to education, social services and healthcare facilities. In this context, the Free Movement Regime between India and Myanmar is worth mentioning.

A Free Movement Regime (FMR) is in place in the Indo-Myanmar border region but restricted to the three points of Moreh (Manipur), Zokhawathar (Mizoram) and Pangsau Pass (Arunachal Pradesh). FMR allows the tribes/ethnic groups residing along the border to travel up to 16 kilometres on both sides of the international border. Mizoram and Manipur also face the problem of illegal and clandestine migration from Myanmar. The Myanmarese frequently cross over to the Indian side of the border in search of economic opportunities and work as labourers, coolies, street vendors and domestic workers.[3] These migrants also constitute the 'floating population', i.e., they come and go as they please without often intending to settle down in India. Thus, the FMR coupled with the divided community ties has transformed migration into a continuous process.

II. Existing Situation of Border Diseases: HIV-AIDS

In India's Northeast, HIV-AIDS constitutes one of the most potent non-traditional security threats claiming millions of lives worldwide. Northeast India is an isolated and mountainous area. It is home to a wide range of different ethnic groups, each with its own distinct culture, traditions and language. Many of these ethnic groups are in conflict with the Indian government, demanding more autonomy or independence. Several ethnic movements have turned into armed struggle pressing for their political demands. Conflict and underdevelopment in the region have propelled drug production and consumption. In India, about 2.17 million people are living with HIV. As per India's National AIDS Control Organisation (NACO) 2017 report, the highest prevalence of the disease has been recorded in India's North-eastern states, namely, Nagaland (1.29%), Mizoram (0.81%) and Manipur (0.60%).[4] Injecting Drug Use (IUD) remains the chief driver of HIVAIDS in these states thereby hinting at the deeper social and economic roots of the disease. In Figure 1 below, it can be noted that the role of migrants or rather single male migrants (SMM) and long-distance truckers (LDT) is being acknowledged to get an estimate of the epidemic among the bridge population in recent years. However, the data remains ignorant about female migrant workers.

Figure 1: HSS 2003, 2007 and 2017

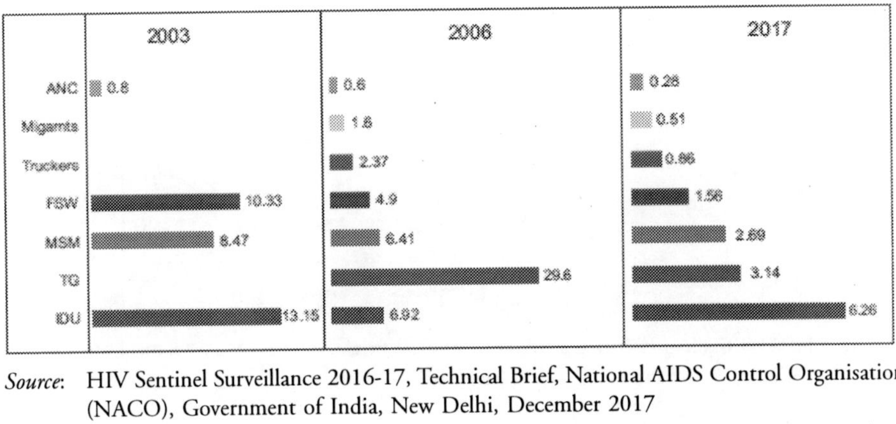

Source: HIV Sentinel Surveillance 2016-17, Technical Brief, National AIDS Control Organisation (NACO), Government of India, New Delhi, December 2017

Manipur is closer to the drug circuits of the Shan Hills and Tiddim Kachin. This provides easy access for smuggling drugs to different parts of the world making Manipur the transit state. Manipur has the highest estimated adult HIV prevalence of 1.15 per cent followed by Mizoram (0.80%) and Nagaland (0.78%).[5] Mandalay, Tiddim Tahang, Homatin, Kheinam and Tamu are the main drug centres in Myanmar. It is from these centres that heroin is smuggled to other parts of the world through Manipur via the towns of Manipur, namely, Behiang (Churchandpur District), New Samtal (Chandel District) and Kamjong (Ukhrul District).[6] HIV related to IUD is high in Thoubal, Ukhrul, Churachandpur, Imphal West and Chandel districts. Some of these districts share the border with Myanmar.

Mizoram, which shares a 404-kilometre unfenced border with Myanmar, serves as a two-way route for cross-border drug trade based in Myanmar. According to newspaper reports in January 2018, around 6.035 kg of heroin, 13,400 methamphetamine tablets and 159,471 tablets of pseudo-ephedrine were seized in 2017 in Mizoram which resulted in the death of 68 persons.[7] Heroin and other drugs are smuggled into Mizoram from Myanmar. While pseudo-ephedrine tablets are being smuggled to Myanmar from India in trucks via Guwahati from where they are taken to Manipur or Mizoram before entering Myanmar. Karimganj and Silchar act as transit points in this regard. In Myanmar, they are manufactured into methamphetamine in clandestine laboratories run mostly by militants to generate funds to procure weapons in the black market. This leaves a dark mark on the security system and the check gates.

Figure 2

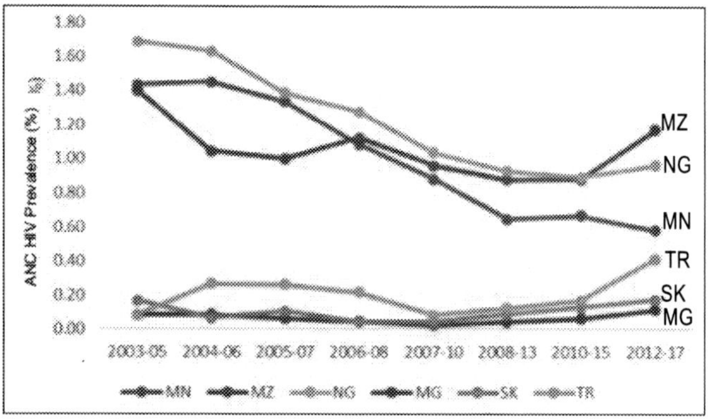

Source: HIV Sentinel Surveillance 2016-17, Technical Brief, National AIDS Control Organisation (NACO), Government of India, New Delhi, December 2017

In Myanmar

Myanmar remains the hub of opium cultivation in Asia, and is the second largest producer and exporter of illicit opium in the world after Afghanistan. Myanmar is an integral part of the Golden Triangle that accounts for the highest percentage of opium cultivation in Asia. The Golden Triangle refers to the region between the borders of Myanmar, Laos and Thailand. Within Myanmar, cultivation of opium is the highest in Kachin, North Shan, South Shan and East Shan. There are reports of new cultivation areas opening up in Sagaing region that borders the Indian states of Manipur and Nagaland.

In 2015, it was estimated that there were 224,794 people living with HIV. The Asian Epidemiological Model (AEM) report estimates that people who inject drugs (28.5%) are the chief reason for this epidemic. In 2016, the Government pledged US$ 15 million for HIV treatment including ARVs and other commodities and US$ 1 million for the procurement of methadone. The Myanmar Health Sector Coordinating Committee (M-HSCC), established as a part of the Nay Pyi Taw Accord in 2013, has the broad mandate as the coordinating body for all public health sector issues.[8]

Figure 3: HIV Estimates and Projections—Myanmar 2010-15

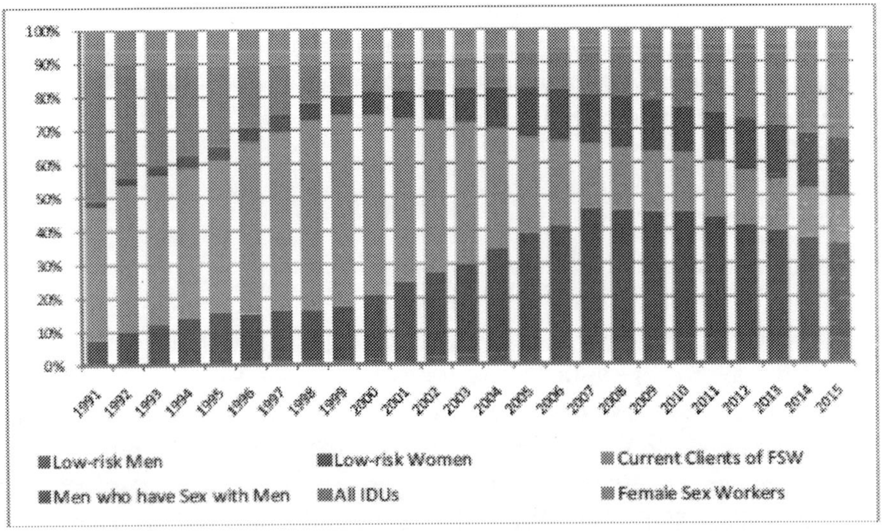

Source: "HIV Estimates and Projections, Asian Epidemiological Model, Myanmar 2010 2015" Strategic Information and M&E Working Group, Technical_and_ Strategy_ Group_on_AIDS, http://www.aidsdatahub.org/sites/default/files/documents/Myanmar_ HIV_ Estimates_2010-2015.pdf

Though a lot of effort is being made to combat this deadly disease, it cannot be ignored that Myanmar has one of the worst health indicators in the world. The public health care system in the country is heavily under-resourced. Discrepancies in the access and coverage of healthcare facilities further account for the poor health indices in the country. Therefore, an effective border health management and disease control strategy is central to the Government of India's vision for greater connectivity and regional integration with its eastern neighbours.

HIV-Hepatitis C (HCV)

Hepatitis C or HCV is an emerging public health threat in Northeast India and Myanmar and has a close association with HIV-AIDS. HCV is a liver disease caused by the Hepatitis C virus. According to the WHO, HIV-affected IUDs are at high risk of contracting HCV if they share needles. There is no vaccine for Hepatitis C. According to a survey conducted by the Indian Council of Medical Research, 98 per cent of HIV-positive people in Manipur's Churachandpur district were co-infected with hepatitis-C. Manipur is among the three north-eastern states where Hepatitis-C is silently killing people. Nagaland and Mizoram are the other two states where the prevalence rate of HIV and hepatitis-C co-infection is very high. The Yaswant Rao Gaitonde Centre for Aids Research Education (YRGCARE), a Chennai-based NGO in collaboration with various NGOs based in Manipur like the Social Awareness Service Organisation (SASO), Care Foundation, Manipur Network of Positive People (MNP+) and Manipur State AIDS Society are currently willingly to treat people with Hepatitis C in Manipur free of cost.[9] Such initiatives will enhance cooperation if it is extended to other states and to people living across the border.

HIV-TB Co-infection

According to the World Health Organisation's latest report on Tuberculosis (TB), India and Myanmar fall under the category of high-burden countries along with Brazil, Cambodia, China, Ethiopia, the Philippines, Uganda and Vietnam. The threat of TB looms large in India's north-eastern states of Nagaland, Mizoram and Manipur. Nagaland has a high percentage of population suffering from TB. As per government estimates, the detection rate of TB in 2014 was 81 per cent as against the national target of 70 per cent and the cure rate was 91 per cent as against the national target of 85 Per cent. While this points to the success of the Department of Health in meeting its target, recent researches present a dismal picture. The link between people who use/inject illicit drugs (PWID) and their chances of contracting TB is increasingly becoming visible, the reasons being poverty, unemployment, malnutrition, social stigma and limited access to health care.

In addressing the challenge posed by HIV-TB co-infection in India, the National AIDS Control Programme (NACP) and the Revised National TB Control Programme (RNTCP) began collaborative HIV/TB control activities in the six high-burden states in 2001. Such joint efforts were further scaled up in 2007 within a National Framework for collaborative HIV-TB activities. By 2012, the intensified HIV-TB package achieved national coverage.[10] A host of other actors such as medical associations, international NGOs and faith-based organizations (FBOs) are engaged in TB control efforts.

Notwithstanding such measures being adopted by both the governments in their respective domains, there has been little effort towards building a systematic framework for cross-border health infrastructure. Except for a few NGOs such as the Centre for Social Development (CSD) that has been working in border areas, there is little or no initiative towards developing cross-border disease surveillance mechanism.[11] On the Myanmar side of the border, health organizations from Arakan, Chin, Kuki and Naga ethnic groups are engaged in providing preventive services and treatment for AIDS in the Sagaing region albeit on a limited basis. However, health workers on either side of the India-Myanmar border hardly co-ordinate with each other. The Assam Rifles that has a formidable presence in the north-east obstructs the activities of Myanmar health workers by intimidating them or arresting them on the slightest suspicion of their involvement in the insurgency.[12] The paramilitary forces whose task is to curb insurgency and drug-trafficking in the border regions wrongly assert their daunting presence in the region by rounding up well-meaning health workers and, in the process, undermine prospects of meaningful cross-border exchanges.

Malaria

Malaria is one of the major infectious diseases threatening millions of lives in Myanmar and India's North-East. In 2014, a research team led by Dr. Kyaw Myo Tun of the Defence Services Medical Research Centre, Napyitaw, Myanmar, and coordinated by the Mahidol-Oxford Tropical Medicine Research Unit (MORU) in Bangkok, Thailand, brought to light the spread of drug resistant malaria parasites in the India-Myanmar border region. The drug resistant parasites were found in Homalin, Sagaing region, which is only 25 kilometres from the Indian border.

Mizoram is the most malaria-prone state of the three North-Eastern states sharing a border with Myanmar. According to media reports, Mizoram and Arunachal Pradesh had the highest deaths per 100,000 population due to malaria between 2013 and September 2017.[13] Lawngtlai district in Mizoram along the Myanmar border is most susceptible to attacks by malaria. Lawngtlai also has a poor rural public health delivery system. In addition, Zokhawthar village in Champhai district is prone to malaria owing to poor sanitation and absence of primary health centres/sub-centres in the region. In the event of a malaria epidemic, Mizoram is likely to suffer the most. According to another newspaper report, mosquito-borne diseases have led to the deaths of 16 persons in a village along the India-Myanmar border in Manipur.

It has been argued in this context that without the Chin migrants being brought within the purview of healthcare facilities, a true assessment of the potency of malaria in the region is difficult to arrive at. The Indo-Burma border region forms a potential site for unmonitored cross-border population movement that can aid the spread of malaria parasites as well. It is this floating population that is most likely to carry malaria vectors from Myanmar into Manipur and Mizoram and vice versa. However, lack of health surveillance of this floating population and absence of coherent health data on migrants residing on either side of the Indo-Myanmar border makes early detection of malaria and other vector-borne diseases nearly impossible and, in the process, complicates disease management efforts.

Another factor that is likely to facilitate the outbreak of vector-borne diseases in the Indo-Myanmarese border region is largely institutional and political. It has as much to do with poor health infrastructure in the border districts and townships as with poor governance and alienation of migrants from mainstream healthcare practices. Researches show that drug-resistant malaria parasites can rapidly multiply in environments lacking proper information on the parasite and without adequate infrastructure to stall its spread. As has been stated earlier, certain border districts in Manipur and Mizoram have already been designated as malaria-prone owing to their location in the Tropical belt, dense forest cover and humid climate. What make the situation worse are low literacy rates and poor healthcare services in the border towns that underscore the socio-economic deprivations faced by the border population, a veritable sign of poor governance. Lack of awareness about diseases because of low literacy rates and under-resourced health care centres expose the local inhabitants as well as the migrant population to the scourge of vector-borne diseases. It has also become known that Myanmarese migrants are often scared of utilizing healthcare facilities offered by the state and local NGOs. A study revealed that the Chin migrants fear availing of the drugs distributed by the Young Mizo Association, a local voluntary association, that is known to harbour a hostile attitude towards them. Without migrants being brought within the purview of healthcare facilities, a true assessment of the potency of vector-borne diseases in the region is difficult to arrive at.

III. India-Myanmar Cooperation in Health Services

In the wake of the political transition in Myanmar and the introduction of multi-party democracy in 2011, former President U Thein Sein prioritised the upgradation of healthcare services. He emphasised the need to seek the co-operation of the local population in implementing health reforms. Since 2013, the Myanmar Government has increased the total expenditure on health from kyat 7,688 million in 2000-01 to kyat 652,745 million in 2014-15.[14]

To implement healthcare reforms, the former Myanmarese President, U Thein Sein, sought financial assistance from India. During his visit to India in October 2011, India signed a Memorandum of Understanding with Myanmar for the up-gradation of Yangon's Children Hospital and Sittwe General Hospital. India offered US$ 7 million for the up-gradation project that was to be managed and overseen by Hospital Service Consultancy Corporation India Ltd (HSCC). India also facilitated the construction of Monywa General Hospital.

The most recent endeavours made in the direction of building up collaboration in the health sector has been the signing of a Memorandum of Understanding between the Ministry of AYUSH, Government of India, and the Ministry of Health and Sports of the Government of Myanmar in the sphere of traditional medicine on 29 August 2016. It is indeed a significant step towards creating a common framework of knowledge and healing practices between the two neighbours.

In 2017, both sides agreed to begin consultations to establish and operate a state-of-the-art hospital in Nay Pyi Taw in association with one of the leading Indian hospital groups based on modalities to be mutually decided.[15] There are some steps that can be further taken for cross-border health collaboration as well as cooperation. The role of state and other institutional actors in laying the groundwork for cross-border disease control strategies needs to be put in place and enhanced in the following ways:

- India is a cost-effective destination for well developed medical facilities. State-of-the-art medical facilities should be established in the North-Eastern states to tap the potential of healthcare tourism.
- Need for adequate political will from the Central government in allocating funds and enabling state governments in implementing health welfare and disease control programmes.
- Need for synergy between local government agencies and civil society groups/ NGOs/ FBOs/UN agencies working in these disease-affected areas in India to prevent and control the spread of infectious diseases on a sustained and long-term basis.
- Civil society groups on the Indian side of the border can forge linkages with NGOs and FBOs in the bordering townships of Myanmar to work out a common framework of disease prevention and control strategy.
- Disease-control programmes may be introduced at district levels, i.e., in

certain specific districts that are prone to communicable diseases.

- There is a need to ensure availability of healthcare to people living in hard-to-reach areas.
- A well-equipped primary healthcare centre (PHC) in the border towns and villages can not only cater to the needs of the rural population in remote areas but also address the health problems of poor Myanmarese who often cross over to the Indian side for treatment.
- There should be a concerted effort towards improving the database for infectious diseases in the border areas before any firm action is taken.
- The infrastructure of border hospitals on both sides should be strengthened to include updated equipment, manpower and diagnostic facilities.

ENDNOTES

1 Brigadier V P Malhotra (Retd.), "*Terrorism and Counter Terrorism in South Asia and India*", Vij Books India Pvt. Ltd., New Delhi, 2011, P. 90

2 Brian D. Gushulak and Douglas W. Macpherson, "Population Mobility and Infectious Diseases: The Diminishing Impact of Classical Infectious Diseases and New Approaches for the 21st Century", *Clinical Infectious Diseases*, Vol.31, No..3, September 2003, pp.776-780

3 Julien Levesque & Mirza Zulfiqar Rahman, "Tension in the Rolling Hills: Burmese Population and Border Trade in Mizoram", *IPCS Research Papers*, April 2008

4 Annual Report 2016-17, National AIDS Control Organisation (NACO), Government of India, New Delhi, Chapter 24 pp. 339-340, http://naco.gov.in/sites/default/files/NACO%20 ANNUAL% 20REPORT%202016-17.pdf.

5 Annual Report 2016-17, National AIDS Control Organisation (NACO), Government of India, New Delhi, Chapter 24 pp. 339-340, http://naco.gov.in/sites/default/files/NACO%20 ANNUAL%20REPORT%202016-17.pdf

6 Moirangmayum Sanjeev Singh and Rajkumar Meiraba Singh, "Cross Border Crime and its Impact in Manipur, India", *International Journal of Interdisciplinary and Multidisciplinary Studies (IJIMS)*, 2014, Vol. 1, No.5, pp. 161-165, http://www.ijims.com/uploads/6123c4cd506070e2d8 bazppd_575.pdf

7 "Drug abuse killed 65 in Mizoram in 2017", *Business Standard*, 15 January 2018, http://www.business-standard.com/article/news-ians/drug-abuse-killed-65-in-mizoram-in-2017-118011500365_1.html

8 National Strategic Plan on HIV and AIDS, Myanmar 2016-2020, *The Republic of the Union of Myanmar*, https://www.aidsdatahub.org/sites/default/files/highlight-reference/document/Myanmar_National_Strategic_Plan_on_HIV_and_AIDS_2016-2020.pdf

9 "Free Hepatitis C treatment facility in Mnp", *Nagaland Post*, 13 May 2017, http://www.nagaland post.com/ChannelNews/Regional/RegionalNews.aspx?news=TkVXUzEwMDExNDQxMA%3D%3D

10 "TB India 2015: Annual Status Report", http://www.tbcindia.nic.in/showfile.php?lid=3166

11 HIV/AIDS work across borders, https://www.oxfam.org/sites/www.oxfam.org/files/manipur.pdf

12 *The Gathering Storm: Infectious Diseases and Human Rights in Burma, July 2007,* Human Rights Center University of California, Berkeley and Center for Public Health and Human Rights Johns Hopkins Bloomberg School of Public Health, http://www.jhsph.edu/research/centers-

and-institutes/center-for-public-health-and-human-rights/_pdf/GatheringStorm.pdf

13 "4 Northeastern States Have Highest Death Rates Due To Malaria", *Fact Checker*, 8 November 2017, http://factchecker.in/4-northeastern-states-have-highest-death-rates-due-to-malaria/

14 Myanmar Health Care System, "Health In Myanmar", Ministry of Health and Sports, The Republic of the Union of Myanmar, 2014

15 "India-Myanmar Joint Statement issued on the occasion of the State Visit of Prime Minister of India to Myanmar (September 5-7, 2017)", Ministry of External Affairs, Government of India, New Delhi, 6 September 2017, http://www.mea.gov.in/bilateral-documents.htm?dtl/28924/IndiaMyanmar+Joint+Statement+issued+on+the+occasion+of+the+State+Visit+of+Prime+Minister+of+India+ to+Myanmar+September+57+2017

III. NORTHEAST INDIA AND ASEAN

15

Look and Act East: View from the Northeast Region and Mizoram

Jagadish K. Patnaik

Against the backdrop of the cataclysmic changes that were taking place in India during 1991, the focus of the foreign policy establishment perforce seemed to shift from West to East. The loss of the Soviet Union as an ally and the difficult economic scenario in Europe and the Americas at that time necessitated to shift our focus towards the East. The economic miracle of the 'Asian Tigers' and the dire state of the Indian economy did impel India to take a serious look into foreign policy priorities. The success of the Association of South East Asian Nations (ASEAN) as a regional economic group in the world market at that point of time was attracting the attention of the national policy makers. Added to that, India's opening of the economy and changing the macro-economic policy for bringing reforms in the country also provided the necessary conditions to strengthen our relations with the countries in the East, including Japan. The more urgent attention, however, was directed towards directly engaging with ASEAN countries bilaterally as well as multilaterally.

It is indubitable that India's foreign policy architecture stands on the edifice of continuity and change. Although there have been paradigmatic shifts from time to time, the fundamental parameters of India's foreign policy do continue and remain unchanged. The introduction of the Look East Policy (LEP) in India's foreign policy in 1991, however, under the PVN Rao government added a new dimension as a sub-text to India's foreign policy discourse. Still more important is that the present dispensation under Narendra Modi has further strengthened the discourse and the policy architecture as well by bringing in the new phase "Act East Policy" (AEP). As it has been opined, "While this does not really signal a departure from the LEP, it does highlight a more nuanced position of acknowledging the need to 'act' or to `get one's act together', to move ahead on the implementation of projects and proposals that have been initiated in principle but are lagging in practice.[1]

This essay has attempted to examine the trajectory of the LEP and the AEP in general as well as in the context of its implications for the northeast region (NER), and specifically the State of Mizoram.

I. Look East Policy: Evolution and Context

Foreign policy in the aftermath of the independence of India was more or less focused on Asia centring on the idea of Asian regionalism and resurgence. In fact, in the mid-40s and 50s of the last century there were some serious efforts to concentrate on Asia. It did not, however, work well to the satisfaction of India. Although India's debut in the international arena had its origin in South-East Asia with Jawaharlal Nehru taking up the initiative for Pan-Asian solidarity, it petered out following the betrayal by China in 1962.[2] There was also a proposal to form an Asian Council in 1967. These postures did not seem to match with the actual work on the ground, mainly from the economic perspective. India's continued membership in the Commonwealth was based on the premise that economic development could be ushered in with collaboration with the Western world rather than with Asia.[3] Further, the economies of Asia were also in the process of developing in the aftermath of decolonization. Added to this, the cold war politics was also largely responsible in maintaining its focus on the West more than the East. This trend continued until the dismemberment of the Soviet Union and the ending of the cold war in 1991. As I.K. Gujral said in one of his speeches in 1996, "The forces of history and circumstances intermittently disturbed this closeness. Colonialism and the Cold War, despite our efforts to come together, drew artificial boundaries between us."[4] Further, the focus during that time was more political rather than economic. Issues like decolonization, neutrality and security were the key motivators for the leaders of Asia and Africa to rally round a common platform.

Against the backdrop of the momentous changes that took place in the international system following the ending of cold war, there was a decisive shift in India's foreign policy paradigm.[5] The shift is vividly palpable in the adoption of the Look East Policy (LEP) by India since 1991.[6] It marked the beginning of the ending of India's South Asia centric image;[7] and provided a new dimension to India's foreign policy paradigm.[8] The paradigm shift in Indian foreign policy is further vindicated by focusing its attention on foreign trade more than it was earlier in the cold war era.[9] As Albert O. Hirschman in his classic *National Power and the Structure of Foreign Trade* demonstrated, foreign trade serves as an instrument of national power.[10] In a still more persuasive way, Richard Cooper in his article "Trade Policy is Foreign

Policy," refers to the intrusion of trade in high foreign policy area. According to him, "Foreign trade and investment policies are traditionally regarded in the category of low foreign policy; the same is true of monetary and financial relations among countries—*although this trend is more pronounced among students of international relations than it is among high government officials.*"[11] The change in the focus from an exclusively security domain to an economic domain in India's foreign policy may not be deliberately part of the quest for increased activism in international relations. It may not be the result of its quest for increased power in the international system. It is definitely a response to the crisis in the international system which witnessed a shift from a bi-polar to a multi-polar international system.

The loss of market in East Europe and the erstwhile Soviet Union as well owing to the declining tension in the European theatre, presented the policy makers with a crisis situation. As is wont, following the crisis in the old paradigm, a new paradigm comes into being.[12] That is how there is a new thrust in India's foreign policy paradigm. In fact, it has been suggested that India did miss the opportunity during the cold war by putting its stakes on the wrong side of the balance in the international system. The ending of the cold war provided the necessary objective conditions for Indian policy makers to set the system right and diversify its focus on the East. There was a change in the macroeconomic policy as well. Rather, the change in the foreign policy and macroeconomic policy has been concomitant.

In fact, the logical fallout of the ending of cold war has been the short shrift to the existing foreign policy paradigm in the South Block that worked for roughly five decades. In keeping with the neo-liberal agenda of the Western world, the low politics of trade and commerce took precedence over the high politics of security. The focus of peace has been shifted from security to development. The development dimension of the state is now linked to liberalization, privatization and the globalization process.[13] The earlier macro-economic policy of mixed economy waned and wafted under the dead weight of sluggish growth.[14] The body polity was witnessing a sort of crisis of governance.[15] In view of these developments, both from within and without, there was the need for a total overhaul of the economic policy architecture. It meant not only India's engagement with the South-East Asian nations or the ASEAN, but also with other Eastern nations such as China, Japan and South Korea.[16] India is also interested to be a part of the Asia-Europe Meeting (ASEM) initiated in 1996. It evinces a keen interest to become a member of the Asia Pacific Economic Cooperation (APEC). As Gujral suggested, "What look-East really means is that an outward looking India is gathering all forces of dynamism—domestic and regional—and is directly focusing on establishing synergies with a fast consolidating and progressive neighbourhood to its East in the

Mother Continent of Asia."[17] The purpose is also to go beyond bilateral relations and participate in institutional arrangements for the economic development and peace and security in Asia.

India's LEP was framed to diversify its trade interest with the South-East Asian countries in general and ASEAN in particular. The emergence of the 'Asian Tigers',[18] and the growth of the Association of South East Nations (ASEAN) as leading economies of Asia provided a further fillip for Indian policy makers to look at the East as a possible avenue for conducting economic transactions.[19] The change in the focus is compounded by the emergence of this region as one of Asia's economic power centres. The North East Region (NER) of India, being closer to the South-East Asian nations rather than the mainland in terms of culture and geographical contiguity, is supposed to gain in large measure.[20] It could serve as a corridor for the ASEAN nations. So far, however, there has been no substantial or tangible gain for the region. The pace of economic transaction has been very low. Despite the border agreement with Myanmar as early as in 1994 and numerous trading arrangements with the ASEAN and other Eastern nations from time to time, there has hardly been any visible impact on the economies of the NER. There might be a number of factors responsible for this. The obvious cause for the negligible impact of LEP on the NER is the lack of any viable economic policy architecture with a suitable policy orientation for the pursuit of trade activity.

II. The Look East Policy vis-à-vis ASEAN and other Eastern Countries

There is no doubt that India-ASEAN relations could be "a reconfiguration of age-old ties that date back 2000 years."[21] Save the hiatus of a few decades, India has been very much present there. The Look East policy that took shape under the stewardship of PVN Rao reinforced India's pursuit in the region. Mr. Rao may not have had the flamboyance, but his down-to-earth and pragmatic outlook did contribute immensely in forging "instant personal chemistry" with the ASEAN leaders.[22] In fact, prior to Mr. Rao's prime ministership, India's relations with the South-East Asian (EAS) nations were subdued. India had some serious ties with states of the former communist bloc—Vietnam, Laos and Cambodia—that were in deep economic and social crisis during the cold war years. This was part of the foreign policy dynamics of the cold war politics. For this reason, India's relations with ASEAN was in a limbo for a while, as it was not possible to accept India's proximity with the Soviet Union and its recognition of the Vietnam-backed government in Cambodia in 1980.

Following the adoption of the LEP, there has been a series of developments that did, ipso facto, testify to the extent of shift in the foreign policy paradigm in

India. The first decade of the adoption of the LEP was confronted with a slow pace of economic reforms and lack of better integration of its foreign and trade policies. As a result, there were doubts about the viability of the "Look East" policy. No doubt, there has been a lot of fanfare associated with the prime minister's annual trips to the region. The first phase of the policy had suffered a slow pace due domestic political compulsions.[23] Frequent change of governments coupled with lack of appropriate direction seemed to be some of the bottlenecks. The second phase, which began after the NDA government took over, provided some boost to the policy. At the ASEAN summit in Bali in October 2003, Prime Minister Vajpayee spelled out new initiatives for economic cooperation, including air and road links. He also outlined a program of free trade agreements with countries of the region. The Indian prime minister signed a deal with Thailand to slash tariffs on a range of goods and offered closer intelligence and military cooperation.

In the second phase of its "Look East" strategy, Mr. Sinha, the then Foreign Minister, pointed to a remarkable transformation in India's attitude towards Asia:

> "*In the past, India's engagement with much of Asia, including Southeast and East Asia, was built on an idealistic conception of Asian brotherhood, based on shared experiences of colonialism and of cultural ties. The rhythm of the region today is determined, however, as much by trade, investment and production as by history and culture. That is what motivates our decade-old 'Look East' policy. Already, this region accounts for 45 percent of our external trade.*"[24]

It is significant that the volume of trade between India and ASEAN countries quadrupled in a span of roughly ten years. India's trade with the world was $ 252.22 billion and ASEAN accounted for $ 21.29 billion which was roughly 8.44 per cent of India's global trade. (See Table 1)

Table 1: India's Import-Export to ASEAN (2015-16)
Values in US$ Million

Sl. No	*Region*	*2015-16*	*% share*	*2016-2017 (April-June)*	*% Share*	*% Growth*
			Import: Region-wise			
1	ASEAN	39,909.60	10.4748	9,547.85	11.3652	
	India's Total Imports	**381,006.63**		**84,009.89**		
			Export: Region-wise			
1	ASEAN	25,154.50	9.5903	6,416.91	9.7910	
	India's Total Exports	262,290.13		**65,538.87**		

Source: Dept. of Commerce: Export Import Data Bank, 20 September 2016

Alongside the increasing engagement with ASEAN in trade and commerce, India has also ventured to go beyond it. There has been a marked improvement in

India-China relations. The volume of trade with China has also picked up to a great extent, although there is much to be done to iron out some of the basic issues relating to the border dispute. There has been a series of dialogues and meetings at different levels going on to settle the long-standing border problem with China. There is no doubt that economic relations between the two countries have far outpaced the progress in political relations. There is a growing realization among the political elites of both the giants of Asia that their increasing bilateral relations with each other will vindicate the furtherance of the "Asian Century." India's achievements in the information technology sector and China's success in manufacturing serve as a catalyst for improving India-China relations. The LEP has really influenced the easing and further strengthening of relations between the two neighbours.

India's relations with Japan and South Korea have also increased to a great extent. There has been a substantial increase in the volume of trade with South Korea in the last ten years. India's exports to South Korea have increased over 300 per cent while imports from South Korea have increased more than five times. Although Indo-Japanese relations have been refurbished as a consequence of the LEP, there is not much improvement in the volume of trade. There is, however, an increase in the interest of Japanese investors to invest in India in recent years. This is owing to India's second phase of the liberalization process as well as change in the thrust in the foreign policy posture.

The latest figures relating to ASEAN trade vis-à-vis India reveal that exports have increased to $ 39,028.41 million and imports to $ 19,455.71 million with a total trade share of 2.6 per cent of the overall trade with ASEAN partner countries. A report from Standard Chartered forecast that Indian exports into ASEAN would rise dramatically over the next 10 years to $ 280 billion a year, up from $ 33.13 billion in the 2013/14 financial year. Two-way trade is currently locked at around $ 80 billion a year.[25]

III. The Look/Act East Policy and North-East India

The states of North-East India are more geographically contiguous to South-East Asia than other parts of the country.[26] The culture, tradition and mores of the people of the NER are more akin to South-East Asia than to the mainland. The cold war politics had a terrible adverse impact on the region. "The partition transformed the region at the crossroad of emerging Asia, into a landlocked outpost of a large continental economy."[27] The economy and society of the region had to suffer due to the lop-sided strategies adopted by New Delhi.[28] Foreign policy was more attuned to security than development. This is due to the internal problems that this region has been afflicted with due to insurgency and separatism. The states of the region, being border states with our neighbours, were victims of cold war rivalry. The Indian government had difficulty in managing the law and order situation as most of the state governments in the region failed to generate support and legitimacy among the people. Consequently, development became the principal casualty. There was a total neglect of the economic advancement of the region.

The LEP, however, opened a window of opportunity for the economic development of the NER. As part of the LEP, there has been a series of measures to make it more workable. Part of these initiatives has been the signing of South Asian Sub-region for Economic Cooperation (SASEC), Bangladesh-India-Myanmar-Sri Lanka-Thailand-Economic Cooperation (BIMSTEC), etc. India has been trying to link up with the Greater Mekong sub-region of which China is a partner along with Myanmar, Thailand, Laos, Cambodia and Vietnam, and has renewed its trade ties with Myanmar. India has also signed a Free Trade Agreement with Thailand. It is said that the NER serves as the 'gateway' to South East Asia. The immediate impact of the LEP on the NER is the signing of the Indo-Myanmar Border Trade Agreement in 1994. This agreement, however, has not made any substantial impact on the economies of the region.[29] Recently, more trading routes, especially at Longwa, Rih and Pangsau Pass, have been opened. The direct land route between India and ASEAN is the 160-km long road linking Moreh in Manipur with Kalewa in Myanmar that was built in February 2001. The international highway that passes through NER-Myanmar-Thailand has not been useful due to safety and other reasons.[30] That is why most of the trade with ASEAN countries is now still transacted through sea routes. This does not in any way help the region. As Sanjib Baruah writes, "The look east policy is making impressive headway. However, there is a danger that it may get delinked from the vision of north-east India as a gateway..., mainland India's ties with south–east Asia were primarily maritime and not continental. Even today, it is cheaper and easier to trade with south-east Asia by sea rather than by land.[31] The government has already set up some Customs posts in the states of Manipur and Mizoram though there has not been any visible improvement in the border trade between India and Myanmar to the extent that it can have some impact on the NER. There is little goods movement across the border though; it hardly affects the economy of the region to any significant extent.

The implications for Mizoram: As a consequence of LEP, a number of initiatives have been taken including infrastructure development projects that will help connect the NER with ASEAN countries. Specifically, in the context of Mizoram, it is relevant here to have a brief discussion on the various proposals that relate to this State.

Rih-Tiddim and Rih-Falam roads: Mizoram has border trade relations with Myanmar with the opening of the Zokhawthar check post connecting with Rih across the border. The Government of India has signed a border trade agreement with Myanmar as part of extension of the LEP; border trade is just at the stage of more of a transit nature rather than having any significant impact on the economic development of the state.[32] In order to strengthen trade activity across the border and make it more functional, two road projects (i) Rih-Tiddim (80.17 km) and Rih-Falam (151.5 km) have been identified and detailed project reports have been prepared and a construction agency has been identified.

Further, the Government of India entered into a Framework Agreement with the Government of Myanmar in April 2008 to facilitate implementation of the project on the Kaladan Multimodal Transit Transport system to the North Eastern states through Myanmar. The DPR was prepared by the Indian consultant, M/s RITES, during 2003.[33] However, the project has missed its deadline of October 2015. It was expected to be completed within its revised project cost of Rs. 2,904 crore. It includes a waterway component of 158 kilometres on Kaladan river from Sittwe to Paletwa in Myanmar and a road component of 109 kilometres from Paletwa to Zorinpui along the India-Myanmar border in Mizoram. On the Indian side, the 99.83-kilometre road from NH-54 at Lawangtalai to Zorinpui in Mizoram has achieved a physical progress of 66 per cent it is likely to be completed by June 2018.

As regards construction of the 109-km Kaladan road in Myanmar, a tender for selection of a contractor was issued in February and the submission of bids is in May, Minister of State for External Affairs, Gen. V. K. Singh (retd) said in reply to a question in the Rajya Sabha.[34]

Along with the economic infrastructure projects that are in place now, there is a need to look into the softer dimensions such as tourism potential, academic intercourse and cultural exchange. These soft resources have enormous potential that can be feasible as an important element of economic and political power. The NER and, for that matter, Mizoram has a vast potential in contributing to this aspect to a large extent. The Act East policy needs to look into these dimensions with greater care alongwith the trade and economic interaction.

Conclusion

The Act East and Look East policies are premised on integrating the NER with mainstream India by linking it with the economies of South-East Asia. The political integration model with India and the economic integration model with the rest of Asia is one direction that certainly holds much promise to a large extent. For this to happen, the mindset in India has to change as well, not just the mindset in the Northeast. The policy makers in the South Block need to hold consultations often with elites, intellectuals and civil society of the region for implementing the Act East policy in its various dimensions. Specifically, in making the soft resources feasible for economic outputs, the people of the region need to be involved in the policy making domain.

ENDNOTES

1 Shankari Sundararaman, Modi in Myanmar: From 'Look East' to 'Act East', *The Indo-Pacific*, Article No.#4742, 17 November 2014

2 As early as March 1947, the Asian Relations Conference was held in Delhi in which 28 delegations including eight sovereign states participated. In January 1949, another conference assembled in New Delhi. In 1955 there was the Bandung conference representing leaders from Asia and Africa.

3 See J. N. Dixit, *India's Foreign Policy and its Neighbours*, Gyan Publishing House, New Delhi, 1998

4 I.K. Gujral, Statement by His Excellency Mr. I. K. Gujral, http://www.aseansec.org/4338. htm, dt. 6/11/2006

5 A paradigm is described as essentially a collection of beliefs shared by scientists, a set of agreements about how problems are to be understood. See Thomas S. Kuhn, *The Structure of Scientific Revolution* (Chicago: Chicago University Press, 1962)

6 The policy was given an initial thrust by the then Prime Minister Narasimha Rao who visited China, Japan, South Korea, Vietnam and Singapore in 1992. India also became a dialogue partner with ASEAN in 1992. In the beginning of this century, India has given a big push to this policy by becoming a summit level partner of ASEAN (2002) and getting involved in some regional initiatives such as the BIMSTEC and the Ganga Mekong Cooperation and now becoming a member of the East Asia Summit (EAS) in December 2005. See Nityanand Deva, India's Look-East Policy, http://www.indianMBA.com, 11/2/2206

7 As Mr. Raja Mohan writes, "the Look East policy in phase two has opened the door for the first time since Independence to break out of the political confines of the subcontinent that have severely limited India's grand strategic options." See his, "Look East policy: phase two", *The Hindu*, October 9, 2003

8 "The Look East policy has allowed India to break the artificial political barriers between the subcontinent and Southeast Asia". See *Ibid*

9 During the cold war, India's multi-lateral relations in South East Asia brought some benefits through serious trade links.

10 Albert O. Hirschman, *National Power and the Structure of Foreign Trade* (Berkeley: University of California Press, 1945)

11 (Italics mine) Richard N. Cooper, "Trade Policy in Foreign Policy." *Foreign Policy* (New York), no 9, winter 1972-73), p. 18, quoted in my book, *India and the GATT*, Asish Publishing House, New Delhi, 1997

12 Thomas Kuhn writes, "All crises begin with the blurring of a paradigm and the consequent loosening of the rules for normal research... Or finally, the cases that will most concern us here, a crisis may end with the emergence of a new candidate for paradigm and with the ensuing battle over its acceptance." See his, *The Structure of Scientific Revolution*, op. cit.

13 For a perspective on the impact of globalization in India, see P.C. Mathur, "Globalization and the Emergent Geo-Economic Polarization in federal India (A Prefatory Analysis)" in S. N. Mishra et al, *Public Governance and Decentralisation* (New Delhi: Metal Publications, 2003); also see B.S. Human, "Impact of Globalization, Liberalization and Privatisation Policies on Governance: the Indian Experience, *Ibid*

14 Arjun Appadorai coined the term 'disjunction' to refer to the collapse of the nation states in the context of the globalization syndrome. See his "Disjuncture and differences in the global cultural economy" in M. Featherstone (ed.) *Global Culture, Nationalism, Globalisation and Modernity* (London: Sage, 1990), pp. 293-311

15 See my article, "Good Governance and Third World Development: Implications for Coalition Politics in India," in *Social Change and Development*, July 2006, pp. 1-17

16 As Sanjib Baruah writes, "Economics has been a prime mover of India's Look East policy. India had ignored the Asian economic miracle in its early phases since the lessons of the export-oriented economies of a few small countries indulged by the West seemed inapplicable to an economy of India's size and ambition. That view, however, was badly shaken by the emergence of China—its spectacular growth since the 1980s that is based on trade and a liberalized economy." See his, *Between South and South Asia: North East India and The Look East Policy*, CENISEAS PAPER 4, (OKDISCD, Guwahati, 2004), pp. 20-21

17 I.K. Gujral Statement By His Excellency Mr. I. K. Gujral, Minister of External Affairs of India, http://www.aseansec.org

18 See Kelly Brian and Mark London, *The Four Little Dragons: Inside Korea, Taiwan, Hong Kong and Singapore at the Dawn of the Pacific century* (Simon and Shuster, 1989)

19 India was invited for the first time to attend the ASEAN plus three (APT) summit meeting in November 2002. New Delhi is ready to consider a free trade agreement with ASEAN. Singapore's Prime Minister Goh Chok Tong reportedly told the APT summit meeting of November 2002 that ASEAN resembles the body of an airplane with one wing made of East Asia and the other of China and India enabling the grouping to establish the ASEAN Economic Community by 2020. Indian and ASEAN finalized a framework agreement in Jakarta, with a FTA expected to enter into force by 2011. The products to be included had yet to be decided on, although agriculture and textiles were to be excluded. Further, India also acceded to the Treaty of Amity and Cooperation (TAC) in Southeast Asia in the 2nd India-ASEAN Summit of October 2003. China signed the TAC at the same time. Also, India agreed to conclude a bilateral FTA with Singapore as a long-term goal in November 2002 and signed a framework agreement for a Thai-India FTA in October 2003. See Syeda Naushin Parnini, "New dynamics of regionalization in East Asia: evolving ASEAN plus three and challenges for Bangladesh," SARID Journal, Vol. 1, Issue 2, 2005

20 The North-East India, consisting of seven states—Arunachal Pradesh, Assam, Manipur, Meghalaya, Mizoram, Nagaland, and Tripura—form an interdependent economic system for historical and geo-political reasons. The region is landlocked, surrounded by foreign countries—Bangladesh, Bhutan, China, Myanmar, and Tibet—with 99.5 per cent of international border and only 0.5 per cent of border with the country. Kedilezo Kikhi, What Ails the North-East? Challenges and Responses, *Sociological Bulletin* 58 (3), September-December 2009, p. 346

21 http://www.ibef.org, dt. 11/8/2006

22 See V. Jayanth, http// www.thehindu.com/2004/12/24/stories/200407541200.htm, dt. 11/6/2006. Incidentally, in the 1995 ASEAN Summit, it was decided to elevate India to the status of full dialogue partner, and the following year India began participating in the ASEAN Post-Ministerial Conference and the ASEAN Regional Forum (ARF)

23 Phase one of the policy was characterized by trade and investment linkages. Phase two is marked by "arrangements for FTAs and establishing institutional economic linkages between the countries of the region and India." The then External Affairs Minister, Mr. Sinha, has also underlined a number of other features that define Phase two of India's Look East policy. See C. Raja Mohan, "Look East policy: phase two", *The Hindu,* October 9, 2003

24 Quoted in Sultan Shahin, India's 'Look East' Policy Pays off, *Asia Times*, October 11, 2003

25 File:///C:/Users/JK Patnaik/Downloads/LOOKEAST/Indian Trade Seen Booming With ASEAN_The Diplomat.htm, dt.1/10/2016

26 This region is ethnically, linguistically, and culturally distinct from the so called "Aryan-Dravidian mainstream' India. This region is home to more than 250 tribes speaking more than 190 languages and dialects and addressing the long-drawn conflicts to preserve ethnic identities and land ownership and other resources is definitely a difficult task. A large number of people from the North-east speak languages belonging to the Sino-Tibetan/Tibet-Myanmarese family of languages.

27 Sushil Khanna, "Economic opportunities or continuing stagnation", http://www.india-seminar.com/2005/550/550%20sushil%20khanna.htm, dt. 13/11/2006

28 According to Jairam Ramesh, with regard to the strategies and policies of the Government of India vis-à-vis the North East "there are four dominant paradigms that stand out"–cultural, security, political and development. For a brilliant analysis of the issue, see his, "North-East India In A New Asia", *Manipur Online*, January 12, 2006

29 Gurudas Das, "Trade Between the North Eastern Region and Neighboring Countries: Structure and Implications for Development," In Gurudas Das and R.K. Purkayastha (eds.) *Border Trade: North East & Neighbouring Countries* (New Delhi, Akansha Publishing House, 2000)

30 Myanmar has an international border contiguous with parts of NER stretching over 1,600 km. It is the land bridge that connects India with SEA nations

31 Sanjib Baruah, "Of Broken Promises and False Starts," The *Telegraph*, April 12, 2005

32 See Paul Songhaulal Songate, Indo-Myanmar Border Trade: A Study of the Socio-Cultural and Political Implications, Ph.D. Thesis (unpublished), Mizoram University, 2010

33 http://mdoner.gov.in/content/introduction-1, dt. 1/10/2016. The construction activities at Sittwe in Myanmar began in December 2010. As of date, the physical progress achieved is 79 per cent (approx.) and financial progress is 65 per cent (approx.), i.e., Rs. 224 crore has been recorded till date. Original time schedule for completion of this component was till June 2013 which has now been extended till June 2014 due to delay in handing over of land at Sittwe and Paletwa, Custom clearances and other approvals by Government of Myanmar

34 http://www.assamtribune.com/scripts/detailsnew.asp?id=apr3016/oth054, dt. 1/10/2016

16

Developmental Implications of the Act East Policy: A Case of Tourist Promotion in Mizoram

K.V. Reddy

The Look East Policy (LEP) of the Indian government was renamed the Act East Policy (AEP) by the Narendra Modi regime in the context of making it the pivot of its foreign policy towards the ASEAN countries. Prime Minister Modi told the world leaders about it being accorded a high priority by turning India's LEP into the AEP.[1] Besides the foreign policy focus, it has certain developmental implications at the domestic level for North East India (NEI) as well. The regional development has been focused accordingly. Among others, tourist promotion in the region has been encouraged in the recent past. As part of the AEP implementation, the backward state of Mizoram is expected to promote tourist development and ensure potential benefits for the local population. More than the tourists that visit it from with and without Northeast India, the local population will have significant developmental prospects.

Various studies have already indicated the prospects of boosting the state economy through promoting eco-tourism, for instance. Eco-tourism has twin objectives. Not only will the state have ensured natural ecological balance, the eco-tourist potential will also be enhanced. Consequently, the economic development of the state and its population could be achieved at one go. While there are numerous ideas being considered for promotion of tourism, certain specific projects can be undertaken at the earliest so that the prospects of eco-tourism can be realized. However, there are certain impediments that affect tourist promotion in the state. This article tries to identify such developmental problems like the Inner Line Regulations (ILR) among others that undermine the development of tourism in the state. Also, the article is an attempt towards enlightening tourists at home and abroad about the unexplored prospects of tourism in Mizoram.

North East India

Northeast India has been attracting national regimes for quite some time. Since the region was 'notorious for reasons of insurgencies and violent movements' for decades on end, attention was rarely given to its development or under-development. The region is rich in mineral resources and hydropower potential. Many states in the region have the capacity to generate surplus hydropower that can be sold in the neighbouring countries. There are many varieties of agricultural products, floriculture products, handlooms and handicrafts, tea products, herbs and medicinal plants, that can be exported with huge returns. Besides, there are huge reserves of oil, gas, coal, limestone and mineral resources. Many of these raw materials are still untapped and can be utilized. As the region is blessed with a huge biodiversity and heritage sites, the tourism industry can flourish in the region. Besides natural resources, educated manpower resources in the region are also plenty that can be used in various developmental projects.

Hence, the Development of the North-Eastern Region (DONER) ministry regarded the NEI as having the potential to develop into India's economic driving force. The region offers unlimited tourist opportunities with rare flora and fauna, scenic beauty, unique performing arts and varied cuisine and handicrafts. With its physical location, a large number of tourists from Asiatic countries can be attracted. Yet, the NEI does not have easy access to social and infrastructure services compared to mainstream India. Physical infrastructure such as electricity, communication, transportation and banking and finance are limited and unevenly distributed among urban and rural areas. Besides, the north eastern region has always been faced with a multitude of problems in the context of peace, governance and development. However, it is only after the formation of separate states that NEI states like Mizoram have achieved social harmony and political peace to a large extent. Besides, Mizoram has emerged as the most literate in the NEI within a decade or so. Given its communitarian value system, the state has advanced sufficient social capital that certainly helped in implementing developmental projects.[2]

Mizoram

Historically speaking, the categorization of the Lushai Hills (erstwhile name of Mizoram) as 'Excluded Area' in 1935 by the Interim Government of India can be the reason for its neglected development *ab initio*. Lately, fluidity of the political situation on the eve of Independence made the local environment worse for any sort of development. Of course, there existed diverse views amongst the tribal leaders particularly in the hill areas of north eastern India, regarding merging with the political organization of the country. Few of them were for joining the Indian Union whereas some contemplated opting for Pakistan. A third view wanted to be part of a 'Protectorate under the British crown'. There was a fourth group that strived for 'free independent sovereign tribal state' status.[3] All these factors contributed to keep the area under the low priority category for infrastructure development in general. Besides, throughout history, the NEI has provided an actual meeting ground of many races and tribal communities. Despite closed international boundaries, these tribal communities continued to preserve social, cultural and economic affinities with their counterparts across the borders more than with those of mainstream India. A significant part of agriculture production in these hills is still characterized by the practice of '*jhum*', cultivation with extremely low productivity. Obviously, the region is comparatively poor and backward in terms of both industry and infrastructures and most of the states including Mizoram rank poorly on India's human development index.[4]

Essentially, T. Sailo's ministry made a few systemic plans for building economic infrastructure in the power sectors. Yet, most of these projects remained unimplemented by subsequent ministries. Thus, the state is more than 50 MW short of its energy requirement. Obviously, due to absence of power, no major industrial activity was possible.[5] For over decades, the people of Mizoram were disheartened with turbulence of all kinds and are now looking for their socio-economic development. Despite its high literacy rate, fertile soil system, rich cultural heritage and a good political environment, the socio-economic development of Mizoram lagged. Lack of good roads, transportation, electricity, communication, industry, infrastructure and unemployment are hurdles in the development of Mizoram. In fact, the economy of Mizoram is normally marked by low per capita income due to inadequate infrastructure facilities, geographical isolation, communication bottlenecks, inadequate exploitation of natural resources l, hydro power potential, forests, lack of industrial base and investment opportunities. Besides, the lack of skilled manpower and trained workers and poor technical knowhow has dogged its economy. Mizoram has witnessed many obstacles and constraints for the growth of its economic development. Its geographical location was inaccessible, without proper transportation links with mainland India. It eventually made her an unexplored locale. Obviously, there are no proper industries in the state and lack of infrastructure and modern technology added to the critical condition.

In any case, to establish any industry or company, whether in the private or public sectors, the first significant thing is capital, but Mizoram has no sufficient capital for the purpose. Mizoram has had no potential to generate capital without help from advanced 'outsiders'. Similarly, skilled labour is lacking in the state. As there are not enough skilled construction workers in the state, Mizos usually employ outside labourers.[6] Above all, problems of connectivity due to regulation of free movements wherein 'outsiders' need permission to enter the state have created problems of investment that affect economic development. Besides, the opening of border trade also brings in other non-security threats and ushers in social, political and economic dynamics especially among the people residing in the border areas. On another account, trade across the Zokhawthar border has its own ripple effect. Along with its benefits, it brought another dimension of non security threats like increase in drug circulation and arms smuggling and other contraband and infiltration of Myanmar migrants into Mizoram.[7]

AEP and Vision 2020

During the course of LEP implementation, declaration of NE Vision 2020 was announced in 2008.[8] Until then the people-to-people relationship hardly received any policy space. The AEP can be considered as a developmental strategy that could be contextualized with the development of the Northeast region.[9] In a way, the AEP could become a key step towards achieving undertaking to formalize border trade, bring back the old routes of mobility in the NEI and create social bonds and age-old ties among the cross-border tribes under the Mizo Accord.[10] Inclusion of the locals also became critical because it is they who, based on their familiarity, who could visualise the ground difficulties and suggest what could be done for intensification of cross-border interaction. According to the DONER Ministry, the local people of both sides could stay in the other country for about three days within a radius of 16 km without visa if their activity is confined only to trade–related issues. There is a possibility of this being extended beyond the border for closer people-to-people exchange and thereby attain non-economic benefits.

The vision document also found that poor infrastructure and governance, low productivity and market inaccessibility, seeding of ethnic and cultural identities, frustration and dissatisfaction from isolation, underdevelopment and distance were responsible for providing a fertile ground for various types of insurgencies that played a destabilizing function in trade expansion, regional cooperation and peace. An eminent economist, Lianzela, reverberated this Vision of good governance, peace and security, good infrastructure, high quality education and healthcare facilities, development of primary sector of the economy besides tourism as vital for the development of the NE region.[11] Thus, Vision 2020 became a vibrant version of

AEP that identified the problems of the region in the post-partition peripheral trap. In India's Act East Policy, there are two contesting points. First, is about the global objective for which India intends to extend its strategic and economic ties with Southeast Asia and East Asia. Second is about the local objective, which the people of the north east region would bargain for an increase in its political and economic domains.[12]

It is repeatedly argued that the mainstream approach towards the NE region had been for tactical use instead of developing it as such. In many ways, this region has been kept as a buffer zone for mainstream India. Every intention of many developmental projects in the region is decidedly doubtful. This can be illustrated by the fact that many of the big development projects in the region were undertaken by the Central Government or its associated external authorities. Obviously, there is always some mistrust in the minds of the local people about the benefits of such mega projects in the NE region. In fact, there developed a negative perception that it was the external companies which were extracting the local resources rather than developing the area. Accordingly, without developing the requisite local business acumen, skill and entrepreneurial spirit, the NE region cannot reap rich dividends from the AEP. Of course, there is an enormous urge to develop infrastructure and human resources in this region. Slowly and gradually, the region needs to get rid of its Centre-dependent development model.

An eminent author on the NEI, Sanjib Baruah, once wrote, 'The look east policy is making impressive headway. But there is a danger that it may be delinked from the vision of north-east India as a gateway..., mainland India's ties with south-east Asia were primarily maritime and not continental. Even today, it is cheaper and easier to trade with south-east Asia by sea rather than by land.[13] There were similar expectations expressed in various circles thereafter. Increasing connectivity, trade and infrastructure investment and greater security cooperation with South-East Asia were the core aims of the 'Act East' policy. Thus, central to such policy was an increased engagement with Myanmar, the closest neighbour at the Eastern door. However, there was hardly any scope to maintain close ties with the Myanmar government or its people.

Yet, these NE states can have massive collaboration in tourism, health sector, education and other service sectors as part of implementing the AEP. Obviously, once the developmental advantages are properly explored the northeast region can grow economically and stand out as the most developed in the region. When this policy is implemented, one can see if the core and the periphery share the developmental benefits or is the other way round possible. According to Immanuel Wallenstein's core-periphery analogy, if the gap between the core and periphery is not bridged, it is the mainstream states that are going to reap the benefits whereby these NE states would be converted as channels of goods for markets in ASEAN countries.[14] Viewed in this backdrop, any initiative under the AEP would certainly include a comprehensive tourism plan for the region with a brand ambassador to characterize the heritage and identity of the Northeast. Hence, there is a need for mega circuit and extra-large destination projects to be undertaken for promotion of the tourist industry in the region.

Developmental Prospects

Unlike the other states in the NEI, Mizoram offers the most peaceful location that is very conducive for tourist visits on a regular basis. Besides, the pleasant climatic conditions will be supportive for visitors to the state. Tourism is also an essential requirement for Mizoram through which economic resources can be generated by utilizing the gifts of nature. In an industrially backward state like Mizoram, tourism has immense potential and prospects. While the local literates can earn better livelihood, the state can generate good revenue. The state is on record of achieving the optimum literacy rate (91 per cent) in the region. Even the women participation rate (WPR) is 26 per cent, which is more than the national average.[15] Even the vision document gave specific attention on gender sensitive governance as the key to inclusive growth. Thus, local governance reforms needed women's effective participation, gender equality including exercise of rights, social control, access to decision making and public voice to defend rights. In other words, not only the locale is gorgeous, but the local populace can also be very gregarious towards its prospective tourists.

Mizoram is an underdeveloped state with no mineral resources for industrial development. Thus, the Mizos can pay attention to tourism like what people in Sikkim did.[16] Mizoram state can generate its own financial resources through tourism. It became critical for implementing the AEP at least for three reasons, viz., relative political stability of the state, higher literacy and Bangladesh's refusal to grant transit permits to India. The Kaladan project[17] was intended to offer multiple opportunities to the state including investment and employment, connectivity and opening NEI to the Bay of Bengal so as to transform the state into a major transit route in the region. Incidentally, Mizoram has had a continental link with Myanmar and Bangladesh that helped the geographical spread of its international trade. So, trade through land routes envisaged by the AEP depends largely on Myanmar and its strategic location. Once the India-ASEAN physical connectivity project like the KMMTP, which envisages a direct trade corridor between Indian ports on the eastern seaboard and the Sittwe port in Myanmar and then through riverine-cum-road transport to Mizoram were completed, the geographical isolation of the NEI will come to an end and the region will play a meaningful role in integrating India with South East Asia.

Besides, the KMMTP essentially has three different stretches involving shipping, inland water and road transport. The longest among them is the shipping segment from Kolkata to Sittwe port[18] in Myanmar. The Government of India is funding this project and it is considered as an important investment of India in its neighbourhood. The completion of KMMTP will play a major role in the economic development of the NEI and it will improve bilateral relations between India and Myanmar. Once completed, the KMMTP will shorten the current time taken to transport goods from Kolkata to Mizoram by three to four days, and the distance by around 950 kilometres.[19] Gurudas Das argued that in spite of adopting a pragmatic approach, India's Myanmar policy has failed to yield the desired results mainly due to the fact that it had not made India's Northeast as the front head of sub-regional cooperation. He identified the lack of economic development in the region as a potential factor hindering effective trade relations with Myanmar in comparison with the Sino-Myanmar border trade. The AEP, to be successfully implemented, requires road and infrastructure development, regional security and peace, local participation in trade and improvement in local production in both agriculture and industrial goods. Thus, building good relations with Myanmar is vital.[20]

Tourist Promotion

Tourism is a good source of revenue and many countries and states have gained from it. Besides, when it comes to tourism or tourists, it simply means more interaction and connection with the outside world and it requires attraction. By making easy access for foreign tourists, and not for fellow Indians, tourist development may become a problem as it will create confusion among the people from the rest of India. Tourism does not cover only foreigners but also those from other states in India. It may be unappealing for mainlanders to explore the state and visit it within a time frame as obtaining a legal permit may become an obstacle to boost tourism in Mizoram. Perhaps, their insecurity is due to lack of confidence towards outsiders. This is a big problem which makes it more difficult to tackle tourist development schemes. Some people even believe that the building of a railway link from Bairabi to Sairang could become a problem for the Mizos as there will be easy connectivity that would lead to bring in a heavy population from outside into the state.[21]

Incidentally, the total revenue generated from tourist promotion from the NEI states is still meagre when compared with their counterparts in mainstream India. For instance, with respect to outbound tourism, a total of 3.1 thousand people living in Mizoram undertook foreign trips during 2010-11. This is 0.03 per cent of the total outbound tourists from India. In 2015-16, the overall share of tourism in the state's Gross Domestic Product (GDP) was 5.27 per cent. And the overall share of tourist-related employment in the state 6.62 per cent. The revenue earned by the department for the same period reached Rs.222.01 lakh.[22] Moreover, the number of tourists in Mizoram declined during the last five years. Not only in Mizoram but also in other parts of the North East, the number of tourists from foreign countries does not increase as expected by various policy framers who dreamt about tourist destination in North East India.[23]

Tourist Potential Spots

Hilly terrain, lush green forests, hygienic climate, rich natural resources bestowed by nature, provide ample prospects for developing tourism. Having at least one attractive tourist spot each in each district, Mizoram has got many famous sites such as, Blue Mountain (Phawngpui Tlang) and Milu Puk (Skull Cave) in Lawngtlai district, Pukzing cave near Marpara in Mamit district, Lamsialpuk near Farkawn village in Champhai district, Phulpui grave and Chhingpouii memorial in Aizawl district, Buddha's image in Mualcheng village in Lunglei district and Rih Dil inside Myanmar near Zokhawthar border in Champhai district are among the many historical sites. Besides, there are also other tourist attractions such as Palal Lake which is a natural lake in Saiha district, Vantawng waterfall in Serchhip district, besides traditional Mizo villages in Falkawn, Hmuifang, Reiek and Aibawk near the state capital, Aizawl. Once these sites are developed and good tourist spots created, many tourists from within the country and abroad can be attracted.

Besides, there are a few major rivers in Mizoram, namely, Chhimtuipui (Kolodyne), Tlawng (tributary of Barak), Tuivai (tributary of Barak), Tuichang; these are hill rivers that flow down the mountains and always present waterfalls in numerous places. These rivers are fresh and clean. The Tlawng River is one of the longest in the state. Tlawng has historical significance for the Mizos as the Ganga has for people in the Hindi belt. The mega Tlawng river project can be made multi-beneficial for the state. These rivers can be used for bottling mineral water and a large-scale industry in this regard could be set up. In a way, tourist promotion leads to industrial development..

Inner Line Regulation (ILR)

The British regime introduced the Inner Line Permit (ILP) system in times of non-governance of the hilly terrains of the NEI and it was continued thereafter by independent India. Yet, its implementation was witnessed more in violation, rather than otherwise. States like Arunachal Pradesh, Nagaland and Mizoram still enforce this practice to check the inflow of illegal migrants into their respective states. Incidentally, a few communities in a couple of other states (Meghalaya, for instance) in the region have also raised such demands in recent times. Yet, the problem of illegal entry could not be addressed in any way. While a lot of hue and cry is being witnessed on account of this politically and administratively associated issue, the influx of illegal migrants continues unabated in these states. An argument stems from issues like ILR which somehow makes tourists reluctant to visit some parts of the region, namely, Mizoram. Although the ILR safeguarded the tribals in many respects, it suffered from many criticism. The practice of ILR is a controversial subject among the locals. From the regional perspective, the ILR works as a protector against assimilation from outsiders and it safeguards the indigenous tribal identity from exploitation, whereas from the national perspective, it endangers the process of national integration by encouraging regional sentiments.

In 2003, permits to non-Indians to visit certain parts of India including Mizoram had been removed by the Central government to boost tourism. Foreigners (Protected Areas) Order 1958 that was practised for more than 50 years in Mizoram, Nagaland and Manipur had been removed by the Central government to permit free movement of foreign tourists with the exception of those from Afghanistan, China, Pakistan and Myanmar. The Restricted Area Permit (RAP) had been provisionally removed to boost tourism in these North Eastern states as it discouraged foreign nationals from exploring these isolated areas. Back in 2007, the three opposition parties—the Congress, Zoram Nationalist Party (ZNP) and Mizo People's Conference (MPC)—submitted a memorandum to the Union Home Ministry opposing the lifting of ILR and RAP as they believed that the government was planning to disband it. But the state government had held it was considering relaxation of the ILR/RAP to boost tourism in Mizoram since there were big hurdles for tourists visiting Mizoram.[24] Hence, the RAP had been provisionally removed by the Central Government, but the ILR is still in practice in the state which still creates certain obstacles for Indians.

Any sort of isolationist policy like the ILR cannot make much change in economic growth as it is tied to employment opportunities in the private sector. The result of isolation and less interaction with the outside world can be found in Mizo society's norms and traditions, which is based on resistance to change. Numerous decades have been passed with the experiences of having complied with the notion of stabilizing the ethnic/tribal identity and culture. Due to the fear of possible changes in its traditions and culture, social development had suffered. Lack of a work culture, resistance to change and a negative attitude towards the external environment are considered as attitudes of scepticism.[25] In fact, interaction and interconnection with other people make it easier to acquire new ideas and develop strategy for the development, economy-wise and otherwise.

Perhaps the time has come for critically viewing the need of ILP in the NEI as well as a ban on land ownership rights by 'outsiders'. These outsiders need the local jobs; the north-easterners also need them desperately. More than the issue of legality of their entry or jobs, it is their illegal activities that could be targeted and eliminated. As the ILR prevents large-scale migration to the state, the local people might enjoy the opportunity to run businesses and secure employment for themselves. Yet, it is doubtful if it boosts economic development or can grow faster without. Since the ILR blocked the free flow of people's movements, economic activities and establishing trade relations with outsiders had become harder. Establishing trade relations with other states and countries is obligatory to boost the local economy. When outsiders/ mainland Indians can establish businesses in the state the state economy can flourish. But as long as the ILR controls their movements, it certainly blocks their free movement, including tourism, which make it harder to establish trade relations and businesses for the others.

Of late, different governments in the state had initiated some projects and implemented various policies for its development for the socio-economic well-being of its people. Yet, the state's economy is still heavily dependent on central funding. Recently, the state has been brought on the rail map of India by connecting Bairabi in the northern foothills of the state with Katakal railway junction in the Cachar plains. Yet, it runs for only 1.5 kilometres within the state boundary. There are now plans to extend the line closer to the state capital, Aizawl up to Sairang by 2019 or so.[26]

Thanks to an airport at Lengpui in Mamit district, Aizawl city also has air connectivity with the rest of India since the early 1980s. Of course, very few flights are operating through it. These two modes of transport however facilitate movement of goods and passengers only on a limited scale. Once other modes of transportation (like KMMTP) are developed and virtual connectivity is established without ILR, then there will be no looking back for the Mizos and Mizoram.

To conclude, due to an emerging healthy political process, more peace and harmony is noticed nowadays in some of the North-eastern states including Mizoram. Due to the homogeneity of Mizo society, the competitive spirit is missing not only in the economic sphere but also in education. New ideas and environments that help create overall development were hardly seen as a result of disconnection from the outside world. But as long as the ILR blocks free movements of 'outsiders' it would discourage potential entrepreneurs and capitalists to invest and set up business enterprises in the state. Due to Mizoram's remote location and backwardness, besides a small population that undermines commercial success, there is a need of protecting the interests of outsiders in establishing big businesses, which will be possible only if there was no ILR. To improve the state's economy, transportation and connectivity need to be established for opening linkages and interconnections with each other. Further, completion of the Kolodyne Hydro-Electric Project–II, KMMTP and the *Namani Tlawng* River Project can also be other tourist destinations.

Tourism is a good source of revenue as many tourism-oriented states gained from its development. Tourism boosts the local economy, which in turn impacts the state development. By making access easy for tourists, Indian or foreign, nature-gifted Mizoram can have an edge over the other states in the NEI. But, at times the issue of Inner Line Permit deters tourists from exploring the state and boost tourism in Mizoram. It is time for the state and non-state actors to ponder over it and do the needful at the earliest. Despite many a challenge, travelling in the state of Mizoram, unlike other tourist spots in the mountainous regions, is painstaking and a little hazardous at times, but it has its own reward. With the development of proper infrastructure and adequate planning, the tourist potential can be explored in the state. As a state that is both violence and pollution-free, Mizoram is the best natural destination for tourists. Yes, it is a win-win situation for both the local youth and tourists.

ENDNOTES

1 Thomas, C.J. (2017). 'Look North-East before Acting East: Synergising North-East with Act East Policy' in edited volume by C. J. Thomas and K. Sarda, *Act East and India's North-East*, Pentagon Press, New Delhi, p. 58.

2 Reddy, K.V. (2017). Northeast in India's 'Act East Policy': A Perspective from Mizoram' in edited volume by Pankaj Jha and Rahul Mishra, *Integrating North East in India's Act East Policy*, ICWA, New Delhi. p. 63.

3 Kyndiah, P.R. (1999). *Pillars of Mizo Society and Thoughts to Share*, London: Cambridge.

4 Samir Kumar Das, *Conflict and Peace in India's Northeast: The Role of Civil Society*, Washington, D.C: East-West Center, Washington, 2007, p. 6.

5 Reddy, K. V. (2016). Developmental Strategies in Mizoram: Emerging Challenges (unpublished project report for the ICSSR, New Delhi, p. 95.

6 Ibid, p. 98.

7 Songate, P. (2010). *Indo-Myanmar Border Trade: The Study of Socio-Cultural and Political Dynamics in Mizoram.* (unpublished doctoral dissertation), Mizoram University.

8 *North Eastern Region Vision 2020*, Ministry of Development of North Eastern Region, NEC, 2008.

9 Reddy, K.V. (2017). 'The Act East Policy Implications and Developmental Strategies in Mizoram' in edited volume by C. J. Thomas and K. Sarda, *Act East and India's North-East*, Pentagon Press, New Delhi, p. 121.

10 Haokip, T. (2015). *India's Look East Policy and the North East.* New Delhi: Sage Publications.

11 Lianzela, in an article on 'Economic Challenges and Opportunities in Mizoram since 1986' in edited book by J. K. Patnaik (2014). *State and Civil Society in Mizoram*, EBH Publishers, Guwahati.

12 Chakraborty, Gorky and Ray, Ashok Kumar. (2014). *The Look East Policy and Northeast India.* Aakar Books, Delhi.

13 Baruah, S. (2003). December 12. 'Look East, but via the Northeast'. *The Indian Express*

14 Wallenstein, Immanuel, 'The Rise and Future Demise of the World Capitalist System: Concepts for Comparative Analysis,' *Comparative Studies in Society and History*, Vol. 16, issue 4, 1974.

15 Reddy, K.V. (2016) *op. cit.*, p. 217.

16 Sikkim used tourism as a source of heavy revenue for the development of the state.

17 Kaladan Multi-Modal Transport Project was the first major project undertaken by the Indian Government in Myanmar. India has finished constructing Sittwe Port in the trouble-prone Rakhine state of Myanmar. Also, the extension of the Aizawl-Siaha National Highway by 90 km to the international border at Zorinpui on the Indian side is nearing completion. In addition, four-lane construction of the 300-km Aizawl-Tuipang highway to ensure faster movement of goods between Sittwe and Aizawl is almost on the verge of completion.

18 Sittwe Port would be linked to Lashio (also in Myanmar) via the Kaladan river transport route. Lashio would be connected to Mizoram via road transport (National Highway 54).

19 Government awards contract for completion of Kaladan Project in Myanmar, 9 June 2017. Retrieved from https://currentaffairs.gktoday.in/tags/kaladan-multi-modal-transport-projects).

20 Gurudas, in his article entitled, 'India's Myanmar Policy: Implication for India's Northeast' in the book edited by Joshua Thomas, C. & Das, Gurudas (2016). *Look East to Act East Policy: Implications for India's Northeast.*

21 Reddy, K.V. (2016) *op. cit.*, p. 100.

22 Ministry of Tourism, G. (2016). *Regional Tourism Satellite Account Mizoram, 2015–16 (Phase III).* New Delhi: National Council of Applied Economic Research (NCEAR).

23 Government of Mizoram (2017). Mizoram Economic Survey 2016-17. Aizawl: Planning & Programme Implementation Department (Research & Development Branch).

24 http: //www.oneindia.come>Home>News>India.

25 Anjan Thakur. (1998). *Sociological Constraints to Industrial Development in North East India,* Concept Publishing House, New Delhi.

26 *The Economic Times* 2017. 'Broad gauge connectivity to all NE state capitals by 2020 on target: Budget 2017,' 1 February 2017.

17

Process of Look East Policy and Its Perspectives in Manipur and Nagaland

Jangkhongam Doungel

ABSTRACT

The paper attempts to briefly trace the genesis of the Look East Policy and process of its development. It attempts to critically analyze the perspectives of the Policy in Manipur and Nagaland with objective observation.

Introduction

The Look East Policy can be described as an offshoot of globalization, privatization, liberalisation and post-cold war phenomena. In fact, it is a strategic shift of India's foreign policy in the post-cold war era. It was initiated and developed during the government of Prime Minister P.V. Narasimha Rao and vigorously pursued by the successive governments of Atal Bihari Vajpayee and Dr. Manmohan Singh. The essential philosophy of the Look East Policy is that India must find its destiny by linking itself more with its Asian partners and the rest of the world and that India's future and economic interests are best served by greater integration with East and South East Asian countries. Further, as India's dependable and reliable partner in all fronts, the erstwhile USSR had already exited from the international political scenario and Russia has normalized her relationship with China, it is prime time for India to act for survival in international politics. Due to this, India has to look towards her neighbouring South East Asian countries for survival in the economy as well as to counteract the growing influence of China in the region. Over and above this, the Gulf War of 1991 also awakened India that she could no longer rely permanently on the Gulf region for supply of her ever-increasing energy demand. Thus, for alternative source of energy and for other strategic considerations, the Asia-Pacific region could be the ideal solution that also prompted the Look East

Policy. Former Prime Minister, Dr. Manmohan Singh has said that the Look East Policy is not merely an external economic policy but also a strategic shift in India's vision of the world and India's place in the evolving global economy.[1] India's main agenda in framing and pursuing the Look East Policy is to establish good diplomatic links and cordial trade relationships with South East Asian countries. The Association of the South East Asian Nations (ASEAN) was established in August 1967 at Bangkok by representatives of Indonesia, Malaysia, the Philippines and Singapore.[2] At present, the member countries of ASEAN comprise Indonesia, Malaysia, the Philippines, Singapore, Brunei, Myanmar, Laos, Cambodia, Thailand and Vietnam.[3]

The Look East Policy was classified in two phases, namely, the first and the second. The first of the Look East policy was from 1991 to 2002 and it wholly concentrated on ASEAN countries and mainly focused primarily on trade and investment linkages. The second phase which began in 2003 is more comprehensive in its coverage, extending from Australia to East Asia with ASEAN as its core agenda. As part of the endeavour to strengthen India's linkages with the East and South East Asian regions as well as to reinforce the Look East Policy, a sub-regional grouping called BIST-EC, comprising Bangladesh, India, Sri Lanka and Thailand was established in 1997. With the addition of Myanmar, Bhutan and Nepal, the grouping came to be known as the Bay of Bengal Initiative for Multi Sectoral Technique and Economic Cooperation (BIMSTEC). In fact, India promotes BIMSTEC to establish economic links with peninsula member countries of ASEAN to boost the economic development of its seven North Eastern states.[4]

In pursuance of the Look East Policy, a border trade agreement was signed by India and Myanmar on 21 October 1994 in New Delhi for the opening of three Land Custom Stations (LCSs) on the Indian side and three LCSs on the Myanmar side. As per the agreement, official border trade began to function with the opening of the Land Custom Station (LCS) in the border town of Moreh in Manipur from 1995 but unofficial border trade did exist even earlier. Along with this, one LCS is also scheduled to be opened at Avangkhu in Phek District of Nagaland[5] but it has not yet materialized. It can also be said that Nagaland is not yet covered by the Look East Policy map as far as the process and initiative of the project is concerned. In Manipur, other than the opening of the LCS at Moreh, a 165-kilometre road was constructed by the Border Road Organisation (BRO) from Tamu to Kalemyo-Kalewa at a cost of Rs. 100 crore.[6] The Mandalay and Railway project is also in the offing. However, it is doubtful to express whether the so-called development works and border trade are beneficial for the local people or not? The nomenclature of the 'Look East Policy has been changed to Act East Policy' by the present NDAII Government in 2014. The reason was stated as to initiate action with regard to pursuance of the policy; however, whether the so-called 'Act East Policy' really activates the required action in the policy for all the North-eastern states in general and Manipur and Nagaland in particular have to be observed. The process and perspectives of the Look East Policy in Manipur and Nagaland can be analyzed as follows.

Border Trade in Manipur and Nagaland in pre-Look East Policy Era

Border trade had existed between Manipur and Burma (now Myanmar) as well as between Nagaland (Naga Hills) and Burma (Myanmar) since the pre-colonial era. The districts of Nagaland that share the border with Myanmar are Phek, Kiphire, Tuensang and Mon. As far as Nagaland is concerned, the border areas in both sides of the territory are inhabited by different Naga tribes. As such, they had a cordial relationship since the pre-British period and their inhabited areas were not demarcated by any international boundary. Therefore, the Nagas regarded all their inhabited areas as their ancestral land and their movements were not restricted. Besides, they interacted and coordinated as people from the same land because they were not separated at that time. However, the coming of British imperialism began demarcating the boundary and they were not free like in the pre-colonial era. British imperialism demarcated the boundary to suit its imperialist design without taking the traditional ownership of the land into account. The situation became complex and critical after independence because the land that they regarded and owned as their ancestral property was divided by the international boundary. The same is the case with Manipur. Churachandpur, Chandel and Ukhrul districts of Manipur share a common border with Myanmar and the border areas in both sides are inhabited by the Tangkhul Naga tribe in Ukhrul district and different tribes of the Zo (Chin-Kuki-Mizo) ethnic group in Chandel and Churachandpur districts and in a small area of Ukhrul district. Like Nagaland, people on both sides of the border had free interaction in the pre-colonial era which ranged from matrimonial, trade, cultural, ethnic and other aspects because they are people from the same ethnic stock and were not divided by an international boundary. Therefore, people from both sides moved freely from one place to another and powerful chiefs collected tribute and revenue freely from both sides of the border. The tribes that occupied both sides of the border areas regarded themselves as sovereign in their areas. Alexander Mackenzie mentions in his book, "The Burman is himself nowhere a dweller in the mountains, though thus girt round with a noble mountain barrier."[7] It is thus clear from this statement that the frontier areas were never in the possession of the Burmese or mainland Indians since in the pre-colonial era and the tribals who there were the owners of the land. Therefore, the tribals who lived in frontier areas regarded their inhabited areas as their ancestral and traditional land and therefore freely interacted as people of the same land.

Mackenzie mentions in his book that the Sootic Kookies (Sukte-Kukies) and Chahsad Kookies (Chahsad-Kuki) kept disturbing the kingdom of Manipur. The Suktes conducted surprised attacks and raids in the present territory of Manipur and collected tribute. As far as the Chahsads were concerned, Tonglhu Haokip was their chief and the location of Chahsad was shifted from the present Churachandpur district (southern region) to the present Ukhrul district (frontier area or eastern region) of Manipur. As the tribal chiefs regarded themselves as owners of the traditional land, they did not pay any importance to other rulers. Therefore, the chief of Chahsad was suspicious of the king of Manipur because Nehlam Haokip, father of Tonglhu Haokip, was arrested by Meitei soldiers of Manipur and killed on 11 October 1855.[8] Likewise Raja Goukhothang, a powerful Guite chief, was also arrested and killed in jail at Imphal. The tribals in the Hill Areas of Manipur regarded the king of Manipur as ruler of only the valley areas of Manipur and did not consider themselves his subjects. In the midst of this ongoing mistrust between Chahsad and Manipur, Tonglhu Haokip, chief of Chahsad, declared sovereignty of the geographical areas from where he collected tribute and tax in 1877 and declared war against the king of Manipur. Tonglhun Haokip was fully supported by all his tributary chiefs on both sides of the border and was assisted by the Raja of Sumjok from Kabaw Valley. However, the Chahsad chief was defeated by the king of Manipur with the assistance of the British. Further, he could be brought to the negotiating table only with the involvement of the British Political Agent because he did not trust the king of Manipur.[9] As the colonial ruler disturbed the independent functioning of the tribal chiefs, there were many military conflicts between the British forces and the tribal chiefs in different parts of the present North East India and Myanmar. Subsequently, the chief of Aisan, Chengjapao Doungel, also declared war against the British authority which came to be known as the Aisan Rebellion of 1910 which was followed by the Kuki Rebellion of 1917-1919.[10]

The British India adopted a 'forward policy' towards the Nagas with the occupation of Kohima on 14 November 1878. This was followed by speedy consolidation of British rule in Naga Hills and the Naga Hills district was established in 1881. Different Naga tribes bravely resisted the British forces but they could not succeed in their political goal. The Angami tribe put up their last fierce resistance against the British forces and besieged Kohima for 11 days in 1879-1880. Thirteen Angami villages were involved in the siege of Kohima but they could not resist the superior British military. Thus, the Naga Hills began to be ruled by the British authority until India's independence.[11] The advent of British imperialism limited the activities of the tribal chiefs because their administered areas were demarcated into different geographical boundaries but they kept on interacting without disturbance. The reason being that the areas inhabited by the tribals were demarcated into different geographical boundaries and people from the same ethnic stock were divided by international boundaries after independence. Thus, different Naga tribes and tribes of the Zo ethnic group were separated by their international boundary without their knowledge or approval.

Myanmar shares 1,643 kilometres of common land border with India in the North East bordering Arunachal Pradesh, Nagaland, Manipur and Mizoram.[12] Of this, Manipur shares 352 kilometres border with Myanmar and Nagaland shares 215 kilometres with Myanmar.[13] Thus, Manipur and Nagaland occupy strategic positions for the successful implementation of the Look East Policy because of their borders with Myanmar. As the frontier areas of both these states adjacent to Myanmar are inhabited by people from the same ethnic stock, there was trading and other relationships in the pre-colonial era. As stated above, people on both sides of the border were not aware of the presence of other forces in the pre-colonial era. Therefore, they moved and interacted freely without any restriction. In fact, this free movement was also respected and maintained by the colonial regime. However, the situation became critical with the division of people of the same ethnic stock by the international boundary after the British Colonialism. Yet, the sentiments of the people could not be completely curbed by the boundary. Other than interacting with their own people across the border, the inhabitants of the border areas also maintained trade relationships with other people of Myanmar such as the Burmese (Myanmarese) and other ethnic groups. This relationship existed in the border areas even in the pre-Look East Policy era but it could be called illegal or unofficial trade. Further, trade relationship at that time was carried on in the form of village-to-village trade and that spirit is still there among the people of the frontier areas. Therefore, what is regarded and known as border trade by people outside the frontier areas was considered village trade by people of the frontier areas and that very spirit still exists.

Perspective of Look East Policy in Manipur

Manipur can be said to be the first state in the North Eastern region to be drawn on the map of the Look East Policy. However, whether meaningful socio-economic development has resulted by the said policy is still doubtful. Manipur already carries baggage of worries in connection with the Look East Policy. Thus, the perspective of the Look East Policy in Manipur is be analysed as below.

Opening of Land Custom Centre (LCS) at Moreh: The Land Custom Stations (LCS) in international borders are notified under Section 7 of the Customs Act, 1962 by the Department of Revenue, Ministry of Finance. Some stations have been selected development as Integrated Check Posts (ICP) by the Department of Border Management, Ministry of Finance.[14] As per the border trade agreement signed by India and Myanmar on 21 October 1994 at New Delhi; three LCSs were scheduled to be opened on the Indian side, namely, Moreh in Manipur, Zokhawthar in Mizoram and Nampong in Arunachal Pradesh. Subsequently, border trade was inaugurated by Lt. General Tun Kyi, Trade Minister of Myanmar and P. Chidambaram, Commerce Minister of India at Moreh on 12 April 1995 at LCS at Moreh and Tamu respectively. Twenty-two items of essential commodities were notified for border trade by Public Notice No. 289(PN)/92-97 on 10 April 1995 which comprised: 1. bamboo, 2. betel nuts and leaves, 3. chillies, 4. coriander seeds, 5. food items for local consumption, 6. fresh vegetables, 7. fruits, 8. garlic, 9. ginger, 10. katha, 11. minor forest products (excluding teak), 12. mustard/rape seed, 13. Onions, 14. pulses and beans, 15. reed Brooms, 16. resin, 17. roasted sunflower seeds, 18. sesame, 19. soyabean, 20. spices (excluding nutmeg, mace, cloves, cassia and cinnamon), 21. tobacco and 22. tomatoes. Later, 18 more essential commodities were notified by Public Notice No. 106(RE-2008)/2004-2009 on 7 November 2008 which included 1. agarbatti, 2. bicycle spare parts, 3. blades, 4. bulbs, 5. cosmetics, 6. cotton fabrics, 7. fertilizers, 8. imitation jewellery, 9. insecticides, 10. leather footwear, 11. life-saving drugs, 12. menthol, 13. mosquito coils, 14. paints and varnishes, 15. spices, 16. stainless steel utensils, 17 sugar and salt and 18. x-ray paper and photo paper. For the expansion of border trade, 22 new commodities were added through Public Notice No. 30 (RE-2012)/2009-2014 on 16 November 2012 which comprised 1. agricultural machinery/equipment/ tools, 2. bicycles, 3. bleaching powder, 4. coal, 5. edible oil, 6. electrical and Electric appliances, 7. fabricated steel products, 8. garments/readymade garments/clothes, 9. handlooms and handicraft items, 10. hardware/minor construction materials and electrical fittings, 11. lime, 12. medicine, 13. milk powder, tea, edible oil, beverages, 14. motor cycles and motor cycle spare parts, 15. other items such as electronic/musical instruments, stationery items, torch lights, 16. plastic items: water tanks, buckets, chairs, plastic pipes and briefcases, 17. rice, wheat, maize, millets and oats, 18. scented tobacco, 19. Semi-precious stones, 20. sewing machines, 21. textile fabrics and 22. three-wheelers/cars below 100 CC.[15]

The Moreh-Tamu Border Trade aimed at the opening of a gateway to South East Asia and the people of Manipur expected economic prosperity from it. Its main objective is the availability of cheap transport to South East Asia through

Manipur. India's initiative in building the Moreh-Kalewa-Kalemyo road linking Manipur with Myanmar and the initiatives for a trilateral highway linking Moreh to Mae Sot in North East Thailand through Tamu and Bagan in Myanmar and a trans Asian railway linking Jiribam South West Manipur to Moreh and Tamu have been taken. As stated earlier, trade relationships existed between the frontier areas of both countries in general and the Moreh-Tamu line in particular even in the pre-Look East Policy era. In fact, the border trade, whether it be legal or illegal, was monopolized by Chinese goods. It should be noted that informal trade with transactions in narcotics increased manifold because many refineries are coming up in Myanmarese territory close to the border with Manipur. Informal trade is now larger than the formal trade which is alarming news for India. It is evident that a trader travelling from Moreh to Dimapur has to cross about 53 check posts and many of them belong to insurgent groups. As such, business is not that beneficial for traders.[16]

Domination of the entire border trade by Chinese goods from the pre-Look East Policy era until now is a diplomatic as well as a commercial irritant for India. Different types of goods from sophisticated electronic goods to vegetable products like garlic and other edible items are brought to Manipur through the Moreh-Tamu transit point from China. Every household in Manipur consumes cheap Chinese manufactured goods because of its quality, durability and affordability in comparison to expensive Indian products. Therefore, whether it is welcome or not, Chinese goods are still monopolising and dominating the border trade. Moreover, the increasing influx of drugs in Manipur has its impact in confronting HIV/AIDS in the state. Manipur happened to be the first state in the North-East to have encountered the problem of HIV/AIDs and it was only due to the free passage of drugs and narcotics across the border through illegal trade. If the illegal narcotic trade continues, all the North-Eastern states are vulnerable to it and the problems faced by Manipur may be faced by the other states too.[17]

Moreh-Tamu border trade can be said to be progressing in official records and many essential commodities were notified with subsequent additions. In fact, the widening of the 110–kilometre-long Imphal-Moreh road into two lanes lane and the completion of the 160-kilometre-long Tamu-Kalemyo-Kalewa road in 2001 were initiated for effective growth of border trade in pursuance of the Look East Policy.[18] Further, the Imphal-Mandalay connecting road and the Trilateral Highway linking Moreh to Mae Sot in North-East Thailand have also been initiated. It is evident that essential commodities continue to be imported and exported but important actors of the border trade are mainly traders of outside Manipur, particularly mainland India. Thus, it appears that the so-called developments and economic benefits are reaped predominantly by them. Even within Manipur, the inhabitants of Moreh border town who are the ancestral landowners are deprived of the economic benefit because of lack of resources and capital. It is an undeniable fact that the people of Moreh benefit only by working as manual labourers. Thus, the result of border trade is not what was expected.

Prospects of border trade in Churachandpur and Ukhrul districts: Chandel, Churachandpur and Ukhrul districts of Manipur border Myanmar. As such, people of the three districts kept on interacting with their own people on the other side and their mobility could not be curbed by any change of government or change in foreign policy because trade in the frontier areas has been existing in the form of village trade before the pre-colonial era. Of the three districts, Chandel is the only one included in the Look East Policy map. As for Chandel district, the focus up until now is only on the border town of Moreh and has not been extended to other parts of the district. This development indicates that even those people who have been maintaining traditional relationships with people on the other side of the border since the pre-colonial era have not yet benefitted directly by the Look East Policy.

Churachandpur district is connected with Chin Hills (now Chin State) of Myanmar at Tiddim. The road which begins at Keishampat, Imphal passes through Churachandpur (known as Lamka locally) and enters Tiddim via Singhat and Behiang; it is popularly known as Tiddim Road. Reports indicate that a new checkpost is proposed to be set up at Behiang[19] but has not been taken up as yet. The Tiddim road is one of the earliest state highways of Manipur the state with the neighbouring country but it is still a *kutcha* road. Besides, no proposal has been made for upgradation, widening or improving it which is one of the important traditional trade routes since the pre-independent era. Further, as the people on both sides of the border are from the same ethnic stock, mobility and relationship could not be curbed completely and continues to be the connecting link for them. If the Look East Policy is professed to be implemented in right earnest for the socio-economic development of the people, border trade is required to be initiated in Tiddim Road which should be brought to the level of international standards. However, no policy for extension of border trade and negligence towards the upkeep and upgradation of Tiddim Road indicate that the Government of India is not that serious about it.

Ukhrul district is connected with Somra Tract of Myanmar and some areas adjacent to Sagaing Division. The frontier areas adjoining Somra Tract in Ukhrul district of Manipur are inhabited by the Tangkhul Naga tribe who are also found in

Somra Tract in Sagaing division of Myanmar while some villages in the border areas particularly in Molvailup are also inhabited by the Thadou-Kuki tribe of the Zo ethnic group. Traditional trade links had been maintained and interactions existed between people on both sides of the border since the pre-colonial era. However, appropriate steps have not been taken up to boost trade and commerce in pursuance of the Look East Policy in the district till now. A proposal is said to have been made by the Department of Customs for opening up border trade at two places in Ukhrul district, namely, Konkan Thana and in some border village within Kamjong sub-division but the proposal is pending.[20] Therefore, like Churachandpur district, Ukhrul district is also not covered by the map of the Look East Policy and its fruit has yet to be reaped.

Perspective of Look East Policy in Nagaland: The tribal areas of North-East India (erstwhile undivided Assam) and Baluchistan were defined in section 311 (1) of the Government of India Act of 1935 as "areas along the frontiers of India or in Baluchistan which are not part of British India or of Burma or of any Indian State or of any foreign State." The Indian State means any territory which is part of British India and the provinces which were ruled by kings or princes under the suzerainty of the British.[21] The present Mizoram, Nagaland, Meghalaya, Arunachal Pradesh, Karbianglong district and North Cachar Hills district of Assam, tribal-dominated areas of Tripura and the Hill Areas of Manipur were categorized as 'Tribal areas' by the Government of India Act of 1935. In fact, the tribal areas of Tripura and the hill areas of Manipur were not classified as Excluded Area or Partially Excluded Areas by the Government of India Act of 1935, yet, they were governed by the spirit of the laws and regulations that governed other tribal areas at that time. The above-mentioned tribal areas were not regarded as belonging either to India or to Burma by the ruling authority at that time and there was no proper boundary demarcation. The present boundary dispute among many North-Eastern states can also be traced back to this colonial legacy. As of now, there are border disputes between Assam and Meghalaya, Assam and Nagaland, Assam and Arunachal Pradesh, Assam and Mizoram as well as Nagaland and Manipur. As such, proper boundary demarcation was not done even after many years of independence because the ruling authority of both India and Burma were said to be guided by section 311(1) of the Government of India Act of 1935.

The process for discussion of the border issue between India and Burma was initiated at a meeting of the two prime ministers, namely, Pandit Jawaharlal Nehru and U Nu, at Kohima in 1953 but it was not revived till 1968. After 15 years of that meeting the process was revived with the visit of Shri M.C. Chagla, Minister of External Affairs, to Burma in January 1967 and the issue of boundary demarcation was agreed to by the two countries. After that, the Indian delegation visited Rangoon on 17 February 1967 and signed a boundary agreement with the Burmese team. After both the countries ratified the agreement, a Joint Boundary Commission was established and its first meeting was held at New Delhi on 6 April 1968. The first phase of the boundary demarcation meeting was completed on 25 October 1968 but it dealt only with the Mizo Hills-Burma boundary. The Manipur and Nagaland boundary demarcation with Burma was scheduled to be done only in the second phase. In fact, the undemarcated boundary and the presence of Naga tribes on both sides of the border was a disturbing factor for the two countries. The principal Naga tribes that inhabited the area were Konyak, Yimchungger, Sangtam, Phom, Haimi, Hlangan, Rangpan, Tsalaw, Tsaplaw, etc. There were incidents of raids and counter-raids between the Naga tribes across the border. In 1953, the Nagas from Burmese territory raided the Naga villages in India and the latter reciprocated in 1967.[22] As stated above, the boundary demarcation of Nagaland and Burma was initiated only in 1968 but relationships existed across the border since the pre-colonial era.

India and Burma signed a trade agreement on 27 March 1970 but it could not be pursued because of the complex political developments in Burma. The two governments also agreed to reactivate traditional trade across Nagaland through five points, namely, Longwa (Mon district) and Lahe village (Sagaing division), Pangsha (Tuensang district) and Anyun village (Sagaing division), Mimi (Kiphire district) and Layshi village (Sagaing division), Avangkhu (Phek district) and Layshi (Sagaing division) and Molbe (Phek district) and Somra village (Sagaing division). However, appropriate steps have not been taken up till now for reactivation of the traditional trade points. Longwa village in Mon district of Nagaland is divided into two by the boundary between India and Myanmar and is at a distance of 42 kilometres from Mon town. The approximate distance from Guwahati to Longwa is 515 kilometres and it will take 12 to 14 hours to reach Longwa from Guwahati. Avangkhu in Meluri sub-division of Phek district is 306 kilometres from Kohima which is the state capital and the road from Kohima to Meluri has already been declared as a national highway. The Directorate of Industries and Commerce, Government of Nagaland, has constructed a marketing shed in the designated trade centre, 5 kilometres from the Indo-Myanmar border, to facilitate trading between Myanmar and the local people. Meluri area in Phek district is designated as a mineral belt by the Government of Nagaland because of the mineral resources such as limestone, marble, etc. Myanmar is interested in obtaining cement from the Meluri cement factory. Good road connectivity between Avangkhu and the frontier area of

Myanmar can enable the export of cement, marble, slate, etc., which will be beneficial for the people of the area.[23] The Indo-Myanmar Joint Trade Committee meeting in October 2008 bilaterally agreed to open a new land customs station (LCS) but it is has not yet been notified under section 7 of the Customs Act, 1962 (52 of 1962). As per the said agreement, an LCS will also be opened in Somara on the Myanmar side but the agreement is yet to materialise.[24] Despite the many prospects which Nagaland possesses for border trade, no concrete steps have been taken up and the state has not yet been demarcated within the Look East Policy map.

Is there any Development from the Look East Policy to the Act East Policy?

The Look East Policy happened to be an ongoing policy of the successive governments since the prime ministership of P.V. Narasimha Rao in 1991 and has been pursued vigorously by all the prime ministers, namely, H.D. Deva Gowda, I.K. Gujral, A.B. Vajpayee, Dr. Manmohan Singh and Narendra Modi. Specialized as it is in coining new terminology, the present NDA II government led by Narendra Modi has demonstrated its oratory skill by renaming the 'Look East Policy' as 'Act East Policy' leading to many questions whether a change of nomenclature would bring about any meaningful change in actual pursuance of the policy or is it merely a show of political oratory? It is evident that each ruling party has pursued the Look East Policy as an ongoing significant policy of the government and no ruling party or government can claim the lion's share of contribution to this policy because it is an ongoing one. It should also be pondered over whether each successive government is serious with the socio-economic development of people of the North-Eastern region in the adoption of this policy or is it over-guided by security consideration? Therefore, proper research analysis is required in this regard for an objective study of the issue.

India's Look East Policy aims at engaging China and other major powers in different aspects of economic and strategic matters both at bilateral and multilateral regional forums like ASEAN and to prevent domination of Southeast Asia by China. It is also expected to enable India in facing non-conventional security challenges such as energy security, security of the sea-lanes of communication and transport, rising incidence of sea piracy, terrorism, natural disasters, illicit trafficking of weapons of mass destruction (WMD) and narco crimes. Further, India's Look East Policy is not a co-incidental phenomenon but a logical outcome of neo-liberal economic reforms. ASEAN countries will also occupy a central position in India's strategy to advance its political, economic and security interests in Southeast Asia in particular and the Asia-Pacific region in general. The Look East Policy simply does not aim at establishing only trade relationships with ASEAN countries. The three important approaches which it adopts with ASEAN countries are an attempt to renew political contacts, increase in economic interaction and forging of defence links as a means to enhance political and strategic interests and understanding. The Government of India has initiated certain steps to enhance its national interest for achieving the above-mentioned targets and aims. It has also been found that tourism is an important industry that can blossom fully and benefit both India and ASEAN countries; however, all the targets and plans would not be achieved without a direct land corridor through Myanmar and North-East India. Consequently, the extension of a land corridor from India to Myanmar going up to Hanoi, direct flights between India and Cambodia and extending flights between Delhi and Bangkok to Phnom Penh and Siem Reap have been proposed. In the midst of these ongoing proposals, the 1,360-kilometres long trilateral connectivity that will connect Moreh in Manipur to Mae Sot town in Northern Thailand through Bagan in Central Myanmar was announced in April 2002. From a strategic point of view in the defence perspective, Chinese military expansion is a common threat to both India and ASEAN countries. Therefore, Southeast Asian nations began looking to India's balancing capacity against China. That is also a diplomatic opportunity for India to contain China. India is also alarmed by continuous Chinese expansion in the Indian Ocean and Chinese military and business involvement with Myanmar.[25] Therefore, India is beseeched with unending problems. It is not a smooth sailing diplomatic journey for India due to the Chinese threat that is hanging like the sword of Damocles.

It is to be pondered now whether the new nomenclature of 'Act East Policy' is really gearing up for constructive action or not? If the present ruling party which is coining new terminology goes on with the above-mentioned objectives and targets of the policy without initiating new ideas for expansion and extension, it is unlikely that it will be an action-oriented policy. It is pointed out that the Look East Policy is concentrated on border trade at Moreh town in Chandel district. However, efforts have been not yet made in other parts of Chandel, Ukhrul and Churachandpur districts. The prospects of Ukhrul and Churachandpur districts where there is ample scope for opening border trade have not been paid any attention and even traditional trade routes have also not been revived. As far as Nagaland is concerned, even the five traditional trade routes that were agreed to be revived are dead. Over and above that, the proposed LCS at Avangkhu in Meluri sub-division of Phek district has also not been pursued properly. As a matter of fact, the seriousness of the present NDA II Government towards activating the 'Act East Policy' should be proved with initiatives with regard to the steps to be taken up in Manipur and Nagaland. If appropriate steps are not taken up to put prospective border areas of Manipur and Nagaland in the Look East Policy map, it should be regarded as lip service of the ruling party. Hence, the seriousness of the present ruling party in taking up certain new programmes and proposals for expansion of the Look East Policy in Manipur and Nagaland should be watched. If not, the Act East Policy has no meaningful contribution for people of the frontier areas.

Conclusion

The Look East Policy is the offshoot of globalization, privatization and liberalization; its emergence is unavoidable in India's foreign policy. It was initiated and developed during the government of Prime Minister P.V. Narasimha Rao and vigorously pursued by successive governments. Even before the adoption of the Look East Policy, frontier areas bordering Myanmar in North East India, namely, Arunachal Pradesh, Nagaland, Manipur and Mizoram have been maintaining traditional trade and other relationships with people on the other side of the border since the pre-colonial era. The reason being that people from the same ethnic stock settled on both sides of the border since the pre-colonial era and were separated by the colonial rulers and after that by the international boundary. However, despite the Look East Policy and despite border trade there is not much impact on the people of the frontier areas because their interaction and relationships cannot be curbed by the international boundary. Manipur has a 352-kilometre long common border with Myanmar and Nagaland has a 215-kilometre long common border with Myanmar. As a result of the adoption of the Look East Policy, an LCS began to function at Moreh in Manipur and Tamu in Sagaing division, Myanmar, since 1995 but no projects of the Look East Policy have been initiated in other frontier areas of Manipur in Ukhrul and Churachandpur districts. As for Nagaland, five traditional trade routes on both sides of the border scheduled to be revived as agreed by the governments of the two countries have not been taken up till now. Besides, LCS proposed to be set up at Avangkhu in Meluri sub-division of Phek district from Nagaland and at Somara in Sagaing division have not been taken up till now. It should be noted that the Look East Policy has been renamed as the 'Act East Policy' by the present NDA II Government in 2014 but whether the present NDA II Government is really serious with activation of the policy should be observed from the action taken with regard to Manipur and Nagaland. Therefore, it should be closely observed whether the so-called 'Act East Policy' is really active or reactivate in Manipur and Nagaland.

ENDNOTES

1 http://www. Goggle.com – 'What is Look East Policy of India' accessed on 9 August 2010

2 Palmer & Perkins, *International Relation,* CBS Publication & Distributors, Pvt. Ltd., New Delhi, 2001, pp. 593-594

3 http://www. Goggle.com, 'India's Look East Policy' by Nityanand Deva, accessed on 10 August 2010

4 http://www. Goggle.com 'What is Look East Policy of India, op. cit.

5 http:www.Goggle.com'Present Scenario on Border Trade and Look East Policy' presented by R. C. Agarwal, accessed on 29 August 2016

6 Yogendra Singh's 'Integrating India's Northeast with Southeast Asia: Infrastructural Dimensions' in '*Beyond Borders-Look East Policy & North East India*' Dilip Gogoi (ed.), DVS Publishers, Guwahati, 2010, pp. 64-65

7 Alexander Mackenzie, *The North East Frontiers of India*, Mittal Publication, New Delhi, 2004, pp. 77-80 & 193-201

8 L. Joychandra Singh, *The Lost Kingdom Royal Chronicle of Manipur*, Prajatantra Publishing House, Imphal, 1996, p. 156

9 Op.cit., pp. 204-212

10 Colonel L.W. Shakespeare, *History of the Assam Rifles*, Tribal Institute, Aizawl, Reprinted 1977, pp. 189 & 224-238

11 Udayon Misra, *North East India: Quest for Identity*, Omsons Publications, Guwahati, 1988, p. 7

12 V. S. Seshadri, *Transforming Connectivity Corridors Between India and Myanmar into Development Corridors,* Research and Information System for Developing Countries, New Delhi, 2014, p. 1

13 Project Report on Problems of Border Areas in North East India : Implications for the Thirteenth Finance Commission, sponsored by the Thirteenth Finance Commission, Government of India, New Delhi, compiled and submitted by Prof. J. K. Gogoi, Prof. H. Goswami and Prof. K. C. Borah, Dibrugarh University, 2009, pp. 168 & 295

14 http://mdoner.gov.in/print/node/1474, accessed on 1 September 2016

15 http:www.Goggle.com'Present Scenario on Border Trade and Look East Policy' presented by R. C. Agarwal, accessed on 29 August 2016

16 Langpoklakpam Suraj Singh's 'Indo-Myanmar Relations in the Greater Perspective of India's Look East Policy: Implications on Manipur' in '*Look East Policy & India's North East-Polemics and Perspectives*', Thingnam Kishan Singh (ed.), Concept Publishing Company, New Delhi, 2009, pp. 159 & 169-171

17 Ibid.

18 V.S. Seshadri, op.cit., pp. 2-3

19 Ibid., p. 185

20 Government of India (Department of Customs), Records and Documents, Customs Office, Aizawl, 12 September 2016

21 B.L. Hansaria, *Sixth Schedule to the Constitution of India: A Study*, Jyoti Printers, Guwahati, 1983, pp. 4-6

22 B. Pakem, *India-Burma Relations*, Omsons Publications, New Delhi, 1992, pp. 107, 109 & 111-121

23 https//www.researchgate.net/publication/241651480, 'Negotiating Transnational Identities on Indo-Myanmar Border – The Trade Factor' by Sukanya Sharma, accessed on 1 September, 2016. p.

24 http://mdoner.gov.in/print/node/1474, accessed on 1 September, 2016.

25 Konthoujam Indrakumar's 'Mapping India's Look East Policy: Shifting Alignments' in '*Look East Policy & India's North East-Polemics and Perspectives*', Thingnam Kishan Singh (ed.), Concept Publishing Company, New Delhi, 2009, pp. 27-28, 35-37 & 41-42.

Contributors

Anasua Basu Ray Chaudhury, Fellow, Observer Research Group, Kolkata.

Debajit Jha, Assistant Professor, Jindal School of Government and Public Policy, O.P. Jindal Global University, Sonepat, Haryana. J.C. Zomuanthanga, Asst. Professor, Department of Political Science, Mizoram University, Aizawl.

Jagadish K. Patnaik, Department of Political Science, Mizoram University, Aizawl.

Jangkhongam Doungel, Department of Political Science, Mizoram University, Aizawl.

Jonathan Zodintluanga, Research Scholar, Department of Political Science, Mizoram University, Aizawl.

K.V. Reddy, Head, Department of Political Science, Mizoram University, Aizawl.

Lalengkima, Research Scholar, Mizoram University, Aizawl.

Lalrinngheta, Research Scholar, Department of Political Science, Mizoram University, Aizawl.

Lily Sangpui, UGC–JRF Research Scholar, Department of Social Work, Mizoram University, Aizawl.

M.N. Singh, National Law University and Judicial Academy, Guwahati, Assam.

Nimmi Kurian, Centre for Policy Research, New Delhi.

P. Lazarus Samraj, Professor, Department of Politics & International Studies, Pondicherry University.

James Ralte, Research Scholar, Department of Politics & International Studies, Pondicherry University.

Pankaj Jha, Professor of Defence and Strategic Studies, Jindal Global University, Haryana.

Pradip Phanjoubam, Editor, *Imphal Free Press,* Imphal.

Ruatdiki Hmar, Research Scholar, Department of Political Science, Mizoram University, Aizawl.

Sunetra Ghatak, Research Associate, ASEAN-India Centre (AIC), Research and Information System for Developing Countries (RIS), New Delhi.

Suwa Lal Jangu, Assistant Professor, Department of Political Science, Mizoram University, Aizawl.

Index

12th ASEAN India Summit, 14, 32
6th Ministerial Meeting, 56
9th East Asia Summit, 15, 32, 163, 198, 207

Act East Department, 147
Agriculture, 86
Andhra Bank, 159
Angkor Wat, 158
Anyun village, 215
Arakan Rohingya Salvation Army (ARSA), 113
Arakan, 134
Arunachal Pradesh, 6-7, 39, 65, 67, 95, 107, 120, 132, 145, 169, 170, 175, 202, 210-11, 214, 218
  Hajong refugees, 37
ASEAN, 15-16, 33, 42-45, 50, 53-54, 63-64, 74-75, 107-8, 118-19, 131-33, 137, 140, 142, 144-46, 148, 150, 152, 156, 159, 166, 183, 185-86, 194, 207
ASEAN Economic Community (AEC), 55
ASEAN Free Trade Agreement (AFTA), 55
ASEAN-India Agreements on Trade in Service and Investments, 33
ASEAN-India Connectivity Summit (AICS), 144
ASEAN-India Free Trade Area, 33
Asia Pacific Economic Cooperation (APEC), 185
Asia World Company, 131
Asia-Europe Meeting (ASEM), 185
Asian Century, 188
Asian Development Bank, 166
Asian Environmental Compliance and Enforcement Network (AECEN), 9
Asian Epidemiological Model (AEM), 173
Asian Highway 1, 130
Asian Highway Network, 57
Asian Network of Sustainable Agriculture and Bioresources (ANSAB), 9
Asian Tigers, 43, 186
Asia-Pacific, 44, 46, 107, 206, 216
ASIDE, 99
Assam, 6, 27, 37, 67, 71, 95, 135-36, 214
Assam Rifles (AR), 102, 175
Assam's Barak Valley, 5
Aung San Suu Kyi, 54, 56, 110, 113, 137, 161
  visited India, 163
Avangkhu, 215
AYUSH, 177

Bai-Perron (BP), 82-84, 92
Bangkok, 130, 175
  Declaration, 56
Bangladesh, 5-6, 8-10, 16, 37-39, 43, 48, 56-57, 59, 95-96, 113-14, 118, 136, 169, 199, 207
Bangladesh-China-India-Myanmar Economic Corridor (BCIM-EC), 4
Bank of Baroda, 159
Banking arrangement, 99
Barter Trade System, 98, 122
Baruah, Sanjib, 34
Bay of Bengal, 32, 56, 108, 114, 132, 158, 160, 165, 199
BBIN Transport Corridor, 56
Beijing, 58, 114
Bhutan, 5-7, 10, 38, 48, 56, 95, 118, 169, 207
BIMSTEC, 3, 32, 45, 53-54, 56-57, 59, 163, 189, 207
Blue Mountain, 201
Bodo Movement, 37
Border *Haat* Markets and Community Services, 150
Border *haats*, 150

Border Road Organisation (BRO), 99, 207
Brahmaputra-Salween Landscape Conservation and Development Initiative, 10
Brazil, 174
BRICS, 57
Bridge, 104, 154
British India, 37, 108, 134-36, 157, 209, 214
Brunei, 207
Buddhism, 53, 60, 108, 142
Buddhist Circuit, 142
Buddhist Culture, 53
Buddhist Links, 142
Buddhist Monk, 132

Cambodia, 6, 8, 16, 32, 53-55, 58-60, 132, 142, 166, 174, 186, 207
Cambodia, Laos, Myanmar, and Vietnam (CLMV), 52-55, 58, 60-61
Captain R. Boileau Pemberton, 137
Central Statistical Organisation (CSO), 70
Centre for Social Development (CSD), 175
Chagla, M.C., 214
Chahsad Kookies, 209
Chakma refugees, 37
Chakmas, 39
Chhimtuipui, 201
Chicken's Neck, 35-36, 48, 150
Chidambaram, P., 211
Chin Hills, 121, 213
Chin Migrants, 176
Chin Refugees, 39
China, 8, 10, 16, 19-20, 38, 44-45, 48, 58-60, 88, 93, 95, 103, 109-10, 113-15, 118, 132-33, 142, 150-52, 169, 174, 185, 217
China North Industries Group Corp, 131
China Power Investment Corporation, 109-10, 131
China's Yunnan Province, 9
Chinese Authoritarian System, 21
Chinese One Belt One Road, 57-59
Chittagong Hill Tracts, 38
Churachandpur, 213
Civil Society, 88, 91, 177, 191
Civil Society Organisations (CSOs), 101, 140-41, 148, 150, 153
Climate Change, 9
Closed Deals, 89
Cold War, 42, 44, 148, 184-86, 188-89
Col HSP John Maxwell, 137
Come to India—Walk with the Buddha, 7
Commerce, 118, 142
Communications, 86
Community, 133
Community-based organizations, 105
Competitiveness, 133
Compound Annual Growth Rate, 64, 159
Congress, 202
Connectivity, 118, 133, 139, 142-44
Construction, 86
Contact, 139
Cross-border partnerships, 8, 48
Cultivation, 121
Cultural Connectivity, 101
Cultural Space, 141
Culture, 118, 142

Das, Gurudas, 108, 200
Deals Space, 89
Delhi Dialogues, 60
Development of the North-eastern Region (DONER), 195, 197
Development-oriented Initiatives, 24
DGCI&S Trade Classifications, 76
Directorate-General of Foreign Trade (DGFT), 122
Discipline-flourishing Democracy, 162
Divergence, 35
Doi Moi, 55
Domestic Violence Against Women, 25
Dr. Kyaw Myo Tun, 175
Dragon's Clasp, 60

East Asia, 15, 22, 33-35, 38, 46, 49-50, 63, 160
East Bengal, 134, 136
East China Sea, 58
East-to-West road, 6
Economic Connectivity, 103
Economic Free Zones, 23
Economic Times, 6

Educational/Training Institutions, 151
Employment, 105
Energy, 23
Environmental Problems, 23
ERIA, 60
Ethiopia, 174
Ethnic Communities, 37
EU, 115, 137
Excluded Area, 195
Export and Import (EXIM), 120, 122

Faith-Based Organizations (FBOs), 175
Fernandes, Walter, 148
Festival/Music Events, 151
First Anglo-Burmese War, 134-35, 137
Fishing, 86
Floating Population, 170
Food Testing Mechanism, 100
Foreign Direct Investment (FDI), 56, 159
Forestry, 86
Fourth ASEAN Informal Summit, 55
Free Movement Regime (FMR), 170
Freshwater Action Network South Asia (FANSA), 9

Games and Sports Activities, 151
Gandhi, Mahatma, 27
Gandhi, Rajiv
 visited Myanmar, 109
Ganga-Mekong Cooperation, 143
Gateway of the ASEAN, 154
Ghosh, Amitav
 Glass Palace, 138
Globalisation, 26
Golden Triangle, 169, 172, 173
Gongsaki, Amb Chuntintorn Sam, 145
Government of India, 17-18, 22, 27, 34, 38, 48, 99, 121, 136, 146, 177, 190, 198
Gowda, H.D. Deva, 216
Greater Mekong Sub-region (GMS), 8, 132
Gross Domestic Product (GDP), 36-37, 63, 65, 67, 201
Gross Value Added (GVA), 69
Gujral, I.K., 184, 216
Gulf War, 206
Guwahati, 5, 22, 143, 147, 172, 215
Gwadar, 58

Hall, D.G.E.
 A History of South East Asia, 136
Hambantota, 58
HDFC Bank, 122
Health Education/Medical Services, 151
Heritage Necklace Circuit, 8
Higher Educational Institutions, 18
Himalayan Conservation Approaches and Technologies (HIMCAT), 9
Himalayan glaciers, 9
Hindu, 53
Hirschman, Albert O.
 National Power and the Structure of Foreign Trade, 184
HIV/AIDS, 169, 170-71, 212
HIV-Hepatitis C (HCV), 174
HIV-TB Co-infection, 174
Hong Kong, 43
Hospital Service Consultancy Corporation India Ltd, 177
Hospitality, 150
Htin Kyaw, 161, 163
Human Resource Development, 55
Humanities, 21, 22

IDBI Bank, 122
Illegal cross-border Immigration and Infiltration, 153
Import Export Code (IEC) Certificates, 98
India, 6-7, 10, 17, 33-34, 42-45, 50, 54, 56, 59-60, 63-64, 75, 109, 114-15, 118, 131, 137, 142, 148-49, 158-59
India's Act East Policy (AEP), 3-5, 15-16, 19-20, 22-24, 26, 28, 32, 33-39, 62, 75, 81-82, 92, 107, 117, 119, 131, 133, 140-41, 147, 156, 183-84, 194, 197-200, 207
India's Bilateral Trade with ASEAN, 65
India's Look East policy(LEP), 3, 14-15, 23, 32, 34, 39, 41, 45, 46, 47, 48, 49, 62, 107, 118, 135, 147, 156, 183-84, 187, 189, 194, 207, 212
India-ASEAN Action Plan, 52, 59

India-ASEAN Engagements, 144, 164
India-ASEAN Music Festival, 142
India-ASEAN Physical Connectivity Project, 199
India-ASEAN Relations, 140, 157, 165
India-ASEAN Soft-power Engagements, 141
India-ASEAN Trade, 64
India-ASEAN Youth Summit, 142
India-ASEAN, 108
India-ASEAN, Export/Import, 74
India-China War, 1962, 95
India-Myanmar
    Land and maritime trade routes, 109
India-Myanmar Border Trade Agreement (BTA), 98, 120
India-Myanmar Border, 96-97, 108, 122, 130, 147, 152
India-Myanmar Cooperation in Health Services, 176
India-Myanmar Friendship Road, 110
India-Myanmar Joint Trade Committee, 216
India-Myanmar Military Interactions, 54
India-Myanmar Relations, 108, 160
India-Myanmar Trade Agreement, 121
India-Myanmar Trade, 97, 120
India-Myanmar-Laos-Vietnam-Cambodia highway, 60
India-Myanmar-Thailand highway, 45
India-Myanmar-Thailand Trilateral Highway, 60, 108, 111, 165
Indian Democracy, 21
Indian Diaspora, 158
Indian Institute of Foreign Trade (IIFT), 104
Indian Institute of Technology, Guwahati, 22
Indian IR, 5
Indian Ocean Community, 44
Indian Ocean Region, 164
Indian Ocean, 45, 114
Indian Overseas Bank, 159
India-Singapore Comprehensive Economic Cooperation Agreement, 159
Indonesia, 53, 65, 108, 207
India-Pacific Corridor, 57
India-Pacific Economic Corridor (IPEC), 58
India-Pacific Economic Corridor, 57
Information and Communications Technology, 55
Infrastructure Development, 55
Infrastructure, 104
Initiative for ASEAN Integration (IAI), 55, 59
Injecting Drug Use (IUD), 171-72
Inner Line Permit (ILP), 201, 203
Inner Line Regulation (ILR), 194, 201-2
Insurgency, 19
Insurgents, 18
Integrated Check Posts (ICP), 211
IT, 60

Jallikattu movement, 25
Japan, 45, 59, 133, 147, 183, 185, 188

K. Subramanyam, 53
Kabaw Valley, 137
Kailash Sacred Landscape Conservation and Development Initiative, 10
Kaladan Multi-Modal Transit Transport Project (KMTTP), 75, 108, 111, 149, 157, 164-65, 199-200, 203-4
Kaladan Multi-Modal Transport Project, 109
Kanchenjunga Landscape Conservation and Development Initiative, 10
Kaptai Dam, 38
Kennedy, John F., 21, 24
Khasis, 34
King Alaumpaya, 136
King Bagidaw, 136
Knowledge Hub, 154
Knowledge, 139
Kolodyne Hydro-Electric Project–II, 204
Konbaung dynasty, 136
Krishna, S.M.,
    visited Myanmar, 163
Kuki Rebellion, 209
Kukis, 37
Kunming Initiative, 134
Kurian, Nimmi, 141

Lahe village, 215

Lamb, Alastair
Asian Frontiers: Studies in a Continuing Problem, 134
Land Custom Stations (LCSs), 98-99, 120, 207, 211, 216-18
Laos PDR, 6, 8, 16, 32, 53-56, 59-60, 107-8, 132-33, 142, 160, 165-66, 169, 173, 186, 189, 207
Layshi village, 215
Layshi, 215
Least Developed Countries (LDCs), 160
Lengpui airport, 203
Letter of Credit (LoC), 122
Liberalisation, 26
Lincoln, Abraham, 20
Literature and Art, 151
Long-Distance Truckers (LDT), 171
Longwa, 215
Lower Burma, 134
Lt. General Tun Kyi, 211
Lushai Hills, 195

Mackenzie, 209
Mackenzie, Alexander, 208
Mae Sot, 164
Mahidol-Oxford Tropical Medicine Research Unit (MORU), 175
Malaria, 175-76
Malaysia, 6, 23, 53, 64-65, 75, 108, 158-59, 207
Manipur, 6, 20, 27, 70-71, 75, 95, 100, 104, 107, 112, 119-21, 130, 132, 135-38, 158, 164, 169, 170-74, 176, 189, 202, 207-15, 217-18
Manipur's Border Trade Zone, 126
Maoists, 19
Maritime Silk Route, 58
Master Plan on ASEAN Connectivity (MPAC), 144
Mayangkhong valley, 136
McMahon Line, 135
Media, 102, 148, 150
Meghalaya, 6-7, 27, 39, 71, 81, 95, 202, 214
Mekong Ganga Cooperation, 45, 53-54
Mekong Ganga Economic Cooperation, 4
Mekong River Commission (MRC), 59
Militant groups, 19
Milu Puk, 201
Mimi, 215
Mining and Quarrying, 86
Mitra, Ashok, 135
Mizo Accord, 197
Mizo Hills-Burma boundary, 215
Mizo Hmeichhe Insuihkhawm Pawl (MHIP), 103
Mizo People's Conference (MPC), 202
Mizoram, 36-37, 39, 65, 95-99, 101-5, 107, 111-12, 118-23, 125-26, 128, 130, 145, 149, 152, 154, 157, 164-65, 169-72, 174-76, 184, 189-90, 194-97, 199, 200-4, 210-11, 214, 218
Socio-economic Development, 119
Mizoram Peace Accord, 96
Mizos, 37
MNCs, 15, 24, 26, 47
Modi, Narendra, 15, 110, 113, 216
visited Myanmar, 163
Molbe, 215
Mongoloid race, 49
Monte Carlo, 83
Moreh, 164
Moreh-Tamu Border Trade, 119, 126, 211-12
Moreh-Tamu, 120
Mukherjee, Pranab, 110
Murring Hills, 137
Myanmar, 6, 8, 10, 15-16, 32, 37-38, 43-45, 48, 54-56, 58-60, 63-65, 67-68, 75, 95-99, 101-04, 107-15, 118-21, 125-28, 130-33, 135, 137-38, 143-54, 156-58, 160-67, 169, 172-77, 186, 189-90, 198-202, 207-18
Myanmar, Democratic Reforms, 151
Myanmar, Foreign Direct Investment, 109
Myanmar, Political Reforms, 161
Myanmar Health Sector Coordinating Committee (M-HSCC), 173
Myanmar Internal Politics, 113
Myanmar-India-Thailand Trilateral Transport Highway, 56
Myintsone Dam, 131

Naga Hills, 136, 208-9
Naga Self-Administered Zone (NSAZ), 112
Nagaland, 20, 27, 71, 95, 107, 120, 132, 169, 171-72, 174, 202, 207-8, 210, 214-18
    Nationalist Socialist Council, 20
Nagas, 37
Nalanda University, 142
Namani Tlawng River Project, 204
National AIDS Control Organisation, 171, 174
National Highway 39, 130
National Human Rights Commission, 161
National Interests, 150
National League for Democracy (NLD), 157, 161
Nay Pyi Taw, 177
NDA II Government, 187, 216-18
NE Vision 2020, 97, 197
Nehru, Jawaharlal, 184, 214
Nepal, 5-7, 10, 38-39, 56, 118, 207
New Silk Road (NSR) initiative, 57
News Asia TV Channel, 150
NGOs, 18, 20, 22, 25-26, 101, 103, 175-76
Normal/Regular trade, 98
North East Frontier Agency, 39
North East India (NEI), 147-48, 196, 199, 203
North East Indian ethnic groups, 34
North East Region (NER) , 63, 67, 69, 75, 84-86, 88, 90-93, 95-96, 98, 108, 143, 146, 149, 153, 186
    Economy, 65
    Export Performance Rank, 71
    Import Competing Performance Rank, 71
    Infrastructure Indicators, 67
    Openness Index Values, 71
    Political Space, 88
    Rent Space, 85-86
    Trade with Myanmar, 68
North East-educated youth, 19
North-East India (NEI), 15-18, 20-22, 24, 26-28, 33, 35-36, 38, 133, 145, 147-48, 188, 194-204
North-East's Youth Forum for Foreign Policy (NEYFFP), 143
North-Eastern Universities, 143
North-Eastern Women, 26
Northern Laos, 133
Northern Myanmar, 133
Northern Thailand, 133
NRIs, 144
NSDP, 67, 82, 83, 84
Nye Jr., J., 35

Open Deals, 89
Opium Cultivation, 172-73

Pakistan, 20, 196, 202
Panchayati Raj Institution, 26-27
Pangsau Pass, 120
Pangsha, 215
PCNSDP, 67, 70-73, 75
Pegu, 134
People Who Use/Inject Illicit Drugs (PWID), 174
Peoples' Republic of China, 114
People-to-people (P2P)
    Connectivity, 142, 164
    Contact, 35, 45, 48, 53-54, 101, 146, 154, 197
    Ties, 149
Positive Humanism, 19
Power Generation, 23
Prabir De, 141
Pradhan, Dharmendra, visited Myanmar, 163
Primary Healthcare Centre (PHC), 178
Privatisation, 26
Promoting Regional Economic Integration, 55
Protect Consumer Rights, 24
Public Health, 170

Radcliffe, Cyril, 37
Raja Goukhothang, 209
Rangoon, 134
Rao, P.V. Narasimha, 45, 97, 109, 186, 206, 218
    Government, 183
Real Estate, 86
Red Corridors, 19
Regional Comprehensive Economic Partnership (RCEP), 55

Registered Manufacturing and Business Services, 86
Religious Institutional Connectivity, 151
Rent sharing, 88
Restricted Area Permit (RAP), 202
Revised National TB Control Programme (RNTCP), 174
Rhi-Tiddim project, 164
Richard Cooper, 184
Rih Dil, 127, 201
Rivers, 149-50
Rohingyas, 113, 133, 138, 152
  Extremist Militant, 113
  Refugees, 113
Russia, 115, 206

SAARC, 45-46
Saving Wetlands Sky High, *7*
Scott, James C.
  Art of Not Being Governed: An Anarchist History Upland South East Asia, 136
Second Anglo-Burmese War, 134
Security, 150
Self-contented, 23
Self-empowered, 23
Self-reliant, 23
Serbia, 115
Seven Sisters, 28, 38
Shakespear, L.W.
  History of Assam Rifles, 136
Shan Hills, 171
Shanghai, 58
SHGs (Self-Help Groups), 103
Siddha/Ayurveda, 25
Sikkim, 38, 65, 75, 84, 86, 95
Silk Road Economic Belt, 58
Singapore, 6, 23, 25, 43, 45, 53, 55, 64-65, 75, 108, 158-59, 207
Singh, Dr. Manmohan, 206, 216
  visited Myanmar, 163
Singh, Gen. Dr. V.K. (Retd.), 16, 190
Single Male Migrants (SMM), 171
Sitharaman, Nirmala, 160
Skill Development, 22
Smart Cities, 23
Social and Environmental Activists, 152
Social Connectivity, 101
Social Science, 21, 22
Social-Cultural Show Parks, 151
Socialist-oriented Market Economy, 55
Societal set-up, 101
Soft Connectivity, 140
Soft Power, 34, 140, 142, 146, 148, 152
Somra Village, 215
Sootie Kookies, 209
South Asia, 58, 111, 119, 143, 145, 151, 154, 160
South Asian Biosphere Reserve Network (SeaBRNet), 9
South Asian Network on Environmental Law (SANEL), 9
South Asian Sub-region for Economic Cooperation (SASEC), 189
South China Sea, 44-46, 56, 58
South Indian Chola dynasty, 158
South Indian Pandyan dynasty, 158
South Korea, 43, 45, 185, 188
Southeast Asia, 6-7, 34, 36, 42-44, 46-50, 53, 55, 57-58, 60, 108, 114-15, 132, 134, 141, 144, 147-48, 154, 157-59, 165-66, 186, 198, 216
Southeast Asian Markets, 49
Southern China, 36
Soviet Union, 21, 43-44, 46, 97, 183-86
Soviet-led communist bloc, 42
Sri Lanka, 7, 56, 207
Status of composite buildings, 100
Storage, 86
Strategy, 150
Swaraj, Sushama
  visited Myanmar, 163

T. Sailo, 196
Tai-Ahoms, 34
Taiwan, 23, 43
Tamu-Kalewa-Kalemyo highway, 110
Technology, 139
Telephone Connectivity, 100
Tenasserim, 134
Thailand, 6, 8, 16, 32, 45, 53, 56-57, 63, 65, 75, 103-4, 107-8, 111, 125, 130-32, 144, 159, 164, 173, 175, 187, 189, 207

Thailand-Myanmar-India highway, 130
The Hindu, 145
the Philippines, 174, 207
The Telegraph, 135
Thein Sein
    visited India, 163
Third Anglo-Burmese War, 134
Three Cs, 126, 128, 142
Tibet, 48
Tibetan Buddhism, 53
Tiddim Kachin, 171
Tiger economies, 55
Tlawng River, 201
Tlawng, 201
Tourism Earth Lung Initiative, 7
Tourism, 6-7, 45, 103, 145, 150, 199-200, 204
    Employment, 36
Tourist Potential Spots, 201
Trade Openness Index, 68
Trade, Hotels and Restaurants, 86
Traditional/Free Exchange Mechanism, 122
Traditional/free exchange, 98
Trans-Himalayan trade, 4-5
Transport Connectivity, 86, 165
Tripura, 37, 39, 70-71, 95, 135-36, 214
Tuberculosis (TB), 169, 174
Tuichang, 201
Tuivai, 201

U Htin Kyaw, 110
U Nu, 137, 214
U Thein Sein, 177
Uganda, 174
Ukhrul, 213
Ukraine, 115
UN Security Council, 114
UNAIDS, 170
UNESCO, 170
UNHRC, 113
Union Solidarity and Development Party (USDP), 157
United Human Rights Commission, 112
United Nations Economic and Social Commission for Asia and the Pacific (UNESCAP), 57
Unregistered Manufacturing, 86
Unskilled labour, 105
Upper Burma, 134
US, 58, 115, 137
    Government, 57
USAID, 58
US-led capitalist bloc, 42
USSR, 44, 97
Utilities, 86

Vajpayee, Atal Bihari, 109, 187, 206, 216
Verghese, B.G., 36
Vietnam, 6, 8, 16, 18, 32, 54-55, 60, 65, 108, 132, 142, 150, 174, 186, 207
Village Council (VC), 101

Wallerstein, Immanuel, Core-periphery Analogy, 47
Wanbao Mining Copper Ltd., 131
Wang Yi, 113
Warehouse, 99
Water Management, 8
Weapons of Mass Destruction (WMD), 216
Weighbridge, 99
Well-connected villages, 23
West, 41, 43, 115, 138, 148, 184
WHO, 170, 174
Women Participation Rate (WPR), 199
World Bank, 147
World Trade Organization (WTO), 55, 97, 174
World War II, 130, 137
WWF, 7

XCAMBODIA, 54

Yandaboo Treaty, 135
Yoga, 142
Young Mizo Association (YMA), 101, 148
Yunnan, 8, 132-34, 146

Zo (Chin-Kuki-Mizo), 208
Zokhawthar Border, 97, 99, 121, 122-26, 175, 190, 197, 201
Zokhawthar Tourist Lodge, 102
Zokhawthar Welfare Association (ZWA), 125
Zokhawthar-Rih, 97, 118-21, 124
Zoram Nationalist Party (ZNP), 202